STUDIES IN
AMERICAN POPULAR HISTORY AND CULTURE

Edited by

Jerome Nadelhaft
University of Maine

A ROUTLEDGE SERIES

Studies in American Popular History and Culture

Jerome Nadelhaft, *General Editor*

Writing Jazz
Race, Nationalism, and Modern Culture in the 1920s
Nicholas M. Evans

Automobility
Social Changes in the American South, 1909–1939
Corey T. Lesseig

Actors and Activists
Politics, Performance, and Exchange Among Social Worlds
David A. Schlossman

Studies in the Land
The Northeast Corner
David C. Smith

First Do No Harm
Empathy and the Writing of Medical Journal Articles
Mary E. Knatterud

Piety and Power
Gender and Religious Culture in the American Colonies, 1630–1700
Leslie Lindenauer

Race-ing Masculinity
Identity in Contemporary U.S. Men's Writing
John Christopher Cunningham

Crime and the Nation
Prison Reform and Popular Fiction in Philadelphia, 1786–1800
Peter Okun

Food in Film
A Culinary Performance of Communication
Jane Ferry

Deconstructing Post-WWII New York City
The Literature, Art, Jazz, and Architecture of an Emerging Global Capital
Robert Bennett

Rethinking the Red Scare
The Lusk Committee and New York's Crusade against Radicalism, 1919–1923
Todd J. Pfannestiel

Hollywood and the Rise of Physical Culture
Heather Addison

Homelessness in American Literature
Romanticism, Realism, and Testimony
John Allen

No Way of Knowing
Crime, Urban Legends, and the Internet
Pamela Donovan

The Making of the Primitive Baptists
A Cultural and Intellectual History of the Antimission Movement, 1800–1840
James R. Mathis

Women and Comedy in Solo Performance
Phyllis Diller, Lily Tomlin, and Roseanne
Suzanne Lavin

The Literature of Immigration and Racial Formation
Becoming White, Becoming Other, Becoming American in the Late Progressive Era
Linda Joyce Brown

Popular Culture and the Enduring Myth of Chicago, 1871–1968
Lisa Krissoff Boehm

America's Fight over Water
The Environmental and Political Effects of Large-Scale Water Systems
Kevin Wehr

Daughters of Eve

Pregnant Brides and Unwed Mothers in Seventeenth-Century Massachusetts

Else L. Hambleton

Routledge
Taylor & Francis Group
NEW YORK AND LONDON

Published in 2004 by
Routledge
711 Third Avenue,
New York, NY 10017

Published in Great Britain by
Routledge
2 Park Square
Milton Park, Abingdon,
Oxon OX14 4RN

Routledge is an imprint of the Taylor & Francis Group.

Transferred to Digital Printing 2005

First issued in paperback 2012

Library of Congress Cataloging-in-Publication Data

Hambleton, Else L., 1944–
Daughters of Eve : pregnant brides and unwed mothers in seventeenth-century Massachusetts / Else L. Hambleton.
p. cm. — (Studies in American popular history and culture)
Includes bibliographical references and index.
ISBN 0-415-94860-6 (hardback : alk. paper)
1. Unmarried mothers—Massachusetts—Essex County—History—17th century. 2. Fornication—Massachusetts—Essex County—History—17th century. 3. Illegitimacy—Massachusetts—Essex County—History—17th century. 4. Puritans—Massachusetts—Essex County—History—17th century. 5. Sexual ethics—Massachusetts—Essex County—History—17th century. I. Title. II. Series: American popular history and culture (Routledge (Firm))
HQ999.U6H25 2004
306.874'32'09744509032—dc22 2004005114

ISBN 13: 978-0-415-64902-5 (pbk)
ISBN 13: 978-0-415-94860-9 (hbk)

For my father, David Knudsen,
and my brother, Eric Knudsen

Contents

Acknowledgments

Daughters of Eve began as a dissertation. I was curious about the ways Puritans construed the intersection of sexuality and gender. I had the source before I had the questions, and finally, some answers that made sense to me. I found that the seventeenth-century Essex County quarterly court records, both in the excerpted published series, *The Records and Files of the Quarterly Courts of Essex County, Massachusetts,* and in the original file papers on deposit at the Phillips Library at the Peabody Essex Museum in Salem, Massachusetts, contained trial records of women prosecuted for bearing illegitimate children and of couples whose first child was born within 32 weeks of their marriage. Extramarital sexual intercourse was criminal behavior: these persons were prosecuted for fornication. I was curious about the rhetoric of extramarital sexuality, words like "uncleanness" and "filthiness," the disparate sentencing patterns, the harsh punishments, and by the way a fornication conviction defined and determined a Puritan woman's life. Often a woman's only appearance in the colonial record is the paper trail of her fornication trial. The defendants left richly detailed depositions attesting to the circumstances under which sexual intercourse had occurred, describing their work situations, hopes, their deep sense of shame and of God's abandonment, and their regrets. Midwives, employers, parents, neighbors, and friends also testified in these cases, providing diverse pronouncements on sexual and gender ideologies. These depositions provide an intimate glimpse into what mattered in the close-knit communities of seventeenth-century Essex County where people aspired to Election but expected to fall short, where Satan lurked in the forest, people lived at close quarters in small, dark houses enduring days of unremitting labor, and pursued satisfaction in the form of loving marriages, healthy children, and improved material comfort. Gossipy, bawdy, sometimes self-righteous, hectoring or matter-of-fact, these depositions are touching representations of our colonial forbears. Some of them rise to the level of great literature, compact novels in three, four, or five sentences.

I felt like I knew these women. Despite the passage of three hundred years, I recognized friends from my small-town 1960s adolescence whose futures were derailed, at least temporarily, by out-of-wedlock pregnancies. There was the familiar dichotomy of good girls and bad girls: the maidservant who had a reputation for allowing familiarities and the high school girl who "put out." I couldn't find them in the secondary literature, though, which argued Puritan liberality on sexual issues and the existence of uncounted and incalculable numbers of couples engaging in extramarital and premarital sexual intercourse. It seemed to me that women, in the abstract, had too much at stake in seventeenth-century Puritan society to embrace extramarital sexual intercourse casually. The old adage about women giving sex to get love and men giving love to get sex is one-dimensional and simplistic, but it survives because it contains a nugget of truth. There are significant gender differences between male and female experiences of sexual intercourse, attitudinally, physically, and practically.

My committee was constructive and always helpful. Barry Levy's iconoclastic approach to colonial American history made all of the classes I took with him interesting and rewarding and his determination to reinterpret early America through the objective use of primary source documents has been my most formative educational experience. Joyce Berkman introduced me to women's history. Her ability to simultaneously nurture and challenge her students has contributed in a large way to my development as a historian. Margaret Hunt made me aware that, while the people I studied lived in Essex County, Massachusetts, they were English men and women and their values, self-identifications, modes of thinking and being were early modern European, not proto-American.

Merril D. Smith has critiqued theories, asked questions that moved my work ahead, and improved my prose. We've exchanged e-mails about what we were making for dinner that night and what our children were doing that reinforced the timelessness of women's experiences and the necessities of life in the present. Parts of chapter eight, "'Playing the Rogue': Rape and Issues of Consent in Seventeenth-Century Massachusetts," appeared first in her edited book, *Sex Without Consent: Rape and Sexual Coercion in America.* I am grateful to New York University Press for permission to use portions of this work.

My mother, Kathleen Knudsen, has taken a keen interest in this book. I would like to thank her for a lifetime of encouragement. Most of all, my husband, Ronald Hambleton, has earned my thanks. I have been inspired by the joy he has taken in his research and by his work ethic.

Preface

"The World Fill'd with a Generation of Bastards": The Puritans and Extramarital Sex

> And if such uncleanness be not punishable til it be proved by witnesses; sin will abound, sinners be encouraged, and the world fill'd with a generation of bastards Which god forbid.[1]

Thus Samuel Jackson, of Scituate, wrote in 1662 when his daughter, Hester, was sent home, pregnant and jobless, after a few months of service in the Boston household of Benjamin Gilliam. When she was convicted of fornication following the birth of an illegitimate child, Jackson took a pragmatic view of his daughter's predicament. He understood why the Puritans of Massachusetts Bay Colony had made consensual sexual intercourse outside of marriage a crime. While Jackson blamed the son of his daughter's employer, Joseph Gilliam, for tempting Hester "to harlot," he knew that Hester was weak, and susceptible to sexual solicitation. Jackson's seventeen-year-old daughter had explained: "He did tempt me often, and at last the Lord left me to the temptation; and so I was undone by him."[2] To Jackson, this was a plausible and sufficient explanation. Hester Jackson was, after all, a daughter of Eve, corruptible, and sexually potent. She and women like her, if not punished for engaging in sexual activity unsanctified by marriage, had the potential to bring about the destruction of all that Puritans sought to achieve in their Biblical Kingdom.

One hundred and four women were convicted of fornication following the births of illegitimate children in Essex County, Massachusetts, between 1640 and 1685. A further 151 couples whose first children were born within 32 weeks of their marriages were also convicted of fornication prior to 1685.[3] Since the numbers of fornication prosecutions are the core of this book's thesis, we need to know something about their validity. Three questions arise immediately. One, do these numbers accurately reflect the number of out-of-wedlock pregnancies, or did some elite, connected, or very lucky women escape prosecution? Contemporary comments stressed the efficiency of the quarterly courts and the thoroughness of community oversight. William Bradford, the governor of Plymouth Colony, wrote: "they are here more discovered and seen and made public by due search, inquisition, and due punishment."[4] An objective measure of prosecutions was obtained by correlating twentieth-century Essex County genealogies with the quarterly court records. It confirmed Bradford's assessment.[5] Two, assuming that these numbers are a fair reflection of the occurrence of extramarital pregnancies, how are these numbers to be interpreted? On average, five single or newly married women were prosecuted each year between 1640 and 1685. In my book, this seems an insignificant number. The vast majority of Essex County women eschewed sexual intercourse prior to marriage. Other historians are not so sure. From Edmund Morgan who wrote in 1942 that "illicit intercourse was fairly common," through David Flaherty who wrote in 1971 of "widespread sexual irregularities" to Richard Godbeer who wrote in 2002 of the "sheer number of sex cases," the consensus seems to be that, as Morgan said, "early New Englanders possessed a high degree of virility and very few inhibitions."[6]

The third question involves the likelihood of pregnancy resulting from a single act of coitus, or, how many sex acts can be extrapolated from this number of prosecuted pregnancies? Women who bore illegitimate children often claimed that they had only had sex once. While not entirely plausible, it is not as risible as it first appears. Women between the ages of twenty and twenty-five, whether married or single, were in their peak child-bearing years.[7] Given cultural proscriptions against coitus with a menstruating woman, women were sexually available 23 days of the month and fertile for five to seven of these days.[8] It can be argued that, for this most fertile of female age groups, the odds of conception could be one in four. While this is undoubtedly high, earlier estimations that the "probability of pregnancy from a single act of coitus was about one in fifty" are far too low, and as mothers have reminded their daughters forever, "it only takes once."[9] The possibility of an untimely pregnancy was more than an abstraction, and in the seventeenth-century it was compounded by the belief, embedded in the legal system, that as long as women did not reach orgasm, they would not conceive.

An empirical examination of the 255 Essex County women who were prosecuted for fornication and their male partners makes Puritan sexual attitudes and behaviors explicit. This group study provides a solid foundation for five theses about women and sexuality in Puritan New England. First, the traditional image of Puritans as sexually repressive and repressed described so evocatively by Nathaniel Hawthorne in the nineteenth-century classic, *The Scarlet Letter*, and espoused today by much of the general reading public, is essentially correct, but too unidimensional. The amount of extramarital sexual intercourse, as measured by fornication prosecutions in the Essex County Quarterly Courts, was remarkably small but Puritans were not inexorably opposed to all expressions of sexuality. Mutually satisfying sexual intercourse was an important component of Puritan marriages for the laudable reason that sexual activity enhanced marital relationships and for the practical reason that Puritans believed the Biblical admonition to "be fruitful and multiply" could not be met unless both husband and wife reached orgasm.[10] Even within marriage, ministers, through sermons and hortatory literature, warned parishioners lest sexual desire for their partners should supercede their primary relationship with their "Heavenly Husband." Conversely, as they urged moderation, they stressed the mutual entitlement of husband and wife to frequent marital sex. Although Puritans extolled the pleasures of the marriage bed, sexual intercourse prior to marriage fell into an entirely different category. It was "uncleanness," "filthiness," and "incontinence." The definition of extramarital sex in negative terms set the stage for stringent and effective law enforcement efforts aimed at suppressing consensual sexual intercourse between single women and single or married men and in repressing youthful sexuality.

Second, women paid a higher price than men for breaking (or being forced to break) the laws that criminalized extramarital sex. Women were held to a higher level of responsibility than men because of a Puritan redefinition of femininity. While the old, implicit ideology had depicted women as the lustful daughters of Eve, unable, as she had been, to practice sexual discipline, a new gender ideology that Puritans sought to promote, conflated femininity with chastity. Protestantism required the idealization of virtuous women as suitable help-mates to Puritan patriarchs. Its very newness, however, required constant, explicit reinforcement. Women who bore children out-of-wedlock or whose first children were born before thirty-two weeks of marriage had elapsed threatened the survival of the ideological redefinition of women as virtuous wives and they were targeted accordingly. Women were prosecuted more often and punished more severely than their male partners.

Women who bore bastards and their partners received very different treatment from the church and the court than their peers who married. Bastard-bearers could not be rehabilitated into the Puritan community with a penitent statement and a fine. They were punished more severely than their male partners in almost every instance between 1640 and 1667 even when both were of equivalent class. An amendment to the Massachusetts Bay Colony fornication law in 1668 specifically excluded men from prosecution for fornication in favor of an assignment of paternity which required a lesser standard of evidence to convict and ensured taxpayer relief from the support of illegitimate children. Bastard-bearers tended to be younger than women who married before their trials; however, they came from all strata of Puritan society. The punishment meted out to these women, and the disparate treatment their male partners received, is central to a broader and more nuanced understanding of Puritan attitudes about sexuality and gender.

Third, many women who violated Puritan fornication laws were forced to do so by rape or circumstances beyond their control; yet these women were victimized and condemned by society anyway. The Massachusetts Bay Colony, for all its vaunted ideals and confirmed accomplishments, like other early modern societies, privileged aggressive male behavior. Women were expected to protect their virtue vigorously, even as they had been indoctrinated to embody desired characteristics of the new femininity; the acceptable young woman was devout, deferent, submissive, silent, and chaste.

One-third (106) of the women prosecuted for fornication were unable to force a marriage to their sexual partner prior to the birth of their children. One of every five women who bore illegitimate children was seventeen years of age or less when she conceived, and given her youth, she was probably not engaged in a courting relationship. A further 28 percent were younger than twenty. Their ages, the fact that 40 percent were identified specifically in the court records as servants, and that 44 percent of the men named as the fathers of their children were twenty-seven years of age or older, suggests that what we are seeing here is the vulnerability of young female servants to sexual predators.

Fourth, Puritan New England established a unique system of sex prosecutions that deviated significantly from judicial regimens in other parts of the British Atlantic world. There was a broader range of criminal sexual offenses and men were prosecuted in greater numbers in New England than in other jurisdictions. Ironically, Essex County men who married their pregnant lovers bore the brunt of prosecutory efforts directed against men. In New England, the criminal act was sexual intercourse; marrying a pregnant woman was an admission of guilt. In contemporary British jurisdictions, the criminal act was bastardy. Sexual intercourse was not the problem, producing a bastard that required support from the public purse, was.

Premarital prosecutions reflect a greater intolerance for sexual activities that went unpunished in other jurisdictions, because in Massachusetts they formed part of a ritual of punishment, redemption, and reintegration central to Covenant Theology. Certain categories of male offenders were punished more severely in Massachusetts and Connecticut than in England and the other British North American colonies where an explicit double standard prevailed. When lewd conduct is included in a simple count of prosecutions of men and women for general sexual offenses, the Puritans appear to hold men to a higher standard of accountability, but the features of Puritan fornication law that made it different were mitigated by the religious rationale for its creation and undermined by a gender system that measured female worth by sexual reputation.

Any presumption of gender-neutral prosecution for fornication breaks down when cases involving single women are considered. Single women who bore bastards were punished with greater frequency and severity than their male partners just as they were in England and the other British North American colonies. One hundred and four single women were convicted of fornication in Essex County between 1640 and 1685; only 35 of their male partners were convicted. Puritan religious and gender ideology guaranteed that the consequences of an illegitimate fornication conviction were graver for women in Massachusetts than in other regions.

Fifth, Puritan sexual behaviors and attitudes were not static. There was considerable change from the initial decade studied to the final decade that parallels the decline in religious commitment and incorporation into the greater Atlantic community. The number of out-of-wedlock pregnancies increased in successive decades at a rate that exceeded the population increase and an initially harsh punishment regimen for both sexes was replaced in the 1660s by monetary fines for women who could afford to pay as an alternative to a public whipping, and the substitution of child-support payments for criminal prosecution for men.

I cannot emphasize too strongly that the persons whose sexual behaviors figure so largely in this work constituted a small proportion of the population of Essex County. Extramarital sexual activity was aberrant; it was anti-social behavior that threatened the entire colony. Puritans demanded and got sexual discipline in Massachusetts. Between 1645 and 1655, fewer than five couples per 10,000 colonists were prosecuted following the births of their first children within 32 weeks of marriage. The comparative rate of illegitimate prosecutions was less than 6 women per 10,000 colonists. While the number of premarital pregnancies and illegitimate births had increased to 18 and 13 per 10,000 respectively between 1676 and 1685, the out-of-wedlock conception rate remained very low.

An out-of-wedlock conception, if followed by marriage, was a rehabilitative event. Women and men whose first child arrived within 32 weeks of their marriage were ritualistically excommunicated and prosecuted for fornication. After the payment of a significant fine and a humiliating appearance in church wrapped in white sheets, husband and wife were reintegrated into the Puritan community. Nothing illustrates more clearly the emphasis Puritans placed on the formation and maintenance of the family unit than the difference in the treatment meted out by the Essex County Quarterly Court to couples who married after conceiving a child and to individuals who were unable to marry or who chose not to marry following the birth of an illegitimate child. Observation of the sentencing of couples who married yields the conclusion that Puritans were remarkably even-handed when it came to the punishment of sexual offenders. However, when women who bore illegitimate children and their partners are included in an analysis of sentencing patterns, it is clear that the court privileged single men who engaged in sexual intercourse as a possible prelude to marriage over their female partners.

There are observable differences not only in sentencing patterns between the two categories of defendants, but in socio-economic status. Many of the women who married within 32 weeks of the conception of their first child were older and more prosperous than women who bore illegitimate children. Male defendants were distinguished not by age differentials, but by economic and marital status. If they were poor, indentured, apprenticed, or already married, there was no possibility of marriage, whatever they may have promised their partners before the commencement of intercourse. That the number of couples who married following an unplanned pregnancy was greater by one-third than the cohort that bore illegitimate children may be an indication that the common expectation was that men would marry women whom they had made pregnant.[11]

This study, while its larger purpose is to discover Puritan attitudes to sexuality and Puritan gender roles around sex, is narrowly focused. It is an empirical analysis of fornication cases prosecuted in the Essex County Quarterly Court between 1640 and 1692. The only sexual activity that is measured is fully-consummated heterosexual intercourse between a single woman and a single or married man that resulted in a prosecuted pregnancy. This is the only possible measure of extramarital sexual activity at a distance of 350 years.

It is a mistake to assume that Puritan women and men had the same sexual attitudes, appetites, desires, and practices as their twenty-first century counterparts. It is a mistake to think that they are even talking the same sexual language that we are. In 1674, for example, a young female servant was ordered to stand before the meeting houses in Salem and in

Beverly wearing a placard written in capital letters: "I STAND HERE FOR MY LASCIVIOUS AND WANTON CARRIAGES" or be whipped. Among her crimes, laughing and giggling at the boys' bed that was in the same room as hers, and riding her master's horse astride.[12] Moreover, reliable birth control measures and the medicalization of pregnancy have revolutionized the way we think about sex and motherhood. Puritan women did not have the luxury of planning when to conceive or the assurance that they would survive a pregnancy. Add to that an ideology that conflated chastity and femininity and made marriageability dependent on a good sexual reputation in a time in which marriage represented a woman's best and only career opportunity.

Beds were social places. It was cold much of the year in New England. Fires were labor intensive and, judging by the number of suits filed over encroachment on woodlots, expensive. Lighting was limited. Furniture was rudimentary for much of the first century of settlement. Beds were warm; the textiles that covered them provided warmth, comfort, and ease. The best bed, occupied by the master and mistress, was located in the parlor for convenience and so all could appreciate the elegance of the bed hangings. Very few people slept alone; a woman could be construed to be issuing an invitation if she slept unaccompanied by other servants. Maidservants often slept at the foot of their employers' bed. Children slept in the same room as well. There was little privacy to be had, even for the master and mistress and few Essex County residents can have grown up without hearing the mysterious muffled sounds of coupling. This was a very different world from ours.

In chapter one, the focus will be the religious imperatives that impelled Puritans to conceive their relationship with Christ in highly-sexualized terms and that led to the gender assumptions that required reinforcement of an explicit definition of femininity as chastity and legitimated a system of laws that punished women based on an implicit knowledge system that conflated women, Eve, and uncontrolled sexual desires.

Chapter two contains the quantitative evidence to support conclusions about women and men who were prosecuted for illegitimate fornication. This includes the extent of sexual activity among single women and single or married men, their ages and their socio-economic status. Chapter three examines the same population; single women who engaged in consensual sexual activity that resulted in the birth of an illegitimate child and a fornication prosecution, the legal background for fornication prosecutions, the Puritan rationale for using the courts to punish moral offenses, the course of a typical fornication trial, sentencing patterns, and child support and custody arrangements.

Chapters four and five provide the human dimension behind the statistics and legalities of the previous two chapters. What was it about these women, what were the circumstances that placed them in a household where they were vulnerable to the sexual importunities of their employer or their fellow servants? What led women, in a society where the strictures against out-of-wedlock sex were so strident and the consequences of pregnancy so awesome, to sexual intercourse in fields, barns, and other territories customarily occupied by men in return for a promise of marriage or under questionable circumstances. Or, to pose the question in a positive light; why did a few women turn away from the opportunities that Puritan marriage offered? In these chapters it is possible to hear most clearly the words of the women themselves, their employers and their neighbors through depositions filed in the course of their trials.

Chapters six and seven deal with women who succeeded in marrying their partners after conception, but before the birth of their first child. These cases were very clear-cut; marriage was an admission of paternity by the man involved. There is little depositional evidence because there are no contested paternity issues, and, because married women lost their individual legal status, in many instances even their identities are subsumed by those of their husbands. Men were reluctant to marry pregnant women, most married in the fifth- or sixth-month of pregnancy, and marriage formation took longer in the final thirty years of the study. Chapter six contains the quantitative data; chapter seven the sociological aspects of premarital fornication.

Chapter eight considers the issue of rape. Technically it was a capital crime, and as such, was dealt with by the Court of Assistants, not the Essex County Quarterly Court. Puritan juries were reluctant to hang men for raping women and only one man was executed for the rape of an unmarried Puritan woman. William Cheney was married: he raped his servant, and he drew his sword on a constable during an escape attempt. More commonly rape cases were dealt with at the Quarterly Court level as assaults. The courts privileged aggressive male sexual behavior, and if a woman conceived as the result of a rape she found herself in court prosecuted for fornication because contemporary legal opinion held that both partners had to have achieved an orgasm to conceive. Moreover, the standards of evidence were high. Conviction in a capital crime required two witnesses, and in the instance of rape, an outcry from the victim.

The conclusions are presented in chapter nine.

The women who violated Puritan sex laws reveal through reconstructions of the circumstances leading up to their trials how difficult it was for a servant working in a Puritan household to negotiate the passage from adolescence to marriage in Puritan Massachusetts. Women are silent in the records of seventeenth-century Essex County. Their births, marriages, and the births of their children appear in the recorded Vital Statistics. Their names might be listed on the rosters of churches but even here they might appear as "Samuel Jaques, his wife." For many of the women who were prosecuted for fornication, their trial and conviction is their only appearance in the historical record. Their stories are heart-rending: from the new mother so poor she had no clothes to wear to court, to the thirteen-year-old who was raped while she and her sister were collecting their mistress's cattle from the Ipswich pasture on a foggy evening, to the servant who was propositioned while reaping with her employer, to the servant who had sex with a fellow employee and then had her nursing baby wrenched from her arms, and to the young woman who tried to balance her favors between suitors to optimize her chance of a good match and ended up pregnant, unmarried and indentured for a further two years to compensate her employer. The often sad and outrageous fates of these women heightens our appreciation of the achievement of the majority of women who navigated safely through the shoals of sexually privileged men, gender calumnies, and sexual arousal to the harbor of matrimony and became the goodwives of legend.

Chapter One

"I Threatened I Would Mark Him": Religion, Sexuality, And Gender Ideology

> The last Christmas Day at night Joseph Mayo came to my bed and would have been naught with me til I threatened him I would mark him that he might be known from honest men: then he said to me do you think yourself better than Hannah Adams, she let me have do with her six times that night & if I would let him, then that would be the seventh.[1]

This deposition represents a defining moment in the articulation of competing gender ideologies in seventeenth-century Essex County, Massachusetts. The speaker, Mary Higginson, spurned Joseph Mayo. More, she said, she would expose him "that he might be known from honest men." Higginson is a true daughter of Zion, a goodwife-in-training. She retained her virtue and outlived three husbands. Hannah Adams, having had sex with Mayo in an upstairs chamber, demonstrated her similarity to Eve. Rhetorically and morally, Mary Higginson held the gender high ground.

Massachusetts Bay was settled between 1630 and 1640 by religious idealists intent on creating a society based on Biblical precepts far from the interference of the established Church of England and the temptations of contemporary English society.[2] It was an ideal site for a social experiment. Its newly arrived population was isolated, homogeneous, and committed to the religious and social goals of radical Protestantism. Puritans brought to the New World a distinctive religious ideology, which had the potential to enhance the institution of marriage and, consequently, married women, because Puritans viewed their relationship with God in marital terms. This potential, however, remained undeveloped because Puritans retained standard early modern English beliefs about gender, accepting the traditional Judaic-Christian interpretation that posited women as the inheritors of Eve's characteristics. The idea that women were innately more prone to sin, in turn, affected the ways in which men and women constructed their religious beliefs and their sexual attitudes. Hannah Adams represented the past: Mary Higginson the hoped-for future.

Sexuality and religion were inextricably linked in seventeenth-century Massachusetts. They were part of the same set of behaviors, determined by spirituality, cultural identity, and social status.[3] The dominant metaphor used to describe the relationship between Puritans, both male and female, and God was erotically charged. It depicted Christ as a bridegroom, the true believer His bride, and stressed the submissiveness due from the bride to his/her bridegroom. The attainment of grace, the goal of all devout Puritans, was described in terms of betrothal to God, and images of marriage permeated all aspects of Puritan religious rhetoric.[4] Edward Taylor, a Congregationalist minister in Westfield, Massachusetts, wrote poetry that was sexual in nature to describe his relationship with God:

> Hence, Oh! My Lord, make thou me thine that so
> I may be bed wherin thy Love shall ly,
> And be thou mine that thou mayst ever show
> Thyselfe the bed my love its lodge may spy.
> Then this shall be the burden of my Song
> My Well belov'de is mine: I'm his become.[5]

Did this erotic imagery translate to ministerial attitudes about the role of sexual activity within marriage? In 1942 Edmund Morgan, in his paradigmatical paper, The Puritans and Sex, cited positive ministerial attitudes toward coitus between married persons. Samuel Willard, the minister of Old South Church expressed a common Puritan belief when he expressed his horror of celibacy, "that Popish conceit of the Excellency of Virginity."[6] Morgan quoted another minister, John Cotton, regarding Puritan views on women:

> Women are creatures without which there is no comfortable living for man: it is true of them what is wont to be said about Governments, *that the bad ones are better than none:* They are a sort of blasphemers then who despise and decry them, and call them a *necessary Evil,* for they are a *necessary Good.*[7]

This phrase is clearly misogynistic. Morgan said of Cotton's assertion: "Here is as healthy an attitude as one could hope to find anywhere."[8] Women's value, to Cotton, depended on their potential utility as domestic workers and sexual outlets. Morgan, however, in his generally positive delineation of Puritan sexuality, added two key Puritan caveats: (1) sex must not interfere with religion, and (2) marriage was the only appropriate venue for sexual intercourse.

More recently, Kathleen Verduin offered a useful counterbalance to Morgan's enthusiastic endorsement of clerical attitudes to marital sexuality:

> [A]mong the clergy- where such attitudes as may properly be termed "Puritan" are no doubt officially and most articulately expressed- sexuality, sometimes even within marriage, is treated with wariness, distaste, even horror, as a virtual invitation to damnation.[9]

Verduin argued that New England ministers linked sexuality with fundamental Puritan fears. John Winthrop articulated this belief when he associated Mary Dyer's stillbirth, the product of her marital sexual activity, with her heresy and wrote with relish to his friends of seeing "horns and claws, the scales, etc."[10] Witchcraft, which excited the imagination of Puritans throughout the seventeenth century, was associated with sexual congress with Satan. Puritan apocalyptic beliefs, articulated in Covenant theology, were triggered by thoughts of the vengeance God might wreak on a land in which sexual misconduct was left unpunished. The very terms used to describe sexual intercourse, "uncleanness," "filthiness," and "incontinence," illustrate the distaste Puritans felt for sexual activity. Cotton Mather wrote tantalizingly in his diary of "inexpressible uncleannesses in the married state."[11] One wishes he had been more explicit as to whether he was referring to specific sexual desires or practices that he was engaging in, however reluctantly, in his personal life or whether he was chafing against Puritan strictures on excessive marital sexual activity or sexual intercourse while his wife was pregnant or breast-feeding. Edward Taylor, a day after his wife's death, lamented that some "strange charm encrampt my heart with spite/ Making my love gleam out upon a toy," to the neglect of God.[12] Perhaps Taylor thought he might have been too heedless of a jealous God. If so, he had been punished for his uxoriousness through the death of a wife who had been reduced to an object, a toy.

As well, in a meditation of Taylor's, "Upon the Sweeping Flood," he wrote: "Into those liquid drops that came/ To drown our carnal love." Taylor asked, "were th'Heavens sick?" that "they shed/ their excrements upon our lofty heads."[13] Taylor drew an explicit link between sexual intercourse and God's destruction of everything living on Earth except for the contents of Noah's Ark. Even if carnal love had been chosen to personify human sinfulness, it is telling that excrement was the representation Taylor chose.[14] If

Taylor had been regarded among his peers as an eccentric cleric, perched on the western frontier of the Puritan world in Westfield, out of the intellectual mainstream of Puritanism, his poetry could be discounted, but he was, unmistakably, in tune with fellow ministers in eastern Massachusetts.

Marriage provided Puritan men and women with a legal and necessary sexual outlet. Continence was as reprehensible to the Puritans as excessive sexual activity, as the ministerial dismissals of Roman Catholic paeans to abstinence indicate. But that in itself is not a ringing endorsement of marital sexual activity.[15] It is dangerous to extrapolate positive Puritan sexual attitudes from the fact that Puritans accepted sexual intercourse as an essential component of marriage. Certainly nothing can be inferred about the frequency, nature or degree of pleasure conferred by coitus from that information.

Primary sources provide the most reliable information about Puritan sexual attitudes because they articulate contemporary ideology on the sexual responsibilities of each partner and the interest of the court in seeing that these responsibilities were met. The mutual duty of husband and wife to provide sexually for each other is articulated in Catherine Ellinwood's 1682 divorce petition. Ellinwood argued that she should be granted a divorce because her husband, Ralph, was impotent. "If the essence of marriage be one man and one woman given together in the oath of God," then she was not married, for her marriage had not been consummated. Her statement attests to the Puritan expectation that sexual intercourse was the right of both marital partners. She was young, and if she was required to remain in her marriage, she would never have the opportunity to "new [know] any man." Thus, Ellinwood asserted her right to sexual intercourse and declared that she would: "choose rather to die than remain in this connection. Pray pity me and set me free."[16] Ellinwood also warned the court that she "had been under many temptations for a long time." Essentially, Catherine Ellinwood was threatening the court by using the ideology of the sexually uncontrollable woman to obtain a divorce. She needed to be free in order to find another husband or she would be driven to adultery.[17]

Ralph Ellinwood claimed that he had been unable to consummate his marriage because he had been bewitched. There had to be witches not far off, he complained, for he had gone two weeks without attempting intercourse, his wife was willing, and still he "fell away like a rag," when he had attempted to consummate his marriage, stormed out of the house in frustration and embarrassment, returned, and tried and failed a second time that night. Ellinwood blamed his wife, too, for his impotence. His inability to have an erection was due to "suspicious words" from his wife and the presence of witches in the neighborhood. Catherine Ellinwood was forced to defend herself against accusations of witchcraft. Five neighbors provided depositions attesting to the virtue of his wife, declaring her to be a woman who had committed no "uncivil carriages."[18] Further, she was subjected to a vaginal examination by three women who determined that:

> in the search of her body and breasts: do find her body abused; by attempt of copulation, or offers that way, as we conceive, but do judge there had not been any evil act of copulation by any man, it seeming plainly to our apprehension that her body was never so entered by any man as to perform the said act.[19]

The Ellinwood marriage was declared "null and void." The decision of the court is worth quoting at length for the light it sheds on the marital sexual duties of husbands and wives:

> Katherine Ellinwood making her address to this Court, complaining of Ralph Ellinwood who was married to her for her husband, was not a man & had never done, nor could perform the duty of a husband to her; or enter her body as is convenient, & ought to be between man and wife: The man being called did own in Court that at present he is not sufficient or able to . . . perform the real duty of a husband in the way of copulation.[20]

The Ellinwood depositions demonstrate that marital sexual intercourse was a defining feature of marriage, but the depositions say much more. Both Ralph Ellinwood and the Court referred to sexual intercourse as "making use" of a woman's body. Both the men who examined Ellinwood and the Court referred to coitus as "the act of generation," the "work of generation," and the "real duty of a husband." The women who examined Catherine Ellinwood declared there had been no "evil act of copulation." It needs to be borne in mind that depositions were legal documents and that the deponents or the clerks may have felt constrained to use a particular terminology, but the language used in these depositions suggests that while Puritans believed that sexual intercourse was an essential part of marriage, they remained suspicious of the inherent power of sexuality. Perhaps, "Puritans valued and even celebrated sexual and friendly union of husband and wife" and certainly, "sexual pleasure could reinforce the bonds upon which the stability of Puritans male-headed households rested."[21] Procreation and sexual pleasure were mutually compatible to Puritans. Sexual pleasure, however, was construed as an instrument of procreation because it was believed that conception would not occur unless both partners reached orgasm. The primary purpose, then, of orgasm, was procreation, not pleasure. Married couples endured a long sexual drought if they followed the proscriptions of the church. Fully-consummated penetrative sexual intercourse was prohibited from the moment that conception was known until the wife had finished breast-feeding, which could be prolonged for 20 months. That this custom may have been adhered to, at least in the final months of pregnancy is suggested by the number of married men prosecuted for fornication whose wives were pregnant when they had sex with another woman. (As an aside, the gender imbalance of punishment for sexual matters is indicated by the adultery statutes. If a married woman had sex with anyone other than her husband it was adultery, technically a capital crime, although customarily pled down to a misdemeanor. It was not unusual, however, to sentence the erring wife and her lover to some time on the scaffold with nooses around their necks both to shame them and to illustrate the beneficence of the court. Married men, with or without pregnant wives, were only subject to charges of fornication.)

The depositions in the Ellinwood divorce also bear on the larger issue of gender identity. Ralph Ellinwood was "not a man" because he was impotent. His manhood lay in his ability to sustain an erection. For Catherine Ellinwood, the obverse was true. Her identity as a woman was posited upon her chastity. The depositions attesting to her virginity were carefully framed. She was a virgin because she had not been penetrated by Ralph Ellinwood or "any man." The Court stated that had she not been a virgin, whether or not Ralph Ellinwood was physically capable of intercourse, she would not have been given a divorce. Puritan gender ideology required that women who had been sexually active remain within the bonds of matrimony in order to prevent the birth of illegitimate children.

Ambivalence toward sexual intercourse was rooted in Puritan theology. First, Puritans believed that life on Earth was merely the temporal precursor to eternal life in Heaven. God had placed human beings on Earth not to enjoy its pleasures but to improve upon His creation. Coitus was necessary for procreation and to the creation of an affective bond between husband and wife, but excessive enjoyment of sensual pleasures brought with it the potential to divert one's focus from his/her primary relationship with God. Second, the doctrine of original sin convinced Puritans of the importance of self-control.[22] From infancy, Puritans were taught submission that they might gain the strength to resist their natural inclination to sin. Sexual arousal and orgasm represented the ultimate loss of self-control and as such were regarded with suspicion. Third, Massachusetts was founded upon a Covenant. Puritans promised to refrain from sin; in return God would see that their New World enterprise prospered. Sexual desire was a powerful threat to the maintenance of this Covenant. Since it was essential to limit sexual intercourse to marriage, in order to enforce compliance, sexual intercourse between single women and single or married men was criminalized.

It is possible to find positive affirmations of the role of sexuality within Puritan marriage. Anne Bradstreet wrote moving poetry depicting an emotional and physical relationship with her husband strong enough to live beyond the grave. But the ambivalence inherent in marital sexual attitudes as demonstrated by the differing clerical views presented by Morgan and Verduin and the imagery in Taylor's poetry foreshadow the difficulties their parishioners will face reconciling natural sexual desires and their hope of salvation. If sex raised troubling issues of conscience for married couples, it was even more fraught for a woman dealing with the consequences of a coerced sexual encounter or for a courting couple whose loss of control had resulted in a premarital pregnancy.

Puritan men and women interpreted their faith differently because each sex had a gendered notion of what constituted honor. The early modern world, and Puritans were clearly part of that world, viewed women as unidimensional creatures. All other facets of their personalities that might make them enviable wives- their housewifery skills, character, or beauty- were subordinated to their reputation for chastity. Women's honor, as a study of slander suits in early modern England has shown, depended upon a good sexual reputation.[23] This was a patriarchal world in which women lacked property rights, with few exceptions. Men needed to be assured that their property would pass to their legitimate heirs. Women understood both the importance of chastity prior to marriage and the necessity of a good sexual reputation after marriage to protect the status of their households.

A man's honor was multifaceted. Men were measured by a combination of factors that included birth, occupation, wealth and character. Prior to marriage, men were expected to be continent but they were not defined by their chastity as women were. A sexual double standard guaranteed that single men faced fewer consequences as a result of detected extramarital sexual activity. Practical and ideological reasons shaped the customary exclusion of men from prosecution in significant numbers for fornication; the impossibility of proving paternity and the physical realities of conception meant that women were more likely to be prosecuted and convicted of fornication. Additionally, male honor was vested in the spoken word. A fornication conviction following a denial of paternity severely threatened male honor because it indicated the defendant had lied and that he lacked the status and power within his community to sustain his lie. If the man in question was married, it was a double humiliation, because he was exposed as a liar and an adulterer.[24] Isaiah Wood of Ipswich, upon learning from his pregnant servant, Mary Sheffield, that she planned to name him as her child's father:

> "told her that before he would abide the shame thereof, he would make way with himself, for his father and wife would never receive him again."[25]

Men's honor could also be impugned sexually through the sexual misbehavior of their wives. To be cuckolded was a source of immense humiliation. The shame lay in not being able to satisfy or to control female sexuality. For this reason, men were often reluctant to marry pregnant women, even if they were the fathers of the children. Marriage represented not only an admission of their own sexual misdeeds, but a possibly troubled future. Men worried that women who could be persuaded to have sex with them before marriage, could be persuaded to have sex with some other man after marriage.

Male and female definitions of honor influenced the manner in which each gender integrated their beliefs about the nature of sin and salvation. Opposing images of women prevailed. There was the "constant reiteration of an image of womanhood in which sexual virtue was the essence of femininity."[26] To be a woman meant to be virtuous. Yet women had been daily reminded that, as the daughters of Eve, they were prone to sin. This view had been succinctly expressed by the sixteenth-century cleric, Hugh Latimer:

> For a woman is frail, and proclive unto all evils; a woman is a very weak vessel, and may soon deceive a man and bring him unto evil. Many examples we have in holy scripture. Adam had but one wife, called Eve, and how soon had she brought him to evil, and to come to destruction.[27]

This was powerful rhetoric, and its import lingered, creating an unenviable dissonance for women. Faced with the generalized anxieties of all good Puritans about salvation, they worried that an envious thought or a surge of sexual desire evidenced the carnal attributes of their gender.

Elizabeth Reis has argued that women, having internalized clerical strictures on Eve's heritage, viewed themselves as the possessors of inherently depraved natures.[28] This belief left women excessively concerned about their state of grace. The commission of a minor sin provided confirmatory evidence of the essential worthlessness of their natures. It may not be too great a leap, then, to extrapolate that a woman who already considered herself dammed might be more likely to experiment sexually, or conversely, a virtuous woman, realizing her hold on salvation was tenuous because of her relationship to Eve, might be less willing to risk her immortal soul by engaging in sexual intercourse prior to marriage.

The majority of men did not generalize damnation from a few sinful acts as a woman might because, however oppressive their childhood, and however limited their adult opportunities, they were part of the cohort of rulers, even if their power did not extend beyond the boundary of their immediate family. Sons of Adam were not freighted to the same degree with the knowledge of their innate corruption as daughters of Eve. Moreover, since material success was correlated to the achievement of grace, some men had more reason for optimism than other men and women.

Gender influenced Puritan religious beliefs in another fashion. Amanda Porterfield has argued that women were religious conservatives.[29] Like Reis, Porterfield believes that men and women experienced Puritan religious ideology differently. Puritan women remained rooted in the traditionally submissive relationship to God that had developed as a specific offshoot of Puritan religious ideology, while men developed a more modern, expansive notion of their relationship to God which coincides with Reis' theory that men and women interpreted the effects of sin differently. Puritan theology equated a woman's marital relationship with her husband and her relationship with God. The submissiveness required of a good Puritan, Porterfield argues, colored women's temporal relationships with men. If, as Porterfield suggests, Puritan men modernized more quickly than women, it is possible to infer that men's sexual attitudes increasingly diverged from those of women over the course of the seventeenth century.[30] While men still wanted to marry a woman with an impeccable sexual reputation, they could rationalize their own premarital sexual experience unimpeded by the fear of damnation, although obviously not all men and all women experienced religion in lockstep according to gender.

Despite the degree of conjecture involved in moving from the notion that men and women might experience religion in a different manner dependent on their gender, as Reis and Porterfield suggest, to a discussion of differing sexual attitudes and behaviors among the two sexes, my data confirm that men and women experienced the religious consequences of extramarital sexual intercourse differently, especially if marriage did not follow conception. Women who bore illegitimate children prepared penitent statements in which they expressed their sense of God's abandonment and asked for their neighbors' prayers to help bring about reconciliation with Him. Men who fathered illegitimate children became more willing to live with a lie as the century progressed. Since paternity could neither be proved nor disproved, men could not be convicted of fornication unless they confessed. Prior to 1660 most men who fathered illegitimate children gave the admission of paternity required for conviction either to redeem their souls or out of a customary expectation. The 1668 amendment to the fornication statute to prioritize collection of child-support payments over punishment was a tacit admission that men no longer felt a religious imperative to cleanse their souls through public confession.

To understand why Hester Jackson, whom we met in the preface, a socially and economically insignificant young woman, presented a threat to the security of Massachusetts Bay, through, as her father had written, her contribution to "a world fill'd with a generation of bastards," it is necessary first to understand the centrality and ubiquity of the Puritan religion to life in seventeenth-century Massachusetts and its impact on gender hierarchy. Puritans, like their early modern contemporaries, believed that women were inferior to men. God had ordained this inferiority when He created Eve from Adam's rib, to be his helpmeet, not his equal.[31] John Milton summed up the Puritan view succinctly in *Paradise Lost:* "he for God only, she for God in him."[32] Men were equipped by their greater physical and intellectual strength to be the dominant sex. Massachusetts Bay Colony was a patriarchal society in which women, children and servants were subordinate to the male head of the household. The political, religious, economic, and social structures of New England were predicated on the maintenance of male authority. If women like Hester Jackson were allowed to act on their sexual impulses, chaos, in the form of households headed by single women and their bastards, would reign.

The assumption that women and men were equal before God was positive, as was the belief that sexual intercourse within marriage was the right and the duty of both partners, each to the other, but the effect of these beliefs was mitigated by other contradictory and strongly-held Puritan positions that had negative implications for women. It was assumed that God created women as lesser individuals, skilled in the housekeeping arts and happiest when within the four walls of their homes. Protestants, and Puritans were no exception, accepted the traditional Judaic-Christian view that women had been cursed in specific ways by God because Eve bore a greater responsibility in the Fall than Adam.[33] Not only had Eve been created second, she had sinned first.

Womankind's punishment, not incidentally, was linked to sexuality. Women were sentenced to bear many children in pain. Moreover, since Eve had demonstrated women's inherent weakness and duplicity by allowing herself to be seduced by Satan and in turn seducing her husband, the secondary position of women in Western European society could be rationalized as a God-given imperative. Women needed to be placed under the authority of their fathers and their husbands for their own protection.

Women who could be persuaded to yield their sexual favors could be persuaded to yield their souls.

Puritans believed they were on a mission from God as the vanguard of Protestantism, the seventeenth-century recreation of Israel, and the purest representation of God's Kingdom on Earth. Governor John Winthrop articulated the Puritan mission in a speech delivered on board the ship Arbella as the Winthrop Fleet neared New England in 1630:

> For we must consider that we shall be as a City upon a Hill, the eyes of all people are upon us; so that if we shall deal falsely with our God in this work we have undertaken, and so cause Him to withdraw His present help from us, we shall be made a story and a by-word through the world.[34]

Covenant theology promised Puritans that in return for obeying His commandments, God would see to it that Massachusetts prospered. But: "should they fail him, they would as infallibly procure losses by land and sea, defeats at the hands of their enemies, and massacre by the Indians."[13] To fulfill their side of the contract, every Puritan was required to live by God's laws and to monitor his/her neighbors' behaviors as well.

God had ensured that His terms would be difficult to meet. Puritans believed that when He created Adam in His own image, Adam had been perfect. When Eve yielded to temptation and persuaded Adam to join her in sin they became demonstrably imperfect. This original sin was inherited by all their descendants who were born in a natural state, innately corrupt and depraved. Puritans felt the full weight of Eve's transgression. Only a select group, "visible Saints," estimated by John Calvin to be fewer than one in five, was assured of eternal life.[35] Strict implementation of laws designed to regulate every aspect of human behavior was required to save the unregenerate majority from the awesome consequences of their own corrupt natures. Thus the doctrine of original sin provided the rationale for the creation and adoption of a legal system in Massachusetts in which secular and moral law was intertwined.[36] To Samuel Jackson and his fellow Puritans, the criminalization of sexual activity outside of marriage was a necessary form of social control.

The low number of illegitimate births and premarital pregnancies attests to the effectiveness of fornication prosecutions as a form of social control in seventeenth-century Massachusetts. Fornication trials, public whippings, and heavy financial penalties reinforced in the minds of the single men and women in attendance the importance of sexual continence. While Puritans sought the internalization of values through the development of a conscience that would act as an internal compass, this was still a society based on honor and shame. It mattered deeply what the neighbors thought.

Fornication prosecutions, in and of themselves, would not be sufficient to deter single Puritans from sexual intercourse. A number of other factors militated against such sexual activity. The most important were religious and cultural imperatives that promoted male and female chastity prior to the wedding night. The homosocial structure of youth networks, the relatively low marriage age, and the ability of most young people to marry limited the number of persons who were unable to wait for marriage or were forced to seek sexual partners outside the prescribed structure of marriage. Practical problems existed: houses were small, with little privacy and constant supervision. There was a curfew; few warm places to meet free of oversight in long, cold winters; dancing and provocative dress were illegal; courtship was regulated; and most young women understood the value of a good sexual reputation.

The belief that anyone would refrain from sexual activity out of fear of going to Hell might seem ridiculous to a historian steeped in the secular values of the twenty-first-century, but Hester Jackson and her contemporaries believed implicitly in the physical actuality of Hell. When Hester Jackson said God had abandoned her before she succumbed to Joseph Gilliam's sexual importunities, she was not delivering a pat excuse. The depositions in the Jackson trial, like the depositions filed for other fornication trials, express frank horror upon hearing of extramarital sexual activity. It was not something that happened every day. For a single woman, engaging in extramarital sexual activity had life-altering implications that they believed extended beyond the grave. Hester Jackson was by no means alone among women in believing that God had abandoned her.

The prosecution of women who bore illegitimate children and their partners, and couples whose first child arrived within 32 weeks of their marriage, while systematized and implemented in a far more comprehensive fashion in Massachusetts, was not a process invented by Puritans in the New World to advance their moral agenda. They adapted a centuries-old system of prosecution developed in the ecclesiastical courts of England. In England, however, fornication prosecutions had selectively targeted poor women who bore bastards since the aim was to control welfare costs. English Puritans had pressed for a broader range of offenses, uniform application of the existing fornication laws and harsher penalties for offenders. Prior to 1640 they tried unsuccessfully to use their parliamentary clout to have jurisdiction over sexual irregularities transferred to the secular courts. During the Interregnum, Oliver Cromwell's government suspended ecclesiastical courts in favor of civil criminal prosecutions for bastardy and fornication.[37]

English ecclesiastical courts did not make a practice of presenting married couples whose first child was born early, nor did they present single men or women for lewd behavior except during the Interregnum. Nevertheless, there was one area of similarity in the composition of cases prosecuted in the English ecclesiastical courts between 1570 and 1640 and in the Essex County Quarterly Courts between 1640 and 1685. Women in England were almost invariably presented by the ecclesiastical courts for bastardy when they bore illegitimate children.[38] The majority of these women were domestic servants. One in five was too poor to pay her fine. Their male partners were less likely to be presented because there was more tolerance for male sexual misbehavior and because of the difficulties inherent in assigning paternity. As in Essex County, most (80 percent) of these men were single.

The superficial similarity is misleading. In England the charge was bastardy, the female defendants were poor, and the primary motivating factor behind prosecution was economic. In Massachusetts, bastard-bearers from all status groups were charged with fornication, not bastardy. Their crime was not that they had produced an illegitimate child that needed support from the public purse, but that they had engaged in extramarital sexual intercourse. In Massachusetts prior to the 1660s, the laws governing sexual offenses were written and administered by men who had been rebuffed in their efforts to reform the English system of prosecution for sexual offenses. The initial impetus, then, behind the criminalization of consensual sexual intercourse outside of marriage was moral, not economic, although clearly Puritans saw no finite distinction between the two issues.

The moral imperative for fornication prosecutions was sustainable in Massachusetts only as long as the number of illegitimate children requiring community support was limited. Prior to 1665, less than one bastard per year was born in Essex County and not all required community support. The 1668 amendment that created a diminished legal standard for assessing paternity was recognition that bastardy was an economic as well as a moral issue. Bastardy removed a productive and youthful female worker temporarily from the labor market and it created a child who required financial support.

Massachusetts was not the only British North American colony that tried to prevent unmarried persons from engaging in sexual activity by making sexual intercourse outside of marriage a criminal offense. The types of sexual behaviors, though, that were criminalized, the motivating factors for the legislation, and the penalties assigned, varied by colony. Not surprisingly,

New England sexual legislation diverged the most from that of customary English practice, the Chesapeake the least. In the southern colonies the motivation for fornication prosecutions appears to have been primarily economic. Whatever legislation existed on the books in other British North American colonies, enforcement was irregular, gender specific, and status dependent.

The Chesapeake provided a very different ideological and physical environment than Massachusetts. Unlike New England, where most settlers emigrated in family groups, the majority of immigrants to the Chesapeake were male indentured servants between the ages of seventeen and twenty-eight and single women were at a premium.[39] Chesapeake planters had a profitable, but labor-intensive staple crop, tobacco. Fortunes could be made through the exploitation of indentured servants, both male and female. Planters were more concerned about losing the services of pregnant female servants and the expenses of raising their children than they were with the moral issues involved. For this reason, judicial activity was directed against indentured servants who bore illegitimate children.[40] These women were charged with bastardy, as in England, because their crime lay not so much in having engaged in coitus, as in producing an illegitimate child which reduced their ability to work and, temporarily, creating another drain on their master's resources in the form of an infant who had to be raised to a productive age.

Cases that were tried as bastardy cases in the Chesapeake might have become premarital fornication cases in New England. The longer lengths of indentures in the Chesapeake meant that the amount of money required to buy out a pregnant woman's remaining time in order to marry her was more likely to be beyond the financial resources of her partner than in Massachusetts. Even bastardy prosecutions, however, were not routine in the Chesapeake. Mary Beth Norton found that women were not prosecuted for sexual offenses unless there were economic consequences. Some instances of bastardy came to light only because the woman's employer sued the father of her child for compensation for lost labor.[41]

Lois G. Carr and Lorena S. Walsh argue that the economic implications of the withdrawal of a pregnant woman's labor meant that the penalties women paid for bastardy might be severe.[42] The traditional sexual double standard ensured that their partners would not be punished.[43] Men with power and property validated their virility at the expense of two years of minimal child-support payments and moderate social embarrassment. For a short period of time, until the practice became illegal, it was to an employer's advantage to impregnate his indentured servant because it would give him a longer claim on her labor. An employer was usually assigned an additional 12 to 24 months of labor as compensation.[44]

Sexual misconduct that did not have economic consequences, such as premarital fornication, which formed the largest category of offense in Massachusetts, was seldom prosecuted in the Chesapeake. In Maryland the situation was further complicated by a religious dispute between Catholic authorities and Protestant settlers about what constituted legal marriage. Premarital fornication was essentially a victimless crime in a society based on individualism where there was no need to defend family values. In one Maryland county, one-third of all immigrant brides were pregnant when they married.[45] When the locally born brides, who benefited from the protection of their families were factored in, the proportion of pregnant brides dropped to one in five.

The loss of sexual reputation inherent in bearing an illegitimate child in Massachusetts that presented an almost insuperable barrier to marriage did not entail the same consequences in the Chesapeake. Women were scarce. They immigrated in fewer numbers to the Chesapeake and died in greater numbers during childbirth because of complications caused by yellow fever. Men who wanted to marry could not afford to be too particular. Nevertheless, while the consequences of an act of extramarital sexual intercourse differed, and the types of sexual behaviors that were criminalized and the penalty for sexual misconduct varied by region, gender, and the decade in which the offense occurred, a generalized philosophical assumption existed throughout the British Atlantic world that coitus prior to marriage presented a moral and an economic threat to the survival of fledgling communities.[46]

Chapter Two

"I Know Thy Condition, Alas, Poor Wench": A Quantitative Analysis of Illegitimate Fornication Prosecutions in the Essex County Quarterly Court, 1640–1665

> Elizabeth Due, Mrs. Endecott's maid, came several times to our house upon her mistresses business, and did complain of Zerobabel Endecott, his unseemly carriage to the maid, as when she was in an inward room at her work he would pull her away her cushion from before her making of lace and would throw her down on the ground.... Zerobabel would have done as much to me I know thy condition, alas poor wench.[1]

Elizabeth Due was, indeed, a poor wench. A recent immigrant, with no relatives in Massachusetts, she worked in the Salem household of Governor John Endecott in 1654. She complained of persistent attempts by Endecott's eighteen-year-old son, Zerobabel, at intimacy. When she became pregnant, the Endecott family acted quickly to free her from her indenture and marry her to a fellow servant. When Due persisted in claiming that the teenage Zerobabel, not Cornelious Hulett, had fathered her child, she was whipped 13 stripes for slander in June, 1654. When that failed to quiet her, she was whipped again in December, this time 20 stripes, a punishment of unprecedented severity, for continuing to slander Mr. Zerobabel Endecott.[2] Cornelious Hulett, whom she testified had never so much as kissed her, was sentenced to 10 stripes, the sentence to be carried out "some lecture day in seasonable weather." Due's sentence was harsh, and exacerbated by her unwillingness to accept release from her indenture, a husband and a father for her child in return for her silence.

She fits the profile of women prosecuted for fornication in Essex County prior to 1665. She was a servant, her partner was part of her employer's household, and her punishment was more severe than that of her male partner, whether Zerobabel Endecott or Cornelius Hulett.

In the 25-year period between 1640 and 1665, an average of one woman per year was prosecuted for illegitimate fornication in Essex County. Even as the number of female defendants quadrupled between 1666 and 1685 to four illegitimate pregnancies per year, they comprised a tiny portion of Essex County women. Clearly Puritans demanded and got sexual discipline from the majority of single women and men. The successful repression of extramarital sexual intercourse placed a severe burden upon bastard-bearers who were punished not only by the patriarchal system but also by isolation from the majority of women who managed the difficult transition from adolescence through courtship to marriage. Their successes enabled them to view the few women who bore illegitimate children as contemptible failures and provided the women's community with the moral authority to police the behaviors of single women.

The amount of sexual activity outside of marriage in seventeenth-century Essex County as measured by the rate of prosecution of women and men following illegitimate births and is shown in Table 1.[3] Essex County women were prosecuted 104 times for fornication following the birth of illegitimate children between 1640 and 1685. Thirteen of these women were convicted twice and one woman was convicted three times. Six of the women were widows, two of whom were convicted twice. With the exception of the five-year interval, 1661–1665, the number of women prosecuted

Table 1 Comparison of Numbers of Women Convicted of Illegitimate and Premarital Fornication in Essex County, Massachusetts, 1641–1685

Year	Illegitimate Fornication (N=104)	Premarital Fornication (N=151)
1641–1645	2	1
1646–1650	2	2
1651–1655	6	5
1656–1660	10	9
1661–1665	3	11
1666–1670	10	16
1671–1675	18	36
1676–1680	24	33
1681–1685	29	38

for bearing bastards increases with each interval. During the same time period, 151 married couples were convicted of premarital fornication. Two main factors determined whether a pregnancy would be illegitimate or premarital. One was the status of the male partner. If he were already married, indentured, apprenticed, or very poor, marriage was impossible. The second factor was the economic status of the female defendant. If it was equivalent to or better than that of her partner, and her family could afford to provide a dowry, an illegitimate pregnancy could be converted into a premarital pregnancy. This was an important consideration to parents who had economic, social and spiritual aspirations for their daughters. Marriage was rehabilitative and a pregnant daughter with a husband could be reintegrated into the Puritan community. Only 20 percent of women who bore illegitimate children between 1640 and 1685 made a subsequent marriage free from the taint of sexual scandal. Even the average female premarital defendant was six months pregnant at marriage; such was the strength of the ideological link between chastity and femininity. Men were unwilling to marry women who could be persuaded to yield their sexual favors prior to marriage, even if it had been to them. The ability to control and/or satisfy female sexuality was a major facet of male honor. Puritans believed women with damaged sexual reputations were potential adulteresses and no man wanted to risk being labeled a cuckold.

Table 2 shows the ages of women and men at the time of their trial. Forty-five percent of the women convicted of fornication whose ages can be established were twenty years of age or less at the time of their conviction. An additional 38 percent were between the ages of 21 and 26. The remaining 17 percent of women who bore illegitimate children were 27 years of age or older upon conviction.

Within the category of women who bore illegitimate children, there are two major subgroups. The first group, comprising almost half of the women (45 percent), was aged twenty years or younger. Since the average

Table 2 Age Distribution of Illegitimate Fornication Defendants at the Time of Their Trials[4]

	Women (N=66)		Men (N=54)	
Age	Frequency	Percent	Frequency	Percent
15–17	12	18%	1	2%
18–20	18	27%	6	11%
21–23	16	24%	12	22%
24–26	9	14%	11	20%
27–29	5	8%	6	11%
30+	6	9%	18	33%

marriage age for women in Essex County was approximately 22, their sexual activity cannot be categorized as occurring within the context of a courtship relationship in which marriage would have been an expected outcome, although marriage was an appropriate remedy, if a husband could be found, for women in the upper half of this age group. Nor can this sexual activity be categorized as adolescents having sex with other adolescents as only 13 percent of the men charged with paternity were twenty years of age or less, while one out of every three men whose ages at the time of their trial can be assessed were 30 years of age or older.[5] For whatever reason these women had sex, whether consensual because they were hungry for affection in an unpleasant employment situation or because they lost control in a petting situation or because they were coerced by someone on whom they were dependent; they were the victims of sexual predators. This was casual, opportunistic sex because, in most instances, their age precluded marriage as a serious consideration.

The second major group of unmarried women convicted of fornication is comprised of the 38 percent of women between the ages of 21 and 26 who bore illegitimate children. It can be reasonably assumed that many of these women hoped to marry their partners. The Massachusetts Bay Colony law code encouraged couples who were expecting a child to marry, and in no five-year interval throughout the period of this study is the number of single women convicted of illegitimate fornication greater than the number of couples convicted of premarital fornication. In each five-year interval between 1660 and 1685, the number of couples convicted of premarital fornication was significantly greater than the number of single women who were convicted. Women of marriageable age who lacked a sufficient dowry may have used sexual intercourse as leverage to secure a husband whose financial resources may have exceeded theirs and who would not, in the normal course of events, be considered an appropriate match.

Their motives, however, for engaging in sexual intercourse need not have been calculated. Sarah Lambert of Beverly was whipped in 1667 and again 12 years later in 1679 for bearing two illegitimate children by Allister Greime, a Scottish prisoner of war who worked at the Saugus Iron Works. Whether Greime was unable to marry because of his prisoner-of-war status or because he had a wife back in Scotland, their relationship was long-standing. Elizabeth Preston and William Bingley of Newbury, both indentured servants, were charged in 1656 and 1658 after the births of illegitimate children. Their relationship persisted. They were married February 27, 1660, 16 weeks prior to the birth of their third child. A third fornication trial ensued.

Many women in the 21- to 26-year age category whose depositions have survived said that their partner had promised them marriage before the commencement of intercourse. Others testified that their partner had promised that he would do them "no harm" or "no hurt." There are three plausible explanations for these phrases, which, while ambiguous today, may have referred to a specific sexual practice in the seventeenth-century (such as a promise to withdraw before ejaculation). Alternatively, it may have been a reference to cultural beliefs (that virgins would not conceive or that a mutual orgasm was required for conception) or cultural expectations (a tacit promise of marriage should pregnancy result from casual consensual sexual activity).

Women in the 21- to 26-year age cohort faced the same problems as women in the younger group. Women in both age categories fell victim to sexual predators who promised marriage in return for sex or to employers who made sex a prerequisite of employment. Neither category of women was immune to the lure of sexual desire. The most salient interpretive factor, moreover, is not contained in the details of the circumstances surrounding sexual activity, or in the identification of individual women, it is that the numbers of women in these two categories combined constituted a tiny proportion of the female population of Essex County.

The sexual double standard meant that the loss of sexual reputation was of greater import for women than men. Marriage, the only viable career option for a Puritan woman, became very difficult to achieve after a conviction for fornication. While four women who bore an illegitimate child married the child's father soon after their trials, only 29 percent subsequently married men other than the father of their illegitimate child.[6] Not all of these marriages occurred under ideal circumstances. Four women married during their second pregnancy and went back to court for a second fornication trial. This time, at least, their marital status mitigated the doubled opprobrium and enabled them to keep possession of their child. Two of the married men who had been convicted of fathering bastards themselves. Four more married other men between the conception of their child and their appearance in court for fornication. Only one in five of women who bore illegitimate children made subsequent marriages untainted by a previous court appearance by one or both of the partners for a sexual offense.

Six of these women married men other than the father of their child within a year. All had families living locally who could provide financial incentives to single men to marry their daughters. Rebecca Armitage of Lynn gave birth to an illegitimate son, Benoni, March 15, 1665. Armitage had been her grandmother's sole heir in 1654. The trustees of the estate had been required to post bond of £180 so it was a sizable inheritance. The will stated that the estate was to be improved by her guardians and turned over to her at age sixteen. Eight months after Benoni's birth, she married eighteen-year-old Samuel Tarbox. Tarbox would not have been in a position to marry at that age, having two older brothers, without Armitage's money. Another woman, Mary Dane, who had been sixteen when she bore an illegitimate child, married her step-grandmother's son when she was twenty. William Chandler was twenty-two at the time, so money must have been forthcoming to make this marriage possible. These marriages illustrate the type of husbands available to women with financial resources and tainted sexual reputations; a teenager and a biddable grandson.[7]

What happened to the women who bore illegitimate children and did not marry subsequently? Information on child custody and child support decisions provided later in this chapter make it clear that most were not engaged in raising their children. In many instances the women disappeared into a relative's or an employer's household. The most positive thing that can be said about their futures is that most did not make a second appearance in court for fornication or other criminal behavior. They appeared infrequently as deponents in unrelated suits, usually as witnesses to commercial transactions involving the households in which they were employed. They seldom appeared in probate documents because they rarely accumulated property in their own right to be transferred and men were the preferred witnesses to official documents.

Deaths were not consistently recorded in seventeenth-century court records. Hannah Hayward of Ipswich, convicted of fornication at the age of sixteen in 1677, died unmarried in 1725. She was described in the Ipswich Vital Statistics as "a very Antient maid." At sixty-five, it is more likely that "Antient maid" was a reference to her single status, indicating how remarkable it seemed to her contemporaries for a woman to reach that age unmarried. The deaths of two defendants, Marra Hathorne and Sarah Avery were recorded in 1676, perhaps as a result of Metacomet's War.

Mary Sheffield provides some clues about the possible fates of women convicted of fornication but the information in her case is anomalous in that the births of her two illegitimate children were entered in the Ipswich Vital Statistics under her name in 1658 and 1662. Usually if the birth was recorded, and it seldom was, it was recorded under the father's name. It is possible that this was because she was a widow and had feme sole status; however, there is no trace of a prior marriage. At her first presentment, Sheffield was whipped.[8] In the second instance in 1662, the father was named and required to pay child support. This time Sheffield was severely whipped. She died intestate 22 years later at John Edwards's house. He had "disbursed money for her in her life time and in her sickness."[9] There is no evidence that she was related to Edwards, or to his wife, so one possible inference is that she worked as their servant until her illness. Her son, James, would have been twenty-six then if he were alive; her daughter, Sarah, had died at twenty-two months.

Public assistance was required for some of the women who bore illegitimate children. Rebecca Outen had an illegitimate child in 1669 when she was Zebulon Hill's servant. By 1673, she was working for Samuel Williams. In 1679, she had a second illegitimate child. At this point she must have become unable to support herself because Richard Tree and his wife, Joanna, of Salem agreed to support her for life and raise her illegitimate daughter until the age of eighteen.[10]

A second fornication defendant, Sarah Lambert, can be traced through the Salem town records from 1657 onward. Over a period of ten years during her childhood she lived in at least six households. She may have been mentally or physically handicapped because the town had to pay more money at each move. It should have been expected that the cost of her maintenance would be reduced as she grew older and was able to contribute her labor to the household in which she was placed. Henry Herrick had received £5 in 1657: Mr. William Brown got £10 in 1666. The following year she had her first illegitimate child who joined her on public support. A second illegitimate child was added to the rolls in 1679. She was still receiving public support in 1696. In 1691, Alister Greime, the father of both her children, was also forced to turn to public relief.

Forty percent of the women who bore illegitimate children were described in the court records as servants. This designation is not, in itself, an indication of low economic status. Their status was dependent on the type of service contract they had signed. Indentured servants, locked into a five- to seven-year contract, often in return for their transAtlantic passage, were at the lowest end of the social and economic scale. They were the most vulnerable, since they often possessed no male relatives in Essex County. Also, since a partner would have been required to buy out the remainder of their indenture, the pregnant servant represented a drain on the suitor's resources, which would not be balanced by a dowry.

Young women who had been orphaned or who came from large families with numerous children and few economic assets with which to dower them were similarly circumstanced. A disproportionate number of women in this category bore illegitimate children and were whipped, as were male indentured servants. While Puritan jurists were prepared to issue a fine in the period after 1660 if there had been a possibility of marriage formation, engaging in sexual intercourse while bound to a long-term indenture usually resulted in corporal punishment for both women and men.

Approximately one-half of the women who bore illegitimate children came from families with middling or higher status. A defining characteristic of pregnant elite daughters, and to a lesser extent the daughters of prosperous middling families, was their youth at the time of their conviction. Despite their elite status, many of them were working as servants when they became pregnant. The difference between them and indentured servants is the length of their service contract, or even the lack of a contract, and the status of the household in which they were employed. The families of these women possessed the financial resources to convert an illegitimate pregnancy into a premarital pregnancy if their partners were single and amenable.

Many of the female defendants who were designated in the court records as servants were accompanied to court by their fathers. Some, like Anne Chase of Newbury in 1670, whose father, Aquilla Chase, could have afforded to keep her at home, had worked for at least three families by age 22.[11] Like many daughters of middling families, she was working in the household of a relative who could be expected to supervise her carefully, when she conceived. Mary Dane, a sixteen-year-old girl from Ipswich who was whipped for fornication in 1654, and who was described as a servant, was the daughter of John Dane, one of Ipswich's most respected citizens. Most girls, by the age of fifteen, were put out, as they would have been had their families remained in England, to a series of households, often those of relatives, usually of equivalent or higher status, to gain the skills they would be required to possess when it came time to manage their own households.

Ninety-nine men were summoned by the judges of Essex County Quarterly Court between 1640 and 1692 to answer paternity charges. Four of these men were summoned twice. They were summoned because a woman, during labor, had told the midwife that they, and no other man, had fathered their child. Thirty-eight faced formal fornication charges. Three had their cases dismissed. Thirty-five men (35 percent) were convicted of fornication, either because the offense occurred prior to 1668 or they were married at the time of their trial. In certain instances, they were convicted because they were indentured servants or apprentices.[12] The selective prosecution of men who were not in a position to marry their partners illustrates Puritan attempts to restrict sexual intercourse to procreative activity within the framework of legal marriage. Furthermore, the prosecutions targeted the weakest men. These were men who presented the least threat to the patriarchal ideal because they were not established members of the Puritan community, either because of their ages or their financial conditions. Moreover, if they were indentured servants or apprentices they had violated their contracts by engaging in sexual activity in the first place, and if they were already married, they had sufficiently violated Puritan norms to make them appropriate targets.

Engaging in intercourse for sensual gratification where there was no possibility of marriage was a sinful indulgence that provoked the wrath of Essex County judges. As long as the possibility of family formation existed, the Court seems to have been more lenient with male defendants. It has been asserted that Puritans rejected the traditional sexual double standard, and this seems apparent from judicial activity in the 1630s.[13] But while the idea that men and women had an equal duty to be chaste prior to marriage may have survived in an ideological sense throughout the seventeenth-century, it ceased to impact the day-to-day administration of justice in Essex County after the initial decade of settlement.[14]

The treatment of male sexual offenders in Massachusetts Bay Colony represented a departure from the traditional double standard. Societies that had a strong sexual double standard, like England or Virginia, had higher illegitimacy rates than New England because men who had property and power could seduce and/or force sexually exploitable servants and slaves without fear of punishment. The low numbers of women who bore illegitimate children or married while pregnant in New England suggests that men perceived the consequences to themselves to be severe enough to depress levels of extramarital sexual intercourse. Religious and cultural strictures on extramarital sexual intercourse, the possibility of public exposure, the lack of opportunity, or a combination of these factors, inhibited most men from sexual intercourse prior to their marriages. If however, they were named during labor by unwed mothers, they were less likely to face formal fornication prosecutions and received more lenient sentences from the Essex County Quarterly Court judges; evidence of a modified sexual double standard. Social disapprobation and the temporary loss of honor were the consequences of fathering a bastard. While in seventeenth-century Massachusetts Bay Colony these were not inconsequential, they were not commensurate with the penalties paid by women.

The age distribution of male fornication defendants (see Table 2) follows a different pattern than the women.[15] Only 13 percent of the male defendants were younger than twenty, while 45 percent of the female defendants fell into this category. The largest group of men charged with paternity included those between the ages of 21 and 26 (45 percent), a time at which their more prosperous peers could begin to anticipate the commencement of marital sexual activity. The second largest category were men over the age of 30 (33 percent), most of whom were already married. The second smallest age group of offenders, those between the ages of 27 and 29 (11 percent) was composed of economically marginal men, who, unlike most of their peers, had been unable to marry.

It is difficult to arrive at an estimate of the economic status of the majority of men charged with fathering illegitimate children. Assessments for town and ministerial rates, which would provide the most accurate index of economic status, survive for only a few towns and for limited time periods, and provide insufficient information for accurate identification. Eight (9 percent) of the defendants are listed as servants in the court records. In addition, there is one slave and one Native American. The most measurable index of economic viability in seventeenth-century Essex County is the ability to marry. Four of the men married their partners within a few months of the trial, and three others married other women between the conception of their illegitimate child and the time their case came to trial. Nineteen of the men (20 percent) were already married when they engaged in coitus with a single woman. Thirty-five percent of the men married later, one-half of these within two years of their trial. We can infer, therefore, that these men possessed the economic assets to marry their partner had they wished to. We must remember, too, that 23 percent of the women were presented unaccompanied by a putative father. In these instances, the court may have chosen not to prosecute any one individual because the female defendant had a poor sexual reputation. Also possible, the father may have been a married man who reached a private financial arrangement with the mother to remain silent when interrogated by the midwife in order to protect his reputation. If this is the case, the percentage of married men fathering illegitimate children would be higher than the 20 percent that could be documented. Forty-six percent of the men named as fathers do not appear to have married in New England prior to 1700.[16] Either they were transients when the child was conceived, left the colony to escape a paternity conviction, died, made an unrecorded marriage, or, most likely, never accumulated enough capital to marry.

Three conclusions can be drawn from the statistics in this and the previous paragraph about the men who fathered illegitimate children: (1) a few Essex County men chose to engage in casual sex with women who were, on the whole, significantly younger than themselves, (2) they engaged in this sexual activity without any intention of marriage, either because they were already married or they were not in a financial position to marry, and (3) sexual activity that resulted in illegitimate children cannot be characterized simply as the outcome of teenagers having sex with teenagers.

Prior to 1668, 27 women and 17 men were convicted of fornication. In 1668 an amendment was passed to shift the burden of supporting bastards from local communities to putative fathers. From this point on, men were responsible for the support of their illegitimate children: "though not to any other punishment."[17] Between 1668 and 1685, 77 women and 15 men were convicted of fornication. After 1668, while the established pattern of conviction remained constant for female defendants, only 19 of the men who engaged in sexual intercourse without the possibility of marriage formation were presented, and four were not convicted.

Despite the fact that enjoining marriage and fines had preceded corporal punishment in the hierarchy of sentencing in the fornication law as written in 1641, whipping was the most common punishment accorded to women and men who bore illegitimate children prior to 1660. Seventy-five percent of the women and 53 percent of the men who were convicted were whipped. However, sentencing patterns prior to 1660 were not as egalitarian as the percentages suggest. There were gradations in whipping sentences. Women were more likely than their male partners to receive a severe whipping (15 stripes). After 1660, women and men were customarily given the option of paying a fine, which varied from £2 to £6, to avoid corporal punishment. It is difficult to arrive at the precise value, in present-day terms, of a fornication fine, but for women it appears to be the equivalent of a year's wages. Given the more limited financial resources of many of the female defendants and their lower salaries, paying a fine meant committing themselves to a longer term of service, since their masters paid it for them. There was an element of self-interest in this for employers. A servant who had been whipped was incapable of performing her household responsibilities for some time afterward. Added to this was the labor lost during pregnancy and childbirth, which was recouped through a lengthened period of employment without compensation. Only 16 women received the less shameful sentence of a fine only. Fourteen of the 16 fines were levied between 1679 and 1685 when 50 percent of the female defendants escaped a potential whipping. Yet, when male and female sentencing patterns between 1660 and 1685 are compared, 20 percent of the female defendants and 78 percent of the male defendants were allowed to pay fines without the added possibility of a whipping.

Table 3 summarizes fornication convictions and punishments in five-year intervals from 1641 to 1685. It shows that women were charged and convicted of fornication with greater frequency than men. Nevertheless, the fact that numbers indicate women paid a disparate penalty for sexual misconduct is not, in and of itself, proof that gender was the major determinant in sentencing. Was it because most women worked as servants and

Table 3 Fornication Convictions for Women Who Bore Illegitimate Children and Their Partners in Essex County Quarterly Court, 1641–1685

Years	Women (N = 104)		Men (N = 35)	
	Convicted	Whipped	Convicted	Whipped
1641–1645	2	2	3	1
1646–1650	2	2	1	0
1651–1655	6	5	5	3
1656–1660	10	5	5	4
1661–1665	3	1	1	0
1666–1670	10	3	5	1
1671–1675	18	3	6	0
1676–1680	24	5	7	2
1681–1685	29	0	2	0

judges deferred to property-owning men of higher status? Or, was it the effect of Puritan gender ideology which ascribed to women inferior status and uncontrollable sexual appetites? In order to determine the weight accorded by the judges to the class and gender of the defendants during sentencing it is necessary to look at the sentences in individual cases and compare the status of both defendants and the decision rendered by the judges in each case.

Class and gender were both important determinants of sentencing patterns, but it is difficult to determine the precise roles they played at a distance of 350 years. The sheer number of the cases and the complexity of individual circumstances make it difficult to quantify these data. Furthermore, judges were likely influenced by information about the defendants that has not survived in the records. They knew the defendants and their families personally. They were privy to local gossip and they were able to observe the defendant's demeanor in court.

Some sentencing patterns are clear. In the 1630s men were punished more severely than their female partners. Between 1640 and 1660, the court punished both partners severely. Men and women of marriageable age tended to pick sexual partners of equivalent rank, a pattern that was replicated in each decade studied. Where the defendants were equal in status the female partner usually received a harsher sentence. In the early years of settlement then, gender appears to be the primary determinant in sentencing patterns. Men bore the brunt of the punishment in the 1630s, women in the 1640s and 1650s. After 1665, the number of women convicted in each five-year period increased rapidly, while men benefited from an amended fornication law passed in 1668. From this point on only men whose sexual behavior egregiously offended Puritan sexual mores were charged with fornication.

The 1668 law that excluded men from fornication charges clearly privileged men. After 1668, if they were single, and were neither indentured nor apprenticed, they were free to engage in sexual intercourse with no other penalty than child-support payments should they be unlucky enough to get their partner pregnant. Their female partner paid child support too if the child was fostered out. In that sense they were treated equally. The female partner, however, was whipped or paid a fine as well. It would seem that gender had become an even more important factor in sentencing fornicators after 1668. In order to determine if this is so, it is necessary to analyze sentencing patterns by decade.

In the first decade of settlement, when it was discovered that a single woman was pregnant, her male partner was assumed to have initiated the sexual activity, and he was punished. Between 1630 and 1639 seventeen men and only two women were charged with sexual offenses in Massachusetts Bay Colony.[19] A typical entry in the Court of Assistants docket book records that: "John Jones, for defiling his wife before marriage was fined 20s8d."[20] Judicial leniency was predicated on the fact that the couple had married by the time of their court appearance. Another Court of Assistants entry shows the length to which the Court went to ensure that the couple married and their desire to preserve the anonymity of the woman:

> John Vaughn, having defiled ____ and refusing to marry her was committed to prison til he should give sufficient security to provide both for the mother and the child, or marry her whom he hath defiled.[21]

If the couple, however, had not married or was unable to marry for some reason, the woman faced the same punishment as her partner. Since Robert Huitt and Mary Ridge had not married by the time they appeared in court in 1632, Ridge lost her anonymity and both were ordered to be whipped.[22]

A case in 1638 foreshadows the Court's treatment of single women who admitted to having engaged in sexual intercourse, however reluctantly. Alice Burwood, a Boston servant, went to the authorities and told them that John Bickerstaff, also a servant, had raped her. Despite the coerced nature of the intercourse as Burwood described it, she was whipped for: "yielding to John Bickerstaff without crying out and concealing it for nine or ten days."[23] It cannot have been much of a comfort to her that Bickerstaff received fifteen lashes to her ten. Her employer was so affronted by her sexual activity and the subsequent stain on her character, and by inference his household government, that a court order was required to force him to receive her back into his house after the whipping.

The first fornication case tried by the Essex County Quarterly Court was the presentation of Robert Coaker and Miriam Moulton of Newbury in December, 1641. They had engaged in sexual intercourse and then had married other persons. It was as Miriam King of Hampton that Moulton was presented for fornication. The court punished Coaker, not King, in coy terms when it rendered its verdict in December 1642:

> Robert Coaker betrothed himself too securely to one maiden, and then contracted with another woman. To be severely whipped."[24]

Besides no mention of fornication in the court's verdict, Moulton was not named; she was categorized as a maiden, and her husband, Thomas King, received £5 from Robert Coaker. Whether the money was compensation for the loss of Moulton's virginity, King's honor, or child support, is not spelled out, but to those involved it must have been so apparent that no explanation was necessary.

This case contrasts sharply with Essex County's second fornication prosecution less than three years later which involved a married man, Edward Flint, whose wife had remained in England, and his servant Alice Williams.[25] Flint's case was referred to the Court of Assistants where he was fined £20 for "having gotten a slut with child."[26] Ten pounds of his fine was given to the town of Salem to ensure that the child would not become the financial responsibility of Salem taxpayers. Williams was fined £5 and whipped. While Moulton had been regarded as a "maiden" and not punished, Williams was called "slut" and punished both corporally and financially. It is true that Moulton was contracted to Coaker and expected to be married to him when they had sexual intercourse, and Williams was a young servant who had sexual intercourse with her older, married master whom she could have no expectation of marrying.[27] The conditions under which the sexual activity occurred should have accorded some sympathy from the court for Williams. Williams was in a dependent relationship: her master was a sexual predator. Flint was forty-one, the brother of Mr. Thomas Flint, a magistrate and deputy to the Court of Assistants. Williams was a teenager, the daughter of a gentleman, Mr. William Williams, who had removed from Salem to Watertown in 1641. Williams, however, was branded a "slut," whipped, and fined. Flint was tried by the Court of Assistants, not the Essex County Quarterly Court that Williams faced, and, unlike his partner, avoided the shame inherent in a public whipping.

This case illustrates the difficulty of separating class and gender when assigning causality to the jury's decision to whip or fine defendants. Did Flint escape a whipping because he was a gentleman, or, at least the brother of an influential gentleman? Probably. Was Williams whipped because she was a servant or because she was a woman, a "slut?" Probably both factors played a role. Governor Winthrop's reaction to the child abuse case involving the daughters of John Humphrey had demonstrated the Puritan belief that even girls were capable of behaving in a sexually provocative manner. Given the general trend of Essex County jurists to hold women to a higher standard of blame in fornication cases over the course of the seventeenth-century, the gender of the defendant mattered.

Why did the greater share of the blame for initiating sexual activity switch from men to women at the end of the first decade of settlement? A number of reasons seem plausible. Ann Hutchinson introduced the Puritan authorities to a new kind of woman. Charismatic, independent, ultimately heretical, her activities challenged their notion of Puritan womanhood and backlash was inevitable. Also, from a legal standpoint, it was clearly inappropriate to punish her husband for her heresies because from the Puritan point of view he was incapable of controlling her. This may have opened the door to punishing women for sexual misdemeanors.

Another possible cause: the details of the child sexual abuse case involving the daughters of John Humphrey, a member of the Massachusetts Bay Colony elite, demonstrated to Winthrop and other Puritan legislators that even young girls could be a source of temptation. Beginning when Dorcas Humphrey was seven, her sister, Sarah, five, they were abused by their father's servants for a period of two years, after which Winthrop reported, "[Dorcas} was grown capable of man's fellowship and took pleasure in it."[28] When her father left the colony, the girls were sent to live with Jenkin Davis, a former servant of Humphrey's, in Lynn. Davis was "a member of the church there and in good esteem for sobriety and piety" whose wife was pregnant and "scrupulous of having fellowship with her husband in that condition." Winthrop reports that Davis fought against temptation but "he was hurried by the strength of lust" and abused the elder daughter for a year.[29] Modern psychological theory suggests that Dorcas may have acted in a provocative manner while in the Davis household because of the prior abuse. Winthrop articulates the Puritan belief that women were innately lustful and that their sexual appetites, once aroused, were uncontrollable. He believed that Dorcas had been the instigator of the sexual activity with Davis. If a ten-year-old child could tempt a church member, what might a fully grown woman be capable of?

Further, the population of Massachusetts Bay Colony increased from 1000 fully committed Puritans who arrived in the Winthrop fleet of 1630 to 20,000 by 1640. Likely, communal cohesiveness lessened as the settlers moved out of their dugouts and wigwams into more traditional permanent structures. New towns were established at a distance from the original settlements, and non-Puritan settlers moved into the colony in greater numbers. Winthrop wrote in his journal in 1640 that:

> as people increased, so sin abounded, and especially the sin of uncleanness, and still the providence of God found them out.[30]

In addition, there had been no written code of laws in the initial decade of settlement in Massachusetts Bay and the Court of Assistants had made their decisions based on the circumstances of individual cases. If the lack of an official legal code had allowed flexibility in their treatment of female sexual offenders, it was lost.

The authorities wanted to execute the Boston servants who had initiated the sexual abuse of Dorcas and Sarah Humphrey, but they lacked the legal authority. This impelled them to write the first formal law code, the *The Laws and Liberties of Massachusetts*, issued in December 1641. The fornication statute stated that:

> It is ordered by this Court and the Authority thereof; That if any man Commit Fornication with any single Woman, they shall be punished, either by enjoining Marriage, or Fine, or Corporal punishment, or all, or any of these, as the Judges of the Court that hath Cognizance of the Cause shall appoint.[31]

The formulators of the Laws and Liberties encouraged fornicators to marry. Where marriage was impossible due to unfinished indentures or a lack of financial resources essential to the establishment of an independent household, or a prior marriage on the part of the man involved, the law provided for public corporal punishment or the payment of a £5 fine.

Carol F. Karlsen argues that the relative scarcity of women during the 1630s ensured that the court would treat them more leniently.[32] Perhaps, however, the court is making a legal distinction. Since the couples who were charged were married by the time of their court appearance, the women were femes covert and their husbands responsible for their actions. Still, there is a definite rhetorical and attitudinal shift at the end of the first decade of settlement. The onus for initiating sexual activity switched from men to women after the decade of the 1630s.

During the 1640s there were only four cases of illegitimate fornication in Essex County, and while all four women were convicted and whipped, only two men were convicted, and one, Robert Coaker, was whipped. In two of the instances where the men escaped a whipping, they were of equivalent status to the female defendant. Clearly, as early as the 1640s the Court believed that women bore greater responsibility for engaging in illicit sexual activity and deserved more rigorous punishment.

The trend to punish female defendants more severely than their male partners is discernable in the 1650s when the number of women convicted of illegitimate fornication increased to 16. The number of men convicted of fornication in the decade of the 1650s remained constant at one-half of the number of women convicted. The larger number of convictions in the 1650s provides an opportunity to address the issue of whether women paid a disproportionate penalty in fornication sentencing because of their class or their gender. In five of the 16 women's cases during the 1650s, no men were presented. It does not appear, however, that the court punished these women unduly for not naming their partner, because two of them escaped with a fine. In two of the 16 cases, men were punished more severely than their female partners.[33] In two more cases, both partners were given the same sentence. However, in 75 percent of the cases where the female defendant named her male partner, the female defendant received a more severe sentence than the male defendant, or the male defendant was not prosecuted. For example, Mary Dane, a pregnant sixteen-year-old servant, was sentenced to be whipped in 1654 after the birth of her illegitimate child.[34] She was also ordered to pay for its upbringing. Her partner, Jeffrey Sknelling, had been fined in 1649 for "defects in watching" and whipped for "divers lies and bound to good behavior for suspicion of filthiness" in 1650.[35] In spite of his previous convictions and the age of the female defendant, he was fined rather than whipped and not required to pay child support. Gender was a more significant factor when determining punishment, since women were more likely than their partners to be charged with fornication, and once charged, received heavier sentences.

When class and occupational status are considered during the decade of the 1650s, the situation becomes more complex. The fact that the pregnancy that precipitated a fornication trial was illegitimate, not premarital, was an indication that the female defendant and her partner, where named, lacked the financial resources to marry. This makes class an inevitable factor in creating a vulnerable population of female servants and poor men looking for a sexual outlet outside of marriage. Fifty percent of both male and female defendants appear to be servants, but, in three of the four cases where both partners can be identified as servants, women were sentenced to be severely whipped (15 stripes) and their partners to be whipped (10 stripes). In the fourth instance, the male partner was bound to good behavior; his partner whipped.

In only one of the 16 cases presented in the decade of the 1650s was there a clear disparity in class between the male and female defendant. Richard Brabrooke was a thirty-nine-year-old married man when he impregnated his servant, Alice Ellis. He was severely whipped; Alice Ellis was whipped and freed from her indenture. Brabrooke was treated with greater severity by the court than his servant and he was ordered to raise his daughter by Ellis in his own household with his wife and legitimate children. Named Mehitabel, she is one of the few children born illegitimately whose life can be traced.

By the age of 16, her stepmother had declared her incorrigible and Mehitabel had been put out to another household. That year, she burned her employer's house down. She claimed that she had been standing outside the house smoking a pipe, and somehow, the house had caught fire. The court, having reason to believe that she was not as innocent as she professed to be, ordered her severely whipped and fined her £40, a sum her father would have been required to pay for her. She married John Downing, 12 years her senior, and one of Essex County's less solid citizens that same year with a dowry consisting of half of Brabrooke's farm. Subsequently, Mehitabel Downing was convicted of drunkenness after she was found passed out in the road. It is probable that other illegitimate children experienced similar emotional problems. Both Mehitabel Downing and her stepmother were jailed for witchcraft in Salem in 1692.

Chapter Three

"Priscilla Was Fined, the Child Died": A Quantitative Analysis of Illegitimate Fornication Prosecutions in the Essex County Quarterly Court, 1666–1685

> Mr. Samuel Appleton, Jr., and Priscilla Willson were presented for fornication, And said Samuell denying it was dismissed, paying half the costs. Priscilla was fined, The child died and Appleton was ordered to pay half the cost to Mr. Purchass.[1]

This terse entry in the Essex County Quarterly Court docket book in 1683 conceals a complex series of events that had broad economic and social ramifications beyond the bare fact that Priscilla Willson, a sixteen-year-old orphan, was convicted of fornication and Mr. Samuel Appleton, a twenty-nine-year-old newly-wed, was not. An examination of the evidence presented in this trial, the verdict, and the outcomes of contemporary fornication trials make possible some conclusions about the nature and extent of extramarital sexual activity in Essex County between 1666 and 1685. One notices immediately that Willson and Appleton met disparate fates at the hands of the judges (one of whom was Appleton's father). Also, that there was a significant age differential. These are all too common features of fornication presentations where an out-of-wedlock pregnancy was not followed by marriage.

Appleton's response to Priscilla Willson's childbirth declaration of paternity and the testimony of two young servants who had seen Appleton climb into a four-poster bed occupied by an ill Willson and pull the bed curtains closed, was to deny the charge. The child's death in its first month meant that Mr. Samuel Appleton's honor could be salved at little cost. He was required to pay one half of the infant's expenses; Willson's grandfather, Mr. Oliver Purchis the second half, and Willson's fine. Appleton was representative of a new ethos developing in Essex County beginning in the 1660s, a transitional decade. He was a church member and an entrepreneur who was engaged in a struggle with Willson's grandfather for control of the defunct Saugus Ironworks. He was a member of the third generation of Appletons to settle in Essex County and he had no scruples about lying to protect his good name and his marriage.

Legislative changes enacted in the decade of the 1660s released men from the burden of a fornication prosecution. It had become difficult to gain a conviction, because few men were willing to admit to engaging in extramarital sexual intercourse. Thirteen women were convicted of fornication in the 1660s. Eleven of the women named a male partner, but only five of the named men were summoned to answer charges of fornication or to make child-support arrangements, although these five were all convicted. Four of the men were fined; the fifth, William Reeves, a servant, was sentenced to be whipped and fined. He argued that, being fatherless, he had not had the proper direction and begged to have his whipping remitted. His partner, Susannah Durin, also a servant, was given the option of paying a £4 fine. At first glance, it seems that the court treated Reeves more severely than Durin, but Reeves "had several other misdemeanors to his account" besides fornication.[2] One other pair of servants was presented. She was whipped; he was fined. It becomes more difficult to separate class and gender as determinants of punishment in this decade, but where class is equivalent, as in the two cases above, all circumstances being equal, women were punished more severely.

Marguerite Dudley bore an illegitimate child in 1664. She was not charged. Her name appeared in the course of a paternity suit against the man she named as the father of her child, Francis Pafat, who fled Essex County, forfeiting a £36 bond rather than face presentation. Dudley was very well-connected. Her father was Andover's minister and her grandfather had been Governor of Massachusetts Bay Colony. Clearly class, in the form of the desire not to embarrass the Dudley's more than necessary, played a role here.

In two more instances in this decade, there was a clear disparity in class between fornication defendants. In these cases, the male partner was of superior rank since the women named their employers as the fathers of their children. In the first case, Mary Sheffield was whipped. Her employer, Isaiah Wood, was required to pay child support. But even here, a clear-cut distinction cannot be drawn as this was Sheffield's second conviction. A good argument can be made on Sheffield's behalf that given the difficulties her poor sexual reputation must have created in securing employment, she had little choice but to yield to Wood in order to retain her job. Clearly, from the Puritan point of view, Sheffield fit their profile of a woman who had had her sexual appetites aroused in an untimely fashion and had become dangerously promiscuous.

In the second case, forty-seven-year-old Henry Jacques impregnated his servant, Elnor Knight. Jacques abused a position of trust because Knight was his wife's niece and her parents undoubtedly considered the Jacques household to be secure. Jacques had been the Newbury constable three years earlier, so he was not without knowledge of the processes involved in a fornication trial. He chose to flee from Essex County, leaving behind a wife and seven children rather than face Elnor's parents and his neighbors after he was summoned to answer charges of fornication. He returned two months later after the court threatened to seize £30 of his estate and disenfranchise him. Like Knight, who had since married Richard Bryer, he was fined. In this instance Jacques and Knight received equal treatment from the court. While Knight was a servant, it is likely that her family was equivalent in status to that of Jacques and Knight had married prior to her court appearance and established herself and her baby within a legitimate family structure.

In 1665, the Court of Assistants was obliged to address: "the seeming contradiction between the Laws titled Fornication and titled Punishment as written in the Laws and Liberties."[3] The punishment section of the Laws and Liberties had placed restrictions on corporal punishment. The law said that "gentlemen" could not be whipped. As well, corporal punishment was only to be used in cases where there was no other applicable punishment: "unless his Crime be very shameful, and his course of life vicious and profligate."[4] Apparently some had felt that the crime of fornication did not rise to the level required for the imposition of corporal punishment against a gentleman.

The 1665 revision stated that fornication was such a grievous offense, "a particular Crime, a shameful Sin, much increasing among us," that nothing in the Punishment section of the law code prohibited quarterly courts from imposing corporal punishment. Even gentlemen were to be whipped if the court deemed the circumstances of their case to be egregious. To reinforce the seriousness of fornication as a crime against the Commonwealth an additional clause was added threatening disenfranchisement as the result of a fornication conviction, although it does not appear that this penalty was ever enforced.

In 1668 the legislature issued a new fornication law. In order to relieve local communities of the support of bastards a procedure was established under which an assignment of paternity could be made.[5] Any man named by a woman during childbirth was held to be the true father and liable for support payments.[6] The assignment of paternity, however, would not be followed by a fornication charge. In this way, men who denied paternity might be assessed child-support payments but would escape a fornication conviction. There was no equivalent judicial relief from prosecution for women. Between the passage of this law and 1685, while 77 women who bore illegitimate children were convicted of fornication, only 15 of their partners were found equally guilty.

A typical case is that of Sarah Wait in 1685. She was fined for fornication, and Joseph Burnam, whom she had accused of fathering her child while she was in labor, was assigned child-support payments, the: "court having great grounds to fear he was not so innocent as he pretended."[7] Prior to 1668, the Court might have charged both Wait and Burnam with fornication, but if Burnam had denied the fact, it would have been difficult, if not impossible, to secure a conviction, and the town of Ipswich might have found itself liable to support the infant. After 1668, despite Burnam's denials, the court could compel him to pay child support and in return Burnam could escape a fornication charge. The 1668 amendment that relieved men who did not marry their partners from fornication prosecutions was an important watershed. Massachusetts chose to prioritize the financial support of bastards over the punishment of men who engaged in sexual intercourse outside of marriage.

One could argue that the decision to go after child support showed Puritan respect for the laws of evidence and their unwillingness to convict an innocent man. A lesser standard of evidence, the woman's childbirth statement, was enough to legally assign child-support payments. One might ask why, if a childbirth statement was credible enough to assign paternity, it could not be used to prosecute men for fornication. Whatever the intent of the amendment, the effect was to place single women at the center of fornication prosecutions and to reinforce in the public mind the popular belief that women, not men, bore the ultimate responsibility for the initiation of sexual intercourse.

On paper, prior to 1668, the fornication laws appear to be equitable. Marriage was officially encouraged, equal punishments were assigned to men and women, a procedure for establishing paternity was outlined, and child support was mandated. In practice, as was demonstrated in chapter two, the system was weighted against single women, particularly propertyless single women, from the 1640s. After 1668, most single women who bore illegitimate children faced a fornication prosecution alone.

Three trends had appeared in the 1660s. First, fewer of the men (50 percent) named during labor by their female partners were charged with fornication than in previous decades in accord with the 1668 amendment. It is clear that while the amendment was not passed until 1668, it reflected a codification of existing practice. However, the amendment should have occasioned references to child support in the court records but child support is specifically mentioned only in the case of Isaiah Wood. While Francis Pafat forfeited a £36 bond when he fled, and William Reeves was required to give Salem £30 to guarantee the support of his child, no child-support arrangements were recorded for the remaining ten women who bore illegitimate children in this decade. Second, the stereotypical female defendant was no longer an indentured servant. At least seven of the 13 women who were convicted of fornication were from established Essex County families. The partners they named were of equivalent status. Third, corporal punishment for fornication decreased. Only three women (one a repeat offender) and one man were whipped in the decade of the 1660s. Most paid fines, the amount varying from 50 shillings to £5. One constant remained. Women were more likely to be tried and convicted. Once convicted, they received more severe sentences.

The 1670s, like the 1650s, presented a dramatic leap in the pace of fornication prosecutions from the previous decade. The number of women convicted in the 1670s increased threefold over that of the 1660s (42 versus 13). Of note, while the number of convictions increased substantially, the class of the fornication defendants compared to previous time periods remained relatively constant. Fifty-two percent of the women presented (22) in the 1670s were servants with few or no economic resources.[8] Fifteen of these 22 servants named their partners and sentencing data are available in thirteen of the cases. Five of the 13 women were whipped. (Although, in three of the five cases, the court had reason; it was the defendants' second presentation for fornication.) Of the 13 men convicted in this decade, only two, both servants, were whipped. One of them had exacerbated his crime by fleeing. The other, Joss, was black; his partner was white. His color, not his gender or status, was the major factor in sentencing. Three other male servants were fined. One was an indentured servant with one year left to serve, and his partner, who was whipped, may have been a relative of his master.[9] Another was an eighteen-year-old youth whose partner had a previous fornication conviction, which would have suggested to the court that he was after recreational sex, not marriage.

Here, as in previous decades, married men were generally held to a higher standard of accountability than single men. One was ordered to be whipped or fined and to return to his wife, an equivalent sentence to that of his female partner. The second married man was Lawrence Clinton, whose troubled marriage to Rachel Haffield brought him into court on a regular basis. He and his partner, Mary Wooden, also received equivalent sentences; both were whipped. Curiously, in a strange turn of events, the whipper, Jonas Gregory, was sentenced to be whipped himself for: "not performing the duty of his office upon Lawrence Clinton."[10] He had not whipped Clinton as forcefully as was customary. Wooden and Clinton married later in Rhode Island.

It may be that married men are not adequately represented in the sample since six female servants did not name their partners. Three of the women, however, were repeat offenders, so it is more likely that they failed to bring a man into court because they lacked credibility. In at least one case, that of Rachel Whinnisk, who had been reduced to begging to support her child, there is evidence of coercion. In 1681, two young wives operating in their female inquisitor role went to the magistrates to depose that they had asked Whinnisk why she did not charge Hugh Alley with paternity to get maintenance for her child. Whinnisk had answered that Alley's two sisters had threatened to burn her if she laid the child to him.[11]

The remaining 20 women (48 percent) who were presented may have worked in other persons' households as servants but they were from families of middling rank. Six of the women had fathers who left estates worth more than £250, held local office, or rank in the militia. Did their fathers' ranks and probable acquaintances with the judges mean that the court accorded them special treatment? Four were given the option of paying a fine and a fifth was sentenced to be whipped and fined because she named a putative father, recanted, and refused to name another. The sixth woman was a widow, Sarah Needham. Her father, Walter Fairfield was a prosperous innkeeper, and she had an illegitimate child with Mr. Philip Parsons.[12] Neither she nor Parsons bothered to dignify the charges with an appearance at court. Each forfeited their bonds for appearance and suffered no further recorded punishment.

Twenty-six women were convicted of fornication between 1681 and 1685.[13] Three more women were summoned, but they, like Sarah Needham, did not appear at court. Three men were presented for fornication during this same period. One, John Tucker, was an eighteen-year-old who had sexual intercourse with his family's servant, Ann Gilbert. This type of sexual activity, where there was no possibility of marriage formation, was just what the court wanted to discourage. Both were sentenced to be severely whipped but their sentences were reduced to fines after Tucker and his mother petitioned the court for a reduction in sentences and begged "their honors prayers for all that god would show up the evil of our ways and turn our hearts to him."[14]

The other two men presented between 1681 and 1685 had their cases dismissed. In the first instance, the dismissal was justified because the female defendant, an eighteen-year-old servant, vacillated in her testimony. While she had finally named Ralph Farnum, the son of a substantial farmer, there was reason to believe her illegitimate child had been fathered by her employer's married son. However, in the second case, that of Priscilla Willson and Mr. Samuel Appleton, there was a considerable amount of evidence against Appleton. Appleton denied the charges and was dismissed on his word as a gentleman. In this instance it is clear that the status of the male defendant was the primary sentencing factor, but this was an anomaly. Appleton was the only male defendant presented between 1640 and 1685 who bore the prefix "Mr." designating him to be a gentleman. That he was presented in the first instance, attested to the influence of the female defendant's grandfather, Oliver Purchis. Three other married men fathered illegitimate children between 1681 and 1685 but none were presented.

Between 1686 and 1692, the court records are incomplete, and in many instances there is no clear disposition of the cases. However, some inferences can be drawn. The trend to hold women more responsible for illicit sexual activity became more pronounced. While at least 34 women were presented for fornication and, where the sentence is known, they were usually fined 40 shillings, only one man, Robert Roe, was convicted of fornication. Roe was prosecuted for the same reason that other men had been singled out for prosecution prior to 1685. His partner, Mary Payne, had a prior conviction for fornication, so the court acted on the assumption that Roe had sexual gratification, not marriage, in mind when he had intercourse with Payne.

Comparative data on fornication convictions and court-ordered child support was obtained by looking at change over time using percentages. Table 4 illustrates that, in general, as the conviction rate for male fornication defendants decreased, the rate at which court-ordered child support was assigned increased, although it never rose above 55 percent in any decade.

At best, during the decade of the 1670s, little more than half of the fathers assumed financial responsibility for their illegitimate children. Between 1681 and 1685, the last period for which convictions and child-support agreements can be counted, both convictions of male defendants and court-ordered child support decreased. Of course, child-support arrangements may have been arranged in private through negotiation, so this is not a reliable statistic. The 1668 amendment that required men to pay child support and allowed them to escape punishment compromised the moral intent of the original law passed in 1641. It is to be hoped that it was an economic success. While child support may have been collected assiduously from that

Table 4 Conviction and Court-Ordered Child-Support Rates for Men Accused of Fathering Illegitimate Children in Essex County, 1641–1685

Years	Number Women Convicted	% Men Named	% Men Convicted	% Paying Child Support
1641–1650	4	100%	75%	25%
1651–1660	16	69%	100%	18%
1661–1670	13	77%	50%	20%
1671–1680	42	79%	33%	55%
1681–1685	26	77%	8%	35%[15]

point on, the Essex County court clerk's summaries of individual cases do not reflect an increased incidence of support payment orders.

A second manner of comparing the punishment of female and male fornication defendants is to look at the cumulative sentences assigned by the court to each sex. Men were more likely to receive the most extreme sentence, a severe whipping (20 percent to 9 percent), but 74 percent of the female defendants were subjected to potential corporal punishment compared with 54 percent of the male defendants. Given men's greater financial ability to pay fines in the first instance, the penalties are more weighted against women than the percentages, skewed as they are, suggest. Between 1630 and 1674 women earned 45 percent less than male farm workers. In the years 1674 to 1694, the wage disparity increased to 52 percent.[16] Thirty-one per cent of male defendants and 20 percent of female defendants were allowed to pay fines without the alternative threat of corporal punishment. It also needs to be borne in mind that the men who were prosecuted were the most egregious offenders of Puritan sexual morality so it should not be surprising that in the aggregate their sentences were more severe (see Table 5).

Three conclusions can be drawn from the sentencing data: (1) women paid a disproportionate penalty for bearing illegitimate children, being more likely to be charged and more likely to be convicted. Only one-third of the men who were named as fathers of illegitimate children were prosecuted for fornication, (2) where class was equivalent, women were punished with greater severity than their partners, and (3) men were more likely than women to be fined and, since they received higher wages, a fine represented a lesser burden to men in terms of the work-hours required to pay it.

Three conclusions can be drawn from the sentencing data: (1) women paid a disproportionate penalty for bearing illegitimate children, being more likely to be charged and more likely to be convicted. Only one-third of the men who were named as fathers of illegitimate children were prosecuted for

Table 5 Sentences Issued by the Essex County Quarterly Court to Male and Female Fornication Defendants, 1640–1685

Sentence	Men (N=35)	Women (N=102)
Severely Whipped and Fined	3%	0%
Severely Whipped	17%	9%
Severely Whipped or Fined	0%	9%
Whipped and Fined	0%	1%
Whipped	14%	18%
Whipped or Fined	20%	37%
Fined	26%	19%
Bound to Good Behavior	6%	0%
Watch Partner's Whipping	0%	1%
No Penalty Recorded	9%	1%
Did Not Appear	3%	5%

fornication, (2) where class was equivalent, women were punished with greater severity than their partners, and (3) men were more likely than women to be fined and, since they received higher wages, a fine represented a lesser burden to men in terms of the work-hours required to pay it.

Five broad conclusions about Puritan sexuality can be drawn from the quantitative data. First, the very low number of convictions does not indicate the existence of a sexually charged atmosphere in seventeenth-century Massachusetts if a sexually charged atmosphere is defined as one in which provocative behavior or sexual innuendo is acceptable behavior.[17] David Hackett Fischer says that relationships between men and women were "highly charged with sexual tension" because the courts assumed that if "healthy" men and women were alone together they would engage in coitus.[18] Unmarried people were carefully watched, as he suggests, but the community oversight suggests not the expectation that unsupervised persons would engage in sexual activity but the depth of Puritan fears about sexual activity between unmarried persons. The old stereotype of Puritans as joyless ideologies may be outdated, but even Edmund Morgan, while depicting Puritans as enthusiastically embracing the delights of marital sexuality, stated that they were "frankly hostile" to sexual intercourse prior to marriage.[19] It is anachronistic to assume that Puritan men and women possessed and expressed the same sexual appetites as twenty-first-century youth who are bombarded by sexual imagery in every aspect of their lives. In a society in which coitus interruptus was the only viable birth control measure and herbal remedies the only abortifacients, 104 illegitimate pregnancies over a

45-year period do not represent a large amount of sexual activity. Moreover, this was a society that actively sought to dampen youthful sexual appetites, placed a high premium on female chastity, and provided few opportunities for engaging in private sexual experimentation away from community oversight. We should not underestimate, either, the religious idealism of the Puritans and their commitment to the creation of a Biblical commonwealth in New England that would serve as an example to the rest of the world. Prior to 1670, less than one woman per year had an illegitimate child in Essex County, and while the numbers increased substantially over the last 22 years of this study, the population increased as well.

Second, women who worked as servants were vulnerable to sexual exploitation. About 40 percent of the female defendants were servants, indicating that in the normal course of events most Puritan women spent some part of their adolescence and early adulthood living in other people's houses. While community oversight was effective in public spaces, and courting activities were bound by accepted rituals, the type of relationships that produced illegitimate children occurred outside the normal course of events. When young women worked away from home learning housewifery skills, doing field work, or serving as household helps either on a short-term employment contract or a long-term indenture, they were in a space removed from both family and public oversight and the very factor that should have ensured their protection, their presence within a well-governed household, made them vulnerable if the household into which they had come was not well-regulated.

While we cannot assume that the 45 percent of women who were twenty years of age or younger were the victims of sexual predators, their age and their acculturation to Puritan religious norms and gender ideology make it a reasonable assertion in most instances. The remaining 55 percent of the women, those who were 21 years of age or older, who bore illegitimate children, were subject to similar conditions as the younger women. Their motives for entering into a sexual relationship, however, were probably more mixed, and their greater maturity may have allowed them to resist undesired sexual contact more assertively.

Third, bastard-bearing was not limited to the poorest segment of Puritan society. Women from all strata of Essex County bore illegitimate children. In each decade, approximately half of the women presented were of middling or elite rank. In most instances where their partners were identified, the male defendant was of equivalent rank to the female defendant. There is little evidence for the existence of a bastardy-prone sub-population of families, although some produced more than their share of illegitimate children. Nevertheless, they were not drawn exclusively from the lowest level of Puritan society. Three

Rowlandson sisters were prosecuted for fornication between 1684 and 1687. Their aunt, Mary Rowlandson, had become an authentic New England heroine when an account of her captivity during Metacomet's War had been published in 1682. Three Bridges brothers, the sons of Mr. Edmund Bridges, were convicted of fornication between 1657 and 1667. In neither instance was bastard-bearing replicated in a previous or future generation.

Fourth, in a period in which marriage represented the only female career opportunity, less than one-third of women who had borne an illegitimate child married subsequently. The loss of their sexual reputation severely impaired their ability to make a match. Those who did marry following a fornication conviction, often secured a husband of lower status than they could have been expected to find had they remained public virgins. Moreover, once married, their female in-laws were not likely to welcome them with open arms, nor was their readmittance to the women's community easy.

Fifth, women were sentenced more severely than men when the male and female defendants were of equivalent class. Moreover, even when male and female defendants were fined an equivalent sum, it required more work-hours for women to pay their fines than men. This is the most convincing evidence that Puritan statements that posited women as the lustful daughters of Eve, capable of the most egregious sexual offenses was more than popular rhetoric or Biblical cant. Puritan justices carried this belief system with them into the real-life world of the Essex County Quarterly Court.

The mechanics of punishment varied, with female defendants falling into two categories in regard to the course of their trials. The first group was composed of women who could afford to post a bond during their pregnancy to guarantee their appearance at Essex County Quarterly Court after delivery. Women with financial resources were able to take a pro-active stance, which was to their advantage since they would be presented by the local grand juryman in any case. Once a pregnancy had become visible and it was apparent that it would proceed to term, the pregnant woman, accompanied by a male relative or employer if possible, made an official complaint before one of the judges of the quarterly court who also served as local magistrates.

At this time, usually in the fifth or sixth month, the pregnant woman and her male representative would be required to post a bond, customarily £10, promising to appear in court after the birth of the child to press their complaint against the man they named as father. Within days, the magistrate summoned the putative father, asked him to confirm or deny the charge, and bound him over to appear in court after the birth of the child. This summons may have forced a marriage in some instances since, of 177 premarital fornication cases between 1640 and 1692, the average length of time elapsed between conception and marriage was six months. However, in cases of illegitimate fornication, the man who had been named invariably denied the charge. After the baby's birth, a grand jury presented the woman for fornication, and both parties were summoned to the next session of the Essex County Quarterly Court. Testimony would be presented by the midwife and the female defendant would be sentenced to be whipped or fined for fornication. Child-support payments, and occasionally a penalty for fornication, would be assessed against the man deemed to be the child's father.

This was the procedure followed by Hannah Adams, the twenty-nine-year-old daughter of a prosperous Newbury farmer. On May 14, 1678, accompanied by her brother, Jacob Adams, she charged that Joseph Mayo had gotten her with child on December 25th last. Mayo denied Adams' claim and was given two weeks to disprove it. In July, Jacob Adams paid £10 to guarantee his appearance to prosecute Mayo on paternity charges, and Joseph Mayo paid £10 to guarantee his appearance in court. Mayo was also ordered to pay 3 shillings per week child support from the birth of Adams' child until his appearance at the next session of the Essex County Quarterly Court.[20]

Adam's assertive stance worked. She had child-support payments from Mayo arranged before the birth of her child and before her fornication trial. But it took money, it took her brother's assistance, and it did not alleviate, in any way, her conviction and sentencing. It was Jacob Adams, not Hannah, who initiated legal action, and it was Jacob Adams, who, in the preliminary skirmishing over posting bond, put up £20, and sent Mayo to jail until he could raise £30. Mayo was at sea, however, when Hannah Adams appeared in court to answer the fornication charge. She was ordered to be severely whipped or fined for fornication. Adams chose to pay a fine, as did her stepsister, Sarah Short, who was presented following Adams at the same session, also for fornication with Joseph Mayo. Short, however, had married Mayo, so there was no question of her being whipped. Mayo forfeited the bonds that Adams' and Short's brothers had forced him to take out to guarantee his appearance. It may have been simpler for Mayo to forfeit his appearance bonds than to face the sisters he had seduced and their irate brothers in court.

Poor, property-less women, who lacked the money to post a bond to guarantee their appearance at the next quarterly court session and to force their partner to appear before a magistrate to confirm or deny paternity, were subject to a different procedure. While in some cases the court records mention postponement of the whippings of convicted female defendants until after the birth of their child, most poor women had to wait passively until childbirth to make a formal assertion of paternity to the midwife and then had to rely on the combined forces of the midwife and a local grand juryman to bring their partner to court. Grand jurymen monitored immoral and criminal activity in their town and forwarded to the court the names of single women who were pregnant or who had given birth to an illegitimate child. The woman, along with witnesses such as her employer, neighbors, and the women present at the birth of her child who could attest to the identity of the father, would be summoned to appear at the next session of the quarterly court where she would be inevitably convicted of fornication. If she had made a declaration of paternity during labor, her partner would be summoned too in order to make financial arrangements for the child.

Women who fell into this second category were often in desperate straits. Hannah Sterling, for example, was eighteen when she became pregnant by Robert Cham, a local servant who was suspected of burglary at the time they engaged in coitus. There was not enough evidence to put him in prison for burglary and he "slipped" away from Essex County. Sterling was the sixth of twelve children, at least nine of whom lived into adulthood. The family moved frequently, living in Haverhill, Rowley and Andover before leaving Massachusetts for Connecticut, suggesting that the family was economically marginal, although an alternative reading of upward mobility is possible. Sterling failed to appear in court to answer her 1686 presentment for fornication and Constable James Davis reported that she "is so poor in clothing she is not fit to go to court."[21] That Sterling lacked sufficient clothing to attend court suggests that she had been cast off by her family and her employer. Hannah Sterling, and women like her, even if given the option of paying a fine to escape the pain and humiliation inherent in a public whipping could not afford to exercise it.

While a whipping could not be avoided, it might be postponed. In 1645, for example, Marie Chandler was ordered to be severely whipped but since her breasts were sore and covered with boils, the punishment was postponed until the following week. In other cases, there is specific mention that whipping was to be deferred until after the baby had been weaned but Chandler was tried in the period when women were prosecuted most severely and three men had been prosecuted with her as putative fathers.[22]

Employers occasionally paid their female servants' fines. There would be an element of self-interest involved in seeing their servant returned to productive labor as quickly as possible and if the servant was indentured they had a considerable investment as well as a possible contractual relationship that committed them to room and board.[23] Yet, it may not have been necessary to pay their fornication fines to gain additional service. In 1672, Mary Parker was ordered to serve her employer, Moses Gilman, for three more years after the expiration of her indenture. Further, her child was to serve

Gilman and his heirs as their servant until he/she reached the age of twenty-one.[24] In 1675, Mary Talbut was ordered to serve her employer, Samuel Hunt, two extra years for the time he had lost during her pregnancy.[25] It is not clear from the surviving court records that either Parker or Talbut escaped corporal punishment because their employers paid fines for them.

Usually fines were due on the day of conviction. In 1686, Sarah Savory was told by Major Saltonstall that if her father brought money to the court beforehand for her fine, it would be "less disgraceful" than if the money were passed in public.[26] Sometimes a fine could be paid in produce. In 1671 Ruth Bowin was given the option of paying £4 in money or wheat.[27] In at least one instance, the judges gave the convicted female defendant until the next session of court to pay her fine.

In one case the court agreed to remit a female defendant's fine. In July, 1657, Martha Lemon was ordered to be whipped or fined following the birth of her illegitimate child, Benjamin Lemon. Her mother appeared in court with her and agreed to pay her fine. That November, "Robert Lemon's daughter's fine [was] remitted at his request."[28] Robert Lemon was a substantial Salem farmer and no partner had been presented with sixteen-year-old Martha. The judges must have been aware of extenuating circumstances in Lemon's case that have not survived in the record, but whatever it was that convinced the judges to return the fine paid by Lemon's mother to her father six months later, it was not a common occurrence. It is interesting, however, that the fine was greater when mother and daughter appeared together in court than when the male head of household returned to court to protest the size of the fine.

Child support is mentioned specifically in only 38 of 126 fornication trials. Seven of these cases make no mentioned of the amount to be paid. Fourteen men paid between two and three shillings each per week. There were various other payment options. In three cases the male partner paid a lump sum to the mother's father or husband. Four men paid bond to the town in which their child resided to guarantee its support. Two babies were indentured and three were raised by their fathers and the wives they had cheated on. In one instance payment was made by an employer, in another payment was made to the employer, and in two instances the existence of a private arrangement is mentioned.[29] It is likely that in the majority of cases where no specific sum was assigned by the court, the parties had made an arrangement prior to their court appearance. A mention of child-support payments in the court records, however, is not a reliable indicator that the mother of an illegitimate child was actively engaged in raising her child. Massachusetts courts regularly removed children from households when they felt that the parents were unfit and who was more unfit, in Puritan eyes, than a woman whose sexual behavior violated standards of femininity. There were also practical issues. It was impossible to work as a servant and raise a child at the same time.

It is ironic that women who lost their opportunity to advance themselves economically through marriage also lost the illegitimate children that might have served as a comfort. Again, from the Puritan point of view, authorities did not want to reward women for bearing illegitimate children. Susanna Durin had her baby stripped and taken naked from her while she was still breast-feeding. She was not allowed contact with her baby, and, William Reeves, her partner, alluded to the "extraordinary fear and restraint" that kept her from their child. He pled with the court that Susanna Durin be allowed to visit with her child, arguing, "can a woman forget her sucking child?"[30]

Durin obviously loved her child; it took legal restraints to keep her away from it. The image of the baby stripped of the clothing that Durin had provided for it and reclothed by a new mother is telling. Even William Reeves understood the strength and immediacy of the mother/child bond. At the same time that Durin was prohibited from approaching her child, Reeves was required to support it financially.

Not all mothers of illegitimate children would have shared Durin's experience of an immediate maternal bond. Added to the natural fears of any Puritan woman facing childbirth, was the realization that the baby they were carrying evidenced to all that they had transgressed community sexual boundaries, that they were not one of God's Elect, and that they had severely limited their future options. The pregnancy would have been burdened by stress as they faced their own feelings of shame, worried about the future, and endured harassment from their neighbors. Deposition after deposition attests to demands to know who the father was. In 1682, four women and one man formally deposed on questioning Elizabeth Gould about "how she came by her big belly?"[31] To one inquisitive 40 year-old matron, Gould retorted that "it was the stick behind the fire."[32] Hannah Adams faced taunts from young men who bet on whether or not she was pregnant and told her that Joseph Mayo, who had bragged of having sexual intercourse with her, had been captured by Turkish pirates.[33] These factors would have complicated the development of an affective maternal bond. In addition, the knowledge that they would have to give up the child after birth may have led the pregnant woman to steel herself against maternal urges when the baby stirred within her.

Depositions concerning the support of Sarah Warr's illegitimate child confirm that women who worked as servants regularly lost custody of children born out of wedlock. Warr and her partner, Josiah Clarke, a recently married man, were presented for fornication in April, 1671, and Clarke was ordered to give the town of Ipswich a security bond guaranteeing that he would pay weekly child support of 2 shillings. He was back in court five months later, petitioning for a reduction in support payments. Since at this time, his payments were reduced to 18 pence a week, and Warr was assessed a fee of 12 pence a week at the same time, both sums to be paid to Mr. Baker: "for the bringing up of the child of Sarah Warr," it appears that Warr's guardian, Mr. Baker, had legal custody of the child.[34] The following May, Clarke asked the court for permission to: "put (the child) out to some honest man until it be twenty-one years of age."[35] In April, 1673, shortly after the child's second birthday, Clarke appeared in court with Henry Greene to apprentice the child to him, and Clarke was freed of any further financial responsibility for his child by Sarah Warr.[36]

Once the child reached two years of age as Warr's had, it could be indentured by the father with the mother's consent, although if she did not consent, the court had the option of freeing the father from further support payments. Richard Woolery had been ordered to pay three shillings in corn per week toward the support of his daughter by Abigail Morse in 1676.[37] Two years later he indentured the child, relieving himself of financial responsibility. Other men sued to have the child- support payments reduced at age two. Isaiah Wood's father-in-law went to court to have the payments made to the keepers of Mary Sheffield's child reduced by one-half in 1662.[38]

In 1672, Mary Parker was required to sign her first illegitimate child over to her employer, Moses Gilman, in a twenty-one-year indenture ("unless the father should choose to redeem it") as well as to serve Gilman an additional three years after her own indenture had expired. The following year Parker was pregnant again, but this time Parker named a father, Teague Disco. The court took a £40 mortgage on Disco's land to insure that child-support payments of three shillings per week would be made. Thus Mary Parker had two illegitimate children, and while she lived in the same house as at least one of them, she had lost the right to exercise control over them or to make decisions about their futures.

Some women struggled to pay the child-care expenses themselves. Part of Samuel Sewall's indignation at the rich Coddington family was that Elizabeth Thurston, the mother of an illegitimate child, was struggling to pay two shillings a week to board her child with a Medfield family while its father, a Coddington scion, paid nothing toward its expenses. The two shillings were her entire weekly wage and left nothing over for clothing for either the baby or herself.[39]

In the rare instance where a mother was able to retain custody of her child, the father was able to use the threat of indenture or the threat to take the child into his own home to force her to accept a reduction in child-care expenses. The Widow Stickney had eight legitimate children between the ages of one and fourteen and one illegitimate child when she declared that John Atkinson, a Newbury feltmaker, had fathered her tenth child, born January 20, 1681. She waited eleven months before charging him with paternity. Over Atkinson's protestations of innocence, he was ordered to pay £8 for the past eleven months and 2s6d per week in the future for child support.[40] At the same session, Atkinson was ordered to pay a fine of 20 shillings for striking Stickney. He asked the court for a reduction in child-support payments since he had a wife and nine children to provide for and would end up in prison since he could not make the payments. If the court would not rebate part of his payments, he asked for the privilege all fathers had, to dispose of the child as he saw fit, lest he be, "kept as a continual slave to her who hath injured me, and impudently and scoffingly insulted me."[41] The court agreed to let Atkinson find a suitable home for his illegitimate daughter, Mary, but the court added the stipulation that Atkinson could not take the child into his own household. Stickney was determined to maintain her daughter in her own household, and refused to allow Atkinson his right as a father to put out his child. She was required to give up further child-support payments after this offer was received.[42]

Prior to 1668, child-support assignments were uncertain. We have seen that sixteen-year-old Mary Dane in 1654 was required to support her child herself.[43] Or, as in Sarah Warr's case, both father and mother might be required to make payments to a third party to pay for their child's expenses. In 1668, the law was passed requiring child-support payments, usually between two and three shillings per week, be assigned by the court to the putative father in lieu of a fornication conviction. Evidently child-support payments were made, just as the 1668 law attested, to guarantee that the child would not be a burden on the town's tax rate. It was certainly not to provide financial assistance to a young mother struggling to raise her child alone outside of the secure structure of the traditional two-parent family.

What happened to illegitimate children who were placed in the care of the town of their birth? Since they were assigned by an annual contract to whichever household agreed to maintain them for the least amount of money, they faced an unsettled future. The Salem town records indicate a difficult and insecure passage for Sarah Lambert's child, who at no point in the record is accorded the dignity of a name, sex, or age. It was likely six years old in 1673. Francis Skerry had been keeping both Sarah Lambert and her child prior to that time, but in April, 1673, the child was given to Thomas Greenslet's wife. In August, the town of Salem agreed to give the

Greenslets half an acre of land in return for keeping Sarah Lambert's child until it was eighteen. The following March, however, Sarah Lambert's child was taken from Thomas Greenslet's wife and placed with Thomas Green's wife. Two years later in 1676, Mrs. Green took in another illegitimate child, one fathered by her own husband. The Greens also agreed to maintain Sarah Lambert's child until it was eighteen in return for up to 40 acres of land. At the same time, the Salem selectmen tried to find passage to Virginia for Sarah Lambert. They did not succeed because she had another illegitimate child in 1679. In March, 1679, Sarah Lambert's child was still with the Greens, but its position in the family was tenuous, because the Greens were asking for more money. In 1680 the Greens were given 50 shillings, "the better to enable him to keep [Sarah] Lambert's child, he being poor & in want." Thomas Green's financial position makes it likely that taking in bastards was a strategy for supplementing marginal family incomes. This could not have been a future eagerly sought by pregnant women for their children.

To summarize, few Essex County persons engaged in fully-consummated sexual intercourse prior to marriage, reflecting both Puritan religious ideology that postulated marriage as an essential precondition to sexual intercourse as well as gender ideology that placed chastity above all other female attributes. Puritans valued self-control. It was proof that the individual lived in a state of grace. Love-making to orgasm, by its very nature, represented the antithesis of control, exposing, in that moment, both women and men to Satanic influences. The power and vulnerability experienced during arousal and orgasm needed to be safely channeled. This required marriage, and a godly sanction, if not downright encouragement to sexual intercourse. What is "be fruitful and multiply," but permission for marital sexual intercourse?[44] Sexual intercourse was to be reserved for marriage, as a reward for achieving maturity and, hopefully, financial stability in an independent household. Puritans espoused status-equivalent marriages, not love-matches. Sexual intercourse and the daily occurrences of life and worship as a couple created, Puritans believed, a lasting affective bond rooted in more than sexual attraction. That the rate of illegitimate and premarital births remained low throughout the period studied indicates Puritan success, not only in New England, but in England during the Interregnum, where the illegitimacy rate dropped to between two and four percent.[45]

Two composite but overlapping portraits can be drawn of women who bore illegitimate children in seventeenth-century Essex County. The first young woman, representing 45 percent of the whole, was twenty years of age or less, worked as a servant, and had family in Essex County. Her partner was older, often married, and many of the relationships were probably predatory (in that they did not occur within the context of courtships). The second woman was twenty-one years of age or older, but also worked as a servant. She was less likely than her younger counterpart to have financial resources and family living in Essex County. She may have expected matrimony as an outcome of her pregnancy but her partner, usually of equivalent rank, either because of poverty, disinclination, or a prior marriage, failed her. There were commonalities as well in the experiences of these two groups of women. All were prosecuted and most lost their children. As well, most lost their ability to make an appropriate marriage elsewhere. Money, the age of the female defendant, and the ability and desire of the male partner to marry, determined whether an unplanned pregnancy would be illegitimate or premarital.

Men named as partners by female defendants also fall into recognizable categories. As many as one-half of the men who fathered illegitimate children probably never possessed the economic resources necessary for marriage. These men may or may not have been optimistic about their ability to marry when they engaged in sexual intercourse. That four of them married their partners within a few months of the baby's birth indicates that a few had reason for hope. The second largest category was composed of men of marriage age who married elsewhere soon after their conviction. One of these men married between the conception and birth of his illegitimate child and within three years almost one-third of the men named during labor as the father of an illegitimate child had married. This group of men made a deliberate choice not to marry the women they had impregnated. The third group, 20 percent of the men who fathered illegitimate children, was already married. Clearly the majority of men who fathered illegitimate children, and some of their female partners, engaged in sexual intercourse without the expectation that marriage would follow.

One hundred and four women and 35 men were convicted of illegitimate fornication between 1640 and 1685. Prior to 1665, less than one Essex County woman was presented each year. This is an extraordinarily low illegitimacy rate. For every three women who were convicted of fornication following the birth of an illegitimate child, one man was presented. Once convicted, women were punished more severely than their male partners. The Essex County Quarterly Court held women to a higher standard of sexual accountability than their male partners.

The quantitative analysis reveals a contradictory feature of New England "sex ways." Male sexual behavior was privileged by the court when it came to the decision to prosecute, convict, and sentence. This type of privileging is usually associated with societies with a flourishing traditional double standard, such as that of seventeenth-century Virginia or

Restoration England and characterized by a high rate of illegitimacy. Yet the illegitimacy rate in Essex County is extremely low. This strongly suggests that Puritans punished women with greater frequency and severity because they believed that women were more at fault than men for the initiation of extramarital sexual intercourse.

There are two possible ways in which Puritans may have rationalized their treatment of women who bore illegitimate children more severely than the men who fathered their children. One is that Puritans accepted the implicit Judaic-Christian belief, deeply ingrained in the communal psyche, which posited women as possessing a powerful sexuality which made them naturally lascivious, and, once aroused, insatiable. The second interpretation suggests that Puritans were anxious to promote their new, upgraded version of women as helpmeets, fit mates for the new Puritan patriarch. Very few women failed to meet the required standard of chastity, but those who did, whether they were the victims of sexual predators, poverty, or human weakness, had to be punished severely because their illegitimate pregnancies provided visible evidence of sexual irregularities that undermined the physical and spiritual foundation of their "City Upon a Hill."

These rationale are not mutually exclusive. Rather, they are complementary. The first, the "lustful daughters of Eve" argument satisfied those in New England who retained traditional, implicit beliefs about women. As well, it provided justification to the employers who had sex with their female servants and emboldened men who promised marriage in return for sex and then reneged on their promises. The low numbers of women who evidenced through illegitimate pregnancies, however, that their actions were driven by uncontainable lusts, is convincing evidence to the contrary. Most women successfully controlled their own sexual behaviors and effectively policed the sexual behaviors of other women.

The second rationale offered, that women were punished more severely than men because a new standard had been set for them that conflated chastity and femininity and an illegitimate pregnancy offered irrefutable proof that they had failed this essential test of womanhood, offers promise. The ability to remain chaste until marriage was predicated on the assumption that Godly young women who had been educated to Puritan values would not engage in premarital sex. Women who had illegitimate children not only placed themselves outside the pale of the Puritan community by having coitus before marriage, they had shown that they were not true women. Both rationales placed the onus upon women to protect their chastity. Both blamed women for their failures.

Chapter Four

"I Am a Poor Destitute Creature": Sociological Aspects of Illegitimacy in Essex County, 1640–1685

> I desire your worships to be as favorable as you can for I am a poor destitute creature & far from all my near friends, though I hope I have some here in New England. . . . and I desire your prayers for me, that I might reform and leave of all such wickedness through God's help who is able to save me.[1]

In this forlorn plea issued in 1682, Mary Reddy asked the court to remit her sentence from a whipping to a fine. No man was presented with her, nothing is mentioned of her infant, nor is anything more known about her beyond the fact that her plea was successful. Depositions such as this, filed to prosecute or support women presented for fornication following the birth of an illegitimate child, open a window into the world of seventeenth-century Essex County and allow an unfiltered view of Puritan sexual attitudes and behaviors. Magistrates, constables, and grand-jurymen speak of warrants and whippings, fines levied, layovers in prison, and judicial process. Employers, parents, and neighbors speak with mixed voices; in disapproval, in defense, in disappointment, in shocked surprise, and, rarely, in sympathy. The women, themselves, speak of promises unkept, shame, poverty, loss, hard work, and humiliation.

Historians of early modern England have constructed elaborate theoretical frameworks to explain the plight of young women like Mary Reddy. These studies generally take two forms; (1) long-term analyses focusing on peaks and valleys in the illegitimacy cycle to determine contributory factors or (2) the community study. David Levine and Keith Wrightson, in a community study of Terling, Essex, concluded that the root cause of illegitimacy was economic instability. Couples initiated sexual intercourse after contract or spousals and then economic disruption forced them to part prior to the marriage ceremony. They provided a comprehensive definition of illegitimacy as a "compound phenomenon" that subsumed the activities of a core of repetitive delinquents, predatory masters, couples whose marriages were delayed, women seeking marriage partners, and transients fathering bastards. The range of persons involved in producing illegitimate children, however, suggests that economic insecurity is not a broad enough conceptual framework.[2] Levine and Wrightson locate their cast of characters, who would have been instantly recognizable to any judge in Massachusetts Bay Colony, within the context of a vigorous popular culture exhibiting the following characteristics: high mobility of adolescents and young adults, a popular culture centered on alehouses rather than church and relative freedom from parental control.

Essex County had the opposite social conditions to those of Terling, Essex; a robust economy, low mobility of adolescents and young adults, a popular culture centered on the meeting house, and a patriarchal family structure. Yet the profile of those convicted of fornication after the birth of illegitimate children is the same, only smaller in size. In Terling, moreover, the illegitimacy rate dropped precipitously from a peak of nine percent of births in the 1610s when the traditional culture, centered on the alehouse, flourished to less than two percent of births between 1641 and 1660, not coincidentally during the period in which Puritans were ascendant. The illegitimacy rate continued to decline until 1685. Levine and Wrightson, as might be expected in an argument centered on economic factors, argue that the Puritan drive to control illegitimacy rose not from a general moral impetus but from the desire to limit demands on the public purse. As more substantial members of the community abandoned traditional cultural values in favor of Puritanism, which stressed self-control and sexual restraint prior to marriage, bastardy became more and more an artifact of the poor. I would agree that economic factors played a role in determining illegitimacy rates, but cultural factors are more important. When the substantial residents of Terling imposed Puritan sexual discipline the illegitimacy rate decreased fourfold.

Peter Laslett's courtship intensity model seems to hold more promise for explaining illegitimate births in Essex County. Though the model is not a perfect fit, key aspects of it can be replicated. Laslett looked at fluctuations in the illegitimacy rate over time and concluded that when the marriage rate went up, the illegitimacy rate increased correspondingly. Also, the age at first marriage decreased. In Massachusetts, where 94 percent of women and

98 percent of men married, as opposed to a 73 percent marriage rate in early modern England, courtship intensity was at a constant peak.[3] It must have seemed as if every young person was engaged in courtship and, once married, procreation.[4] There would be an inevitable spillover of illegitimate births. Laslett, however, correlated illegitimacy with the fact that younger, poorer women entered the marriage market in prosperous times, engaged in sexual intercourse after contract, conceived, and then the marriage market failed for some reason, not necessarily economic. Laslett also emphasized the importance of locality persistence (cultural factors, including courtship expectations, which, in Essex County, included premarital chastity) to explain illegitimacy rates. The part of the courtship intensity model that posits a positive correlation between marriage rates and illegitimacy rates can be used to explain the existence of illegitimacy in Massachusetts, while locality persistence can be applied to explain why the rates remained so low.

In early modern England the processes of marriage formation and the defining moment at which a legal marriage had been concluded varied by class and region. In some regions, at some times, and in some status groups, sexual intercourse customarily began after spousals and before the church ceremony. A promise to marry issued in the present tense, before witnesses, was enough to legitimize a sexual union. It took the passage of the Hardwicke Marriage Act in 1753 to systematize marriage practices in England. There was no comparable ambiguity in Massachusetts. Sexual intercourse was allowable only after first, permission to marry had been officially granted by both sets of parents or a magistrate in lieu of parents and second, the completion of a civil ceremony conducted by a licensed official.

Puritan New England needs a theory of illegitimacy that incorporates the economic, religious, and cultural realities of life in the New World. Given the low rate of illegitimacy in seventeenth-century Massachusetts, any theory advanced should be couched in positive terms. In Puritan Massachusetts, where economic conditions favoring marriage formation existed in combination with religious ideology that stressed premarital chastity and a secular law system that punished sexual offenders severely, the illegitimacy rate was low. The desire to conform to social norms, the conflation of chastity with femininity, the identification between self control and sexual control, and a high marriage rate combined to limit extramarital sexual intercourse.

Male sexual exploitation was the major engine for illegitimacy in Massachusetts. Fifty-five percent of men prosecuted for fathering illegitimate children in Essex County were either already married or married another woman within five years. They chose to have sex although they were unable, in the case of married men, or unwilling, in the case of men who married elsewhere soon after, to legitimize their children, let alone to marry a woman who lacked the prime attribute of her gender, sexual virtue. The remaining 45 percent never married in Essex County, indicating that they were too poor to marry or transient. Women knew that an illegitimate pregnancy would mean public shame, financial and/or corporal punishment and reduced marriage opportunities. Consequently, the incentive for women to engage in sexual intercourse outside of marriage was small. This is not to say that every one of the relationships that resulted in illegitimate children was exploitative or that women never sought out or took pleasure in extramarital sexual intercourse. Some relationships were motivated by feelings of love and in these instances couples usually found a way to marry later.[5] The expectation in early modern England and New England was that if a courtship resulted in pregnancy the couple would marry.[6] In Massachusetts, where there were few economic barriers to marriage, most did. Of course, every society has its core of delinquents, predatory masters, lusty widows, transients looking for a temporary relationship, young men willing to promise marriage in return for sexual intercourse and young women hoping that sexual intercourse will bind a man to them, and seventeenth-century Essex County was no exception. As in Terling, Essex, these categories of people bore or sired bastards. As the population of Essex County increased and the religious fervor of successive generations decreased, the illegitimacy rate gradually rose. More of the women presented were poor, or servants, or both, during the last two decades of the seventeenth-century, but for 50 years, between 1630 and 1680, the illegitimacy rate in Puritan Massachusetts reached an unparalleled low.

One way to determine if the observed extramarital sexual activity represented a departure from the norm is to compare the months in which married women and single women conceived.[7] If the pattern is similar, it would indicate a degree of community acceptance of out-of-wedlock coitus. Figure 1 below shows modest fluctuations in the months married women conceived.

From a low in February, marital conceptions rise through the spring and summer months, falling again in the autumn and reaching a secondary peak in December and January.[8] Fluctuations in the cycle of extramarital conceptions are more dramatic. The first peak comes in April at thirteen percent, not coincidentally the month in which it became warm enough for couples to escape the confines and oversight of the Puritan household to engage in sexual intercourse out-of-doors. Extramarital conceptions continue to occur at a higher rate than marital conceptions until August. In September as harvest gets underway, extramarital conceptions peak again at the same high level observed in April.

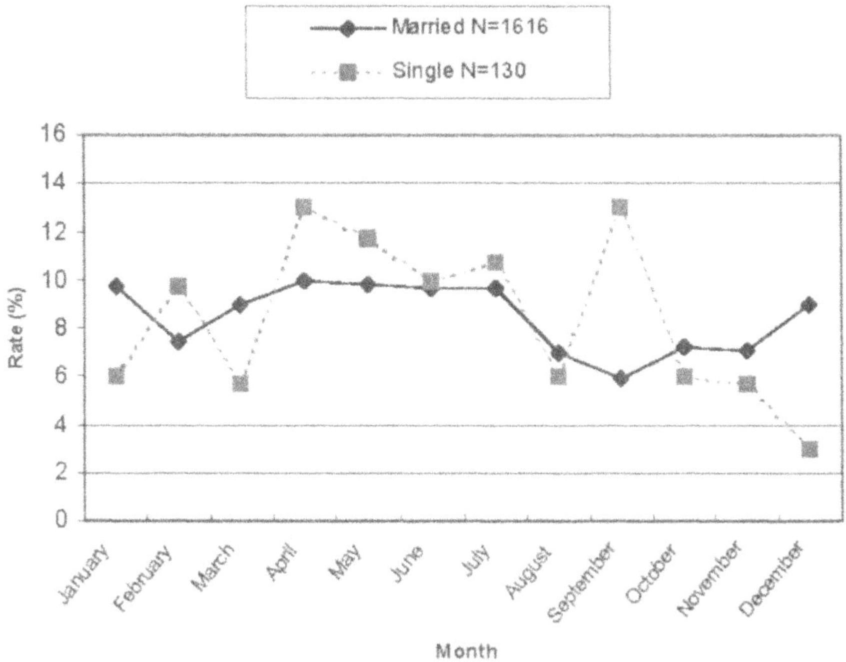

Figure 1 Time of Conception: Married and Single Women in Essex County Massachusetts, 1640–1685

Two obvious conclusions can be drawn from this pattern. First, opportunities for illicit sexual activity were limited in the winter months, while marital sexual intercourse became more frequent as evidenced by the secondary peak in conceptions in December and January. Two, much of the extramarital sexual activity occurred in the open air or in barns and other outbuildings that were not heated in the winter or the conception rate would not increase so dramatically when the weather got warmer. The April and September peaks are not unexpected. April offered the first real opportunity to find comfortable privacy out-of-doors or in outbuildings removed from direct supervision. By August, when the rate of married women who became pregnant exceeded that of single women for the first month since March, the population that was ready to become sexually active had had four months in which to conceive. The September peak may be related to a combination of factors. Harvest activities brought women into the fields to work. This placed them in the male sphere and may have made them more vulnerable. Also, most Puritans married in the winter months, the most popular being November and December.[9] Many of these weddings represented the culmination of courtships begun that summer, and, perhaps, with a commitment to marry made or expected by some women, some couples engaged in sexual intercourse fueled by alcohol and harvest-time exuberance prior to their winter wedding or in the expectation that a winter wedding would occur.

The two months of the fewest recorded numbers of extramarital conceptions are November and December. Since these were the two most popular months for marriage, possibly extramarital conceptions that occurred in these months were masked by subsequent marriages. There are, however, at least two alternate explanations. One is that the populations most likely to engage in extramarital sexual intercourse were marrying in these months and chose to wait until after marriage to initiate sexual intercourse. Two, women who might have been persuaded to engage in sexual activity by a promise of marriage or to secure a promise of marriage knew by October that unless financial negotiations were already underway between their families and their suitors' families, a marriage that winter was unlikely.

In one sense, however, comparing conception patterns of married and unmarried women is like comparing apples and oranges. The frequency with which they engaged in sexual intercourse was likely to be very different and frequency increased the likelihood of pregnancy within a given month because of enhanced opportunities for conception. Women who bore illegitimate children often cited the fact that they had engaged in coitus only one time. While this apologia needs to be accepted with caution, it is no more far-fetched than David H. Flaherty's oft-cited observation that "widespread sexual irregularities" existed, of which prosecuted pregnancies represented only "the most visible manifestations."[10] Women between the ages of 20 and 25, whether married or single, were in their peak child-bearing years.[11] It can be plausibly argued that, for this most fertile of female age groups, the odds of conception were one in four. Recent studies have shown that women are fertile for five to seven days of each 28-day menstrual cycle.[12] Given cultural proscriptions against coitus with a menstruating woman, women were sexually available 23 days of the month, and fertile for five to seven of these days. While live births would have been limited by spontaneous abortions or miscarriages, the possibility of an untimely pregnancy was more than an abstraction, and in the seventeenth-century, it was compounded by the belief, embedded in the legal system, that as long as women did not reach orgasm they would not conceive.

Knowing when extramarital sexual intercourse occurred regularly provides a clue to where couples were finding sufficient privacy and reveals more than just information about location. The "where" provides important information about parental oversight, employment patterns, workplace conditions, employer/employee relations, ideas about privacy, and male/female sexual dynamics. It can also tell us something about the quality of the sexual activity that occurred. Information that is absent from the record tells us something too. What is most apparent is that extramarital sexual intercourse took place in a variety of locations that attest to the inventiveness and fortitude of Puritans determined to engage in coitus.

Much of the information about the locus of sexual activity is derived from midwives' depositions. It was their responsibility to interrogate unmarried pregnant women during labor to ascertain the father of the child. Consensual intercourse was most likely to occur within the well-defined parameters of women's territory when parents and employers were temporarily absent or busy. Seventeen-year-old Hester Jackson testified that she and her master's son had had intercourse first when she was making up a bed in an upstairs chamber in the late afternoon, and again the following week at approximately the same time of day while his parents were absent. She added that although he had approached her many times after that, once while she was milking, and "tempted her to lie with him for money," she refused because she had developed a guilty conscience.

Non-consensual intercourse occurred after dark and out-of-doors in men's territory; barns, pastures, fields, and in the woods. On a March evening in 1669, twenty-two-year-old Anne Chase was traveling from the house in which she worked as a servant to her lodging. She was raped by her employer's brother, John Allen, who followed her from the house and "forced her against the [fence]rails, and she being in a sore fright was unable to call out."[13] In 1680, nineteen-year-old Sarah Lambert was raped "about 8 o'clock on a moonlit night . . . in Mr. Nathaniel Roger's pasture."[14] Both women were convicted of fornication subsequently. John Allen was neither prosecuted nor ordered to pay child support, but John Hunkins, who was already maintaining one bastard, was ordered to pay child support for Lambert's baby.

The level of detail available in the two cases above is lacking in most fornication prosecutions, either because it was never collected, or, more likely, it has not survived. Information about where and how often intercourse occurred is lacking in all but 26 of the 136 cases. Not surprisingly, the most commonly cited location in which sexual intercourse took place, in seven of 26 cases, was an employer's household, exemplified by the account of Hannah Souter of Marblehead, when she was presented in 1690 for fornication. Although she refused to name the father of her child, the local constable and the requisite second witness testified that when they arrived with an arrest warrant they had discovered her "lying under the bedclothes" with her employer, Mr. Philip Parsons, "the said Hannah Souter's arms under the head of the said Mr. Philip Parsons."[15] Souter was fined and Parsons was required to pay child support and lost his license to keep a public house in Marblehead. Souter and Parsons were not unique. In the seven instances in which the employer's household was cited, the master himself was the most frequently named partner, followed by his son and fellow servants.

In only one instance does a single woman state that she had been sexually active in her parent's house, and she claimed to have been raped by a neighbor's son after offering to show him her parent's new bedchamber.[16] Women who lived at home with their parents, like Susanna Bowden of Marblehead in 1688, attested that sexual intercourse occurred not in their parent's house but out-of-doors and that it had been preceded by a promise of marriage. Bowden said:

> that time which she judges he got her with child was sometime in the latter end of August last past in the upper end of the pasture where her father dwells.[17]

One possible benefit of engaging in sexual intercourse in a field in April, as Mary Rowlandson did, or in August, as Susannah Bowden did, is that it offered privacy, an attribute lacking in seventeenth-century Puritan Massachusetts where community oversight was expected and where households were crowded and one room opened into the next. The degree of acceptable oversight is indicated by the activities of fifty-year-old Clement Coldham of Gloucester who went to great lengths to uncover an affair between a fifty-two-year-old widower, John Pearce, and a forty-two-year-old widow, Jane Stanwood. Hearing that Pearce was reputed to fetch the Widow Stanwood to his house at night and that she had been observed returning home in the morning, Coldham peered through the window of Pearce's house as the pair shared a meal and undressed. He listened to their love-making, and when they had fallen asleep, set off to fetch the town constable, Anthony Day, and Deacon Stephens.[18] Day called, "Fire! Fire!" and asked John Pearce if he wanted to be burned in his bed. When the couple emerged from the house, Coldham deposed, Stanwood was only half dressed. No one accused Coldham of being a peeping Tom; he was being a good citizen. Pearce and Stanwood were ordered to be whipped or fined 20 nobles for fornication.[19] They married a week later, thus enabling the continuation of their sexual relationship.

Widows and widowers had more privacy in which to engage in illicit sexual activity than other people. Although some widows' households still contained young children, it is apparent from the depositions in Sarah Stickney's case that her suitors were not inhibited from approaching her bed by the presence of children already in it. Stickney testified that her children were frightened and cried out when Samuel Lowell approached her bed.[20] Nor was Samuel Appleton deterred by the presence of two other women in the room in which he engaged in coitus with Priscilla Willson in 1683.[21] He gained sufficient privacy by shutting the bed curtains.

As the depositions in Mary Talbut's fornication case illustrate, servants employed subterfuges to create private time in which to engage in sexual intercourse.[22] They pretended illnesses to stay home alone and unsupervised. Sunday morning was a popular time to court female servants left at home to tend to their master's young children. With attendance at Sunday meeting compulsory, it was one of the few times couples could find privacy in which to conduct illicit relationships. In 1676, a sexually active widow, Remember Salmon, took advantage of her parents' absence to meet with a married man, Thomas Green. Her niece and a neighbor, entering the house immediately after the lecture, found her in bed and Thomas Green sitting by the bedside smoking tobacco.[23]

Putting out adolescent children for employment in the houses of acquaintances and hiring unrelated adolescents to serve in one's own house in return were common in seventeenth-century New England. An analysis of the financial status of female fornication defendants in Essex County indicates that while some female servants were poor, or orphaned, or both, or were recent immigrants, other women with documented work histories had prosperous parents living in the same community, as did their partners. Martha Rowlandson's sexual experience is typical of that of economically vulnerable young women who lived away from home. Her father had died four years earlier when she was sixteen and her mother had remarried. She was employed as a spinster by Philip Rowell of Amesbury in April 1687 when she described the circumstances under which she had conceived to her midwife, Lidia Mackrest:

> There being a meeting of company at night at John Prouse's house & the said Samuel George going home with her he desired her to lie with him and promised her marriage if she would lie with him & so she consented and lay with him near Wm. Barns' house: between it and Rowells & that she lay with him twice at the same time upon the ground[24]

Samuel George, 16 years her senior and not officially courting her, denied that he had fathered the child who died ten days after its birth. Rowlandson's sister, Elizabeth, had been tried for fornication three years earlier, naming a local doctor as the father of her child, and her twin sister, Mary, had been tried for fornication the previous summer. Her sisters' known sexual activities, combined with her lack of a dowry limited her marriage opportunities and left her susceptible to a false promise of marriage from George in return for sexual favors. Four years later Rowlandson married. This might have been a coup, given her family's sexual reputation, but she married Ralph Ellenwood, her sister Elizabeth's brother-in-law, who had been divorced for impotence in 1682. Ellenwood was no bargain as a husband. He had been declared physically incapable of intercourse, rendering him as unsuitable to make a claim to manhood as Rowlandson was to enter the sisterhood of respectable Puritan goodwives.

Given that the house was also the workplace in seventeenth-century Massachusetts, it is instructive to examine the conditions under which young women lived and worked. With unrelated adults living in many Essex County households, and in some instances sleeping in the same bedrooms, the potential for illicit sexual relationships to develop was considerable.[25] It was essential that domestic order be maintained, but clearly some employers did not exercise the same oversight over their young male and female employees that they applied to their own children. Depositions given during the fornication trial of Susanah Durin and William Reeves in the Salem Quarterly Court in June, 1668, illustrate the vulnerability of young women to sexual pressure from their fellow servants in unregulated households.[26] Reeves and Durin both worked in the Cromwell household. Part of the problem, in this instance, lay in the gendered division of labor. Reeves worked for Mr. Cromwell, Durin for Mrs. Cromwell and Mrs. Cromwell was unable, or unwilling, to prevent Reeves' pursuit of Durin. Two neighboring women testified that whenever the Cromwells were away, Durin would beg one of them to come over and sit with her, because "she could not abide to be with him alone." A friend of Reeves, Thomas Ives, testified that Reeves had asked him: "What aileth our maid, for as soon as I come in at the door, she either runneth into the other room or into the chamber?" Ives further testified that Reeves had procured a love potion to slip into Durin's drink.

The frequent absences of the Cromwells from their household, the inability of Mrs. Cromwell to assert authority over her husband's servant, and Reeves' persistence exposed Durin to what would be considered today as sexual harassment in the workplace. Nevertheless, in a seventeenth-century context, Reeves was engaged in an aggressive courtship which he hoped, his deposition stated, would culminate in marriage. The onus was on Durin to protect herself from his overtures. That she failed is apparent from her pregnancy and subsequent fornication conviction.[27]

Depositions filed in fornication cases offer the opportunity to learn that the ordinary citizen of Essex County, while not going to the same lengths as Clement Coldham had to root out illicit sexual activity, nevertheless harbored a strong degree of animus toward sexual activity between unmarried persons. Even women who found themselves pregnant and unmarried, while they might be flippant or defiant when speaking to friends and inquisitive neighbors, spoke to the court of their remorse and shame. In the remainder of this chapter, we will listen as a group of young men talk about sex; an elderly woman warns a young man away from her servant; and a forty-six-year-old man lies to his shocked neighbors about the circumstances in which his servant had become pregnant. All illustrated with their words what Puritans said and thought about illicit sex.

Puritans assumed that when people of the opposite sex were together alone it was to have sexual intercourse. In 1654, "William Holdred's wife" was presented for unseemly carriages with John Chator, a terminally ill man who had been bedridden for the past two years. Holdred had been discovered lying across Chator's bed by his wife.[28] Isabel Holdred was a married woman in her late thirties and, although she was known to be subject to fits, and her own husband, William Holdred had accompanied her to Chator's house, she was presented. Chator was in no shape to be making advances, and Holdred had experienced a fit while she was nursing him. The court accepted her defense; they "found no censure on her" but that she was presented in the first place seems, from the distance of the twenty-first century, to be a ludicrous overreaction to finding two wholly respectable adults alone together.

The Holdred prosecution had an interesting genesis. The previous year, William and Isabel Holdred had complained to the court that they had uncovered a sordid neighborhood tale.[29] Alice Chator, John Chator's wife, they had learned, had committed adultery with her husband's servant, Daniel Gun, and had agreed to marry him if her husband died. The accusation against Isabel Holdred, under circumstances that make it certain it was Alice Chator who complained, should have led the court to assume that the charges were retaliatory and unfounded. That they dignified the charge with a court proceeding indicates the strength of Puritan ideology about the power of female sexuality.

The attitudes concerning their sexual activity expressed by young women charged with fornication indicate an acceptance of personal responsibility for the situations in which they found themselves. None blamed their partner, or stated that they had been coerced; all stated they believed themselves to be wicked. Three penitent statements were filed during the March 1682 session of the Essex County Quarterly Court meeting at Ipswich. One of them was that of Mary Reddy, who led off this chapter. At the same session, Joannah Smith was sentenced to be whipped or fined for fornication with William Smith. An abject Smith also asked to be fined rather than whipped. Her plea was successful. Smith was fined £3 and court costs after pleading that her "natural wicked inclination" and her subjection to "the temptations of the adversary and his wicked suggestions" had led to her disgrace.[30] A third penitent statement was presented by Elizabeth Gould who also had her sentence reduced to a fine and court costs.[31] Mary Reddy, Joannah Smith, and Elizabeth Gould were presented together.[32] Their depositions bear a common pattern. Each stated they deserved their punishment; that they had sinned; that they had brought dishonor on themselves and their friends. They described themselves as the most debased of women. Whether or not they truly believed their rhetoric, it is obvious that it was what the court expected to hear. Their statements reflected official Puritan beliefs about women and sex.[33] While Joannah Smith mentioned that she had been tempted by the Devil, none of them state that they were seduced by a man. Tellingly, none of them even mention their partner. They accepted their society's dictum that they had been responsible for the sexual activity.

In 1691, Elizabeth Batten of Salem was presented for fornication with her employer's son, John Dolbear.[34] Essentially the rhetoric was the same, with one major exception. Batten wanted her partner to accept some responsibility. Batten may have been trying to force a marriage, but other depositions in the case suggest that Dolbear's parents vigorously resisted child-support payments, and it is equally likely that Batten was trying to ensure that the court order Dolbear to meet this financial responsibility.

While the number of surviving penitent statements such as Batten's is limited, and there appear to be only these four left in the Essex County court files, there is another way to determine whether or not they represented a heartfelt expression of the defendant's remorse. Depositions filed by midwives often indicated that the female defendant expressed penitence during labor, when, Puritans believed, women spoke the truth because no one would risk her immortal soul by lying when facing possible death in childbirth.

Outside the courtroom different attitudes might be expressed. In 1674 two young women described the pregnant Mary Talbut as "laughing much in the time of her speaking, as merry as if she were not in such a condition as she is judged to be."[35] They were incensed that she did not appear to have a proper appreciation of her plight. Talbut's response appears to be entirely human, however. The women had been taunting the nine-months pregnant Talbut as the three gathered at the public well to collect water about the supposed father's refusal to marry her.

Not all women were appropriately deferent to the court. In 1690, Hannah Souter ignored her first summons and demanded to know her accusers. They were the selectmen of Marblehead who, "judging it the duty of the Select men to take notice of such wicked facts," formed a deputation and went to see her.[36] Souter refused to name the father of her child, "however it pleased God to deal with her."[37] Sarah Stickney also indicated her contempt of the court process. She told a neighbor in 1681, following one of her two fornication trials in which she had been fined both times that "the Court did not regard the sin so they could get the money."[38]

Given the court's focus on female sexual activity, it is difficult to locate documentary evidence of male sexual attitudes. Thirty-year-old James Mirrick reported to the court that Samuel Lowell had claimed fornication to be a "sin no more than to smoke a pipe of tobacco in the street, for that was a breach of the Law, and the other was no more."[39] However, Mirrick was anxious to paint Lowell as the possessor of non-traditional sexual attitudes as both were suspected of being Sarah Stickney's sexual partners. Mirrick claimed that although he had been solicited by Stickney, he had told her that he "darest not do it."[40]

It is even more difficult to locate cases in which the men involved were punished more severely than their female sexual partners. The interrelated cases of two brothers, Edmund and Hackaliah Bridges, are singular in this respect. It is notable that they were tried in 1657, a time when the court was more even-handed in its assessment of responsibility for the initiation of sexual intercourse. It is difficult to imagine an equivalent prosecution occurring even ten years later.

Edmund and Hackaliah Bridges were the sons of Mr. Edmund Bridges of Ipswich.[41] They had previously been convicted of petty theft and lying and Hackaliah Bridges had been acquitted of fornication with Sarah French the previous year.[42] In depositions supplied by their friends, the brothers bragged about their sexual activity and indicated their willingness to share their sexual partners with their friends who expressed surprise and disbelief, but not disapproval. All of these men were young, which may explain the unguarded nature of their conversations. Edmund was 20, Hackaliah probably eighteen. Their friend, Samuel Younglove, also aged 20, testified that:

> Edmund Bridges mowing with him the last mowing time he told me that he had frogged Mary Browne divers times & also Mary Quilter. I told him I could not believe it and he vowed John Allen had seen him frog Mary Browne. He also said he had frogged divers others else where I told him again I did not believe it that he should do so for fear it would come to light. He said that he could do it so it should never take effect.[43]

John Allen admitted that he "came down and looked in the door and saw them go to the table and there Edmund flung her down and got upon her."[44]

Edmund's brother, Hackaliah Bridges, was equally informative about his sexual activity. Another youth, John How, who had been regaled by Hackaliah with details of his sexual activities with Mary Quilter, "spoke to him about this business in the prison, & he bid me hold my peace for he was resolved to deny it and knew they could not whip him unless [he confessed] they can prove it or I confess it.[45]

Some basic conclusions can be drawn from these depositions. First, Browne and Quilter were interchangeable objects in the minds of the Bridges brothers. There are no protestations of affection. They were willing to share both the women and their expertise with their friends. The young men who testified against them did not raise religious objections, nor did they express the view that the Bridges brothers were exploiting Mary Quilter and Mary Browne by gossiping about them or offering to share their sexual favors. When John Allen crept down the stairs to watch, he was motivated by curiosity or voyeurism, or both, but not moral outrage. First the young men expressed disbelief, an indication that the Bridges brothers' sexual activity was not the norm. Then they expressed fear of detection—that their activities would "come to light." This could not have been religiously based, since God was all-knowing and would have been aware of the sin as soon as it had been committed. They were afraid that they would be exposed by an unplanned pregnancy as fornicators, unable to control their sexual appetites, and out of conformity with community sexual mores. While they might have been intrigued by the Bridges brothers' conversations, and they were curious, shame was a powerful deterrent. Parental wrath, perhaps the loss of their patrimony, and the costs associated with a court prosecution and child support also deterred these youths.

John How's deposition shows why, in many instances, men were able to escape the consequences of extramarital sexual activity. When Mary Quilter got pregnant, her fornication conviction was inevitable. Hackaliah Bridges hoped to escape a conviction by refusing to confess. If he did not confess and no one testified against him, he could not be whipped. However, Bridges had told too many people, and public opinion had become so aroused against him, that had How wanted to remain silent, he could not. It indicates, though, that men knew if they did not admit to paternity they could not be convicted of fornication.

It is obvious from these depositions that young men talked about sex. Edmund and Hackaliah shared their sexual experiences with four of their friends and, as attested, "divers others." All of them understood the meaning of a colloquial and descriptive term for sexual activity, "frogging." Of course, the boasting of the Bridges brother, while it must have made the time spent mowing or walking from place to place pass faster, possessed a large element of braggadocio. Their claims that they knew how to avoid pregnancy were wishful thinking, and their attempts to proselytize the youth of Ipswich failed.[46]

The Bridges brothers were sexual predators. Neither was old enough to seriously consider marriage. Both of the women were young servants, and vulnerable. Quilter was seventeen. Her father had died three years earlier, and her mother had to mortgage her dower interest in the family home to pay the Quilter share of the money paid to the town of Ipswich to indenture Mary's baby to a third person.[47] Both Mary Quilter and Hackaliah Bridges were severely whipped for fornication.[48] Edmund Bridges was also severely whipped for fornication.[49] Mary Browne received a mild sentence by the standards of the Essex County Quarterly Court. She was required to "stand by and see him whipped." Browne's moderate punishment indicates mitigating factors that do not survive in the court record.

The depositions related to the youthful sexual activities of Edmund and Hackaliah Bridges provide the clearest evidence of the existence of an adolescent culture in Essex County in which youthful sexual experimentation occurred. Still, there is no evidence that this activity was widespread. Earlier in the decade of the 1650s, another series of prosecutions suggest group sexual experimentation might have occurred, but no depositions survive. In 1654, Elizabeth Osgood, the daughter of William Osgood, who operated a mill in Salisbury that employed local youths, was sentenced to thirty lashes for fornication with Barnabas Lamson.[50] At the same time, James George was fined for "wanton dalliance and lascivious carriage with a young wench," and John Ash was whipped for "filthy, lascivious carriages divers times with a wench."[51] Both men were employed by Osgood's father. Given that women were regularly sentenced to ten lashes in the 1650s, a sentence of thirty lashes may indicate three offenses. This is slim evidence on which to mount a theory that there was a viable appositive adolescent culture in Essex County as Roger Thompson argues existed in neighboring Middlesex County, Massachusetts.

Thompson discovered in Middlesex County a "youth culture, which took an earthy interest in sexual matters and spurned the models of obedience, reverence and continence advertised by their elders." He views their activities as "passing phases" and suggests that economic independence, marriage and parenthood conferred sober adulthood upon rebellious youth. Further, he says, the perils of childbirth brought women, and through them their husbands, into a nearer communion with God. He states that "sexual curiosity and experimentation may have been the precursors, even essential precursors, to spiritual stocktaking and rebirth."[52] In Thompson's Puritan world, teenagers rebelled, and then voluntarily chose to accept their parents' values as they entered adulthood. This is a necessary conclusion for Thompson, because he discounts the body of historical evidence that concludes that New England's social organization was patriarchal in nature.

Essex County depositions, while identical in nature and content to Middlesex County depositions (some individuals recur in the depositions filed in both counties during the seventeenth-century), do not document the existence of a similar widespread adolescent culture in Essex County.[53] On the contrary, most parents, with the exception of Mr. Edmund Bridges, Sr., seem to have maintained control of their adolescent children.[54] It needs to be remembered, too, that Hackaliah and Edmund Bridges were not merely rebellious teenagers acting upon healthy sexual appetites but convicted petty thieves and liars who had violated other Puritan standards of morality. The depositions in the Bridges cases do not indicate an "earthy" interest in sex. The tone of the depositions is surprise, disbelief, and prurience. The predominant reaction of the Bridges brothers' confidants is not admiration, or a desire to emulate their activities, but fear of discovery.

Testimony presented in cases involving older men engaged in fornication clearly illustrates three facets of Puritan sexual attitudes: (1) the Puritan disapproval of extramarital sexual activity, (2) the general inclination of the Puritan community to act as inquisitor in cases of suspected sexual misconduct and (3) the loss of male honor involved in a paternity charge. Forty-eight-year-old Henry Jaques of Newbury was accused of fathering a child on his wife's niece, Elnor Knight, who worked as a servant in his household. He asserted his innocence by mouthing the general view that such an act would be "filthiness" and by proclaiming his fidelity to his marriage vows, even as his own son, also named Henry, came under suspicion.[55] Jacques spoke indignantly about a "bold woman" who had rendered him too sick to eat at a neighborhood dinner by, "saying I hear that your maid is with child & you got it: is it true? Or is it not true?"[56] The "bold woman" felt she had the right to interrogate Jaques, but she also knew the propensity of Puritans to resort to the court if they had been slandered so she was careful not to tell Jaques directly who she had heard the story from until she gained his promise not to sue either herself or Goody Swett, who had passed the rumor to her.

Jaques had lost not only his appetite, but his good name, he complained to Anthony Moss. Moss suggested that, "if it be so that you know yourself clear in this business you should do well to clear yourself in the public meeting or before some Grave Godly person."[57] If Jaques felt his honor had been threatened, he could restore his reputation by responding to the charges publicly. That Moss thought such a course to be necessary indicates the importance Puritans attached to possessing a good name and the damage a paternity charge could inflict on a man's reputation. Francis Thorla also deposed to Jaques' feeling that his name had suffered. Since Jaques had touched Thorla's baby's head and sworn that he was no more the father of Thorla's baby than he was of the child "his servant was then big with," Thorla was inclined to be sympathetic. He reminded Jacques that "he might have more peace to suffer unjustly than justly." How much more Jaques would suffer, Thorla implied, if he were truly the father, not just the reputed father, of Elnor Bryer's baby.

Jaques was not the only substantial citizen who feared the effect of a paternity conviction on his reputation. In 1681 John Atkinson said that an assignment of paternity would "disgrace him and his family."[58] Both men were convicted, and both men took desperate measures to avoid their fates. Jaques fled Newbury in 1666 when faced with an arrest warrant, leaving behind his wife and children. When he learned that the court was prepared to seize £30 of his estate and disenfranchise him, he returned and was fined. Jaques could afford to pay the fine; he did not flee because he feared financial ruin. He fled because his shame, embarrassment, and loss of honor rendered him temporarily incapable of facing his family and his neighbors. John Atkinson spent years in court trying to clear his name, consumed by a public vendetta against Sarah Stickney, the mother of his illegitimate child, because she had impugned his honor.

On December 15, 1687, Samuel Sewall reflected in his diary on the sermon that Increase Mather had preached earlier that day on the topic of fornication. Mather had, "shewed that Good Men might fall into such scandalous Sins as might bring temporal Wrath and ruin upon themselves and upon their posterity.[59] The "temporal wrath and ruin" mentioned by Sewall was why Jaques and Atkinson were so anxious to avoid fornication prosecutions. From Sewall's viewpoint, the inherent shame affected not only the man involved, but his descendants. The implications were serious. Moreover, Sewall seems to be suggesting that any "Good Man" might fall victim to the lure of female sexuality.

Increase Mather's son, Cotton, also an eminent minister, had reason as well to reflect on the effect of a fornication accusation on all members of an otherwise estimable family when he wrote in his diary:

> "Oh! Dreadful Case! Oh, sorrow beyond any that I have met withal! What shall I do now for the foolish Youth! What for my afflicted and abased Family?"[60]

This impassioned outpouring followed the discovery that a "Harlot big with Bastard' had accused his scapegrace son Creasy of paternity. Mather kept Creasy inside for the next few weeks to keep him out of the constable's reach, giving him sermons to read, and, all the while, reminding himself to maintain a Christian calm in the face of multiple provocations.

Another type of attitudinal data was presented by neighbors and other interested persons who testified at fornication trials. In 1674, seventy-year-old Ann Reading was forthright in her opinion about what happened to unmarried persons who engaged in sexual activity; "whoremongerers and adulterers God would judge."[61] In 1683, Priscilla Willson's neighbors attested that Willson had never displayed "any immodest or uncivil behavior or wantonness" prior to the time when she had "greatly dishonored god and her relations together with herself by committing fornication."[62] Willson's fornication conviction was so heinous that her neighbors no longer perceived her as a virtuous young woman but as a disgrace to her family.

It is clear from the depositions that Puritans mistrusted female sexuality. The most virtuous woman, such as Isabel Holdred, discovered in spuriously suspicious circumstances might be presumed to have betrayed her husband. Young women like Joannah Smith and Elizabeth Batten expressed shame at their trials. While it may have been feigned, or a rote expectation of the court, they also expressed penitence during labor, which can be taken as an honest expression of their feelings. Young men, as a group, avoided coitus, although for some the major motivation for abstaining may have been fear of getting caught. For older men like Henry Jaques and John Atkinson, a paternity conviction brought with it a loss of honor. Given, moreover, the representative views of Essex County's substantial citizens, religious leaders, and the people next door and the hierarchical nature of Puritan society, it is difficult to imagine that an appositive culture espousing the sexual attitudes that the Bridges brothers were imprisoned and whipped for, Jaques and Atkinson punished for, and Goody Quilter mortgaged her house in behalf of, flourished. Members of the Puritan community as a whole expressed their disapproval when unmarried persons engaged in sexual intercourse and believed that persons who engaged in sexual activity were hell-bound.

Chapter Five

Listening to Women's Voices: Summaries of Selected Fornication Cases, Essex County, 1640–1685

After 1650, witnesses in Massachusetts Bay Colony courts were required to provide written depositions of their testimony prior to the trial. These depositions survive only in a minority of fornication cases. They provide documentary evidence on a person-by-person basis of the relationship between the defendants, the circumstances in which illegitimate pregnancies occurred, childbirth rituals, and details about work routines. The most common surviving document is the magistrate's paperwork prior to trial in which he recorded the female defendant's complaint and the accompanying denial (in the majority of cases involving an illegitimate pregnancy) of paternity by the male defendant. Depositions filed by midwives are the second most common surviving record, reflecting the legal role the midwife played in recording the female defendant's childbirth declaration of paternity. The third most common survival, and the most detailed in terms of describing sexual activity, is the female defendant's deposition recorded during her pregnancy at the time she visited the local magistrate to lay a charge of paternity.

The rarest type of deposition, probably because it never existed in most cases, is a detailed statement from the male defendant explaining why he believed he was innocent or discussing the circumstances under which the sexual act occurred from his point of view. The lack of surviving documentation from male defendants supports my contention that they were not the major targets of fornication prosecutions. The fact, however, that very few men appear to have filed depositions may be a case of least said, soonest mended. Beyond denying paternity there was no need for them to make a statement to the court, and since the whole procedure, for them, was so freighted with situations in which loss of honor was implicit, the incentive would have existed to leave the least record possible.

Depositions will be used here to reconstruct three representative fornication cases in detail. Mary Talbut is the prototypical servant who engaged in a sexual relationship with another servant following a public courtship and a promise of marriage. Priscilla Willson represents young women who were the victims of older, sexual predators under possibly coerced circumstances, and Sarah Stickney is the stereotypical lusty widow. A fourth case is included, that of Sarah Kenney, whose pregnancy resulted from an incestuous relationship, because it is so atypical and at the same time does suggest the range of Puritan sexual behaviors.

MARY TALBUT

The depositions in this case provide evidence of courting behavior, which included spending time together, paying joint visits to other households, and bundling. As in most fornication cases where the male defendant denied paternity, there are two irreconcilable versions of the relationship. What is clear is that twenty-four-year-old Obadiah Wood was wildly enamored of Mary Talbut. One witness deposed that he had heard Wood say "he would have Mary Tarball dead or alive. This I heard him say more than once."[1]

According to nineteen-year-old Mary Talbut, their sexual relationship began when they were fellow-servants in the Ipswich household of Daniel Hovey in January of 1674, as "her master and dame were asleep when they came home." That June, after she had commenced service with Samuel Hunt, Talbut went to Magistrate Daniel Dennison and told him that she was six months pregnant by Obadiah Wood. Talbut described many instances of sexual activity in her deposition. She claimed that:

> Another time on a sabbath day when she stayed at home with the children he came to her in the fore-noon and lay with her, and another time he pretended to be ill on Saturday night & rose not till master and dame were gone to meeting and that sabbath day also he lay with her and since she lives at Goodman Hunts, he came to her into the barn in the evening while she was milking and would have lain with her but she refused.... Further, she saieth that he hath often assured her and promised her marriage & drawn her to promise him. Since she has been with child she has acquainted him with it and he did not disown it.[2]

Obadiah Wood was summoned, denied Talbut's accusation, and was required to post bond of £40, later raised to £50. Samuel Hunt posted a £5 bond on Talbut's behalf, which was later raised to £10.

Talbut documented a private sexual relationship and a public courtship in her deposition. They had engaged in sexual intercourse at least four times. It is not clear where the first act of sexual intercourse occurred.

It may have been out of doors, beside a bridge Talbut describes, but it was January and the master and mistress were asleep when they came home, so it may have been in Wood's bed. It was not in Talbut's bed, since she slept at the foot of her mistress' bed. The couple then engaged in subterfuge to gain time alone in the Hovey household until Talbut wished to discontinue the relationship and asked her master to sell either her indenture or Obadiah's indenture to another employer. After Samuel Hunt had purchased her indenture from Hovey, she said, she had refused to have intercourse with Wood although he had sought her out.

Wood had also courted Talbut publicly. This public courtship, by Talbut's account, included coming to talk to her as she lay in her bed at the foot of Mistress Hovey's bed. A neighbor testified that Talbut and Wood had visited her house twice together in the evening and gone away together.[3] A second neighbor, twenty-one-year old Elizabeth Foster, testified to an occasion when Talbut had encouraged Wood to join them in bed. Foster said:

> She said she would lie with me and so we went to go to bed. And locked the door and Mary before she went into bed she went and unlocked it again and after we were abed Obadiah he came up and put out the light and I asked Mary where Obadiah was and she said on the bed by me and I told him several times that I would complain to the Major and bid him keep clear of us. He said he did not fear us and after a while he went from the bed.[4]

Wood continued to visit Mary Talbut after she went to work for Samuel Hunt. His attentions were so flagrant that her new employer's mother-in-law warned him off. She said:

> Obadiah Wood did constantly frequent the company of Mary Talbot from the time she came to live with my son Hunt, till it was discovered that she was with child which we feared would be, by reason of his great and constant familiarity with her notwith-standing all of our warning of him and forbidding him and telling him whore mongerers and adulterers god would judge.[5]

Hunt's mother-in-law was not the only person to warn Wood away from Talbut after she had gone to work at the Hunts. Her mistress, Elizabeth Hunt, was very explicit about her reasons for wanting Wood to stay away from Talbut. She did not want to lose any of her servant's labor to pregnancy. She testified:

> One lords day night in May last he came and was in her company when I saw them in the evening and I saw such familiarity between them I was

> forced to speak and bid him go home and keep out of her company unless he thought he could pay for her time and forewarned him of coming any more in such a way but he still stayed with her and seemed not to regard me nor what I said. At length I saw him sit astraddle her over her leg and chuck her under the chin and so he sat a good interim of time then I spoke to him again as much as I could say with modesty but he regarded me not til his own time served him to be gone.[6]

Elizabeth Hunt's deposition is remarkable for what did *not* happen. She had no authority over Obadiah Wood. He did not respond to her orders that he leave. Nor did he respond to the request or the threat of Elizabeth Foster when she asked him to leave her bedroom, nor did he pay attention to Talbut's employer's mother's "warning of him and forbidding him." It would seem that there were limits to female authority, even within the household. Moreover, Hunt feels these limits. She said "as much as she could say with modesty." This suggests that in male/female discourse, despite the fact that Wood was on her land and acting in a sexually provocative manner with her servant in front of her, she could not displace Wood without departing from appropriate Puritan norms of femininity. Nor does Talbut reject Wood's advances. At this point, though, she was five months pregnant and dependent on Wood to buy out her indenture and to marry her.

Thirty-year-old Judith Browne testified to Obadiah's attitude toward premarital sexual intercourse. Her testimony, suggesting as it did that Wood considered premarital sexual intercourse to be a prerequisite of any woman he planned to marry, placed her in Mary Talbut's camp after Wood learned of her pregnancy and disavowed her:

> The same night Samuel Griffin was married she heard Obadiah Wood ask him if he never lay with his wife before he was married which the said Samuel denying by rebuking him. The said Obadiah said he would never marry while he lived unless he had laid with his bride before and said it was no sin, for they were married in heaven before & it was only to please men they were married here.[7]

Another defendant, a rival of Wood's, twenty-six-year-old Seth Story, attested as well to Wood's belief that he and Talbut were married in the eyes of God. He deposed:

> Some time last winter Obadiah Wood and I wrought together about the time that Obadiah Wood was in love with Mary Talbut, I the said Seth Story heard Obadiah Wood often say that he was resolved that he would have Mary Talbut dead or alive. None should hinder him of having her for he said that he was married to her. . . . Moreover Obadiah bade me remember how John Leigh fared at court for meddling with other folks.[8]

John Leigh had conducted an adulterous affair with Sarah Roe while her husband was at sea. The strict standards required for an adultery conviction, since it was a capital crime, could not be met so Leigh was severely whipped and fined five pounds and Roe was sent to the House of Correction for thirty days for "unlawful familiarity." Wood's suggestion that Story's attentions to Talbut were adulterous since she was married to Wood in the eyes of God is a further indication Wood had fathered Talbut's child.

Talbut's side of the case, then, was that Wood had pursued her, promised her marriage, threatened off her other suitors, and declared to people that he considered himself to be married to her. He had openly courted her, and during this courtship, and while they were mutually employed at the Hovey's, she had engaged in sexual intercourse with him. At the same time, she had asked Daniel Hovey to sell her indenture, and when she had moved to Samuel Hunt's house she had broken off her relationship with Wood. Unfortunately, she later discovered that she was pregnant. When she told Wood of the pregnancy, he fell out of love abruptly and broke his promise to marry her. Wood's rhetoric about spiritual marriage was not strong enough to survive the inevitable shame of disclosure with the attendant trial, parental opposition, and community disapproval.

Wood presented an alternate version of events. He had loved her, but she had scorned him and engaged in sexual activity with other men. His friends, whose approval was an important part of seventeenth-century match-making, opined that she was making a fool of him. The child she carried, he claimed, was not his. His statement provides a unique view into the mental world of a male fornication defendant. First he proclaims his innocence:

> Ye poor petitioner cannot but be deeply sensible of the Righteous hand of God against him in bringing such a great trouble and affliction upon him by the accusation of Mary Talbet laying that to his charge, which he knows in his heart that he is totally innocent of, and does not doubt, but one day he shall be so found, before the Righteous Judge of Heaven & Earth for that he did contrary to the advice of all his friends and especially his father (whose counsel and command he ought to have attended in matters of this nature) setting his affections upon one, who has thus requited him for the good will he sometimes bore to her. Your petitioner cannot deny but that by his familiarity with her formerly during the time he made love to her, he has given opportunity to her, the said Mary, to accuse him as well as others to suspect him as guilty, yet he most humbly requests so much favor from you that you would be pleased to consider of such allegations that he is able to produce in his own defense, which he humbly engages shall be as free from reflecting on others as the circumstances of the thing will bear. And if upon a view of what shall be alleged against him, and for him the Honored Court

> shall see meet to determine anything that may be matter of suffering to him, he shall with all humility quietly submit thereunto & endeavor to improve himself.[9]

He admitted to courting Mary Talbut, said that he should have listened to his father and his friends, and promised to be a better person even if the court found him guilty. He mounted a typical defense. He blackened Mary Talbut's character and named a number of other potential fathers:

> No witness can be produced of his frequenting her company at any unseemly time, place, or manner otherwise than is usually found by such as are making love to single persons of her sex. During her abode in this town she has been known to be much given to the company of young men. And did affect the company of some others more than my self although it is not my desire to leaven suspicion of them, as if they were guilty of that which I am charged with. That about the time when this fact was done I was earnest suitor to her, and was always contemned and scornfully used by her as many can witness therefore it cannot be supposed that I was admitted to unlawful familiarity, when I desired lawful marriage with her and could not obtain it, until the estate she was now brought into put her in a necessity to seek that as a cover to her folly where she hopes her attempt will be most successful, by former advantages given to her by my familiar carriage with her & living awhile in the house with her. She has sometimes been known to have been out all night without the knowledge of her master & Dame, when I can prove I was not in her company, as was in feb. last when her master Hovey searched his barn and cow house, but could not find her till morning, and I only was seen to come along with her from John Dane's house and was at my lodging within a quarter of an hour and kept there all night. She was out of Samuel Hunt's house all one night in harvest time when I was at my master's house at home all that night. She has used sundry expressions before sundry persons that might render her accusation of me in all probability to be false, as to Ann Cotton, Elizabeth Haraden, Sarah Hely. It is known that one night about the 12th of January, when Seth Story walked with her near the river to Steven Cross his house when she was there all night, Samuel Bowden that sojourned at the said Crosses the very next day told me that he could get her away from me and a dozen such men as I was, and said at last that she was a common whore, and I was a fool if I did bear any affection to her. Many such expressions as these were used at my brother John Frink's house by the said Bowden the very next day, which, with other things I observed, were the reasons I took of my affections wholly away from her ever after that time.[10]

Wood claimed that he had ceased to court Mary Talbut in January, the month her child was conceived, when he learned that she was seeing other men; not later, as Talbut said, when he learned she was pregnant. The Hunts, her current employers, however, had testified that he had been making a nuisance of himself as late as May, hanging around their house in pursuit of Talbut. Clearly his deposition is not as frank and open as he claimed.

Damaging testimony was presented against Mary Talbut. It is difficult to determine credibility at this distance, but some qualifications can be made. First, a common defense was to connect the female defendant with another man who might plausibly be accused of fathering the child. In this instance there were two credible candidates. The first was Seth Story. Two young men deposed that they had seen Talbut and Story engaged in, if not intercourse, heavy petting:

> The deposition of Thomas Burnam, jr., and Thomas Waight, jr., aged about twenty years. These deponents testifieth and saieth that about the last Indian harvest in ye 73 as we were coming in the way from Thomas Burnam's on Saturday in the evening at the twilight by the way side in Daniel Hovey's cowyard which was about fifty or sixty rods from any house we saw Seth Story and Mary Talbut lying on the ground she on her back & Seth Story lying on her breasts & when Seth Story saw us he turned off from the said Mary Talbut & rose up and shook her coat & her clothes were loose and unbraided & these deponents further testify that we have seen the aforesaid Seth and Talbut together several times since in several places before the said Talbut came to live at Goodman Hunt's and after she came to live at Goodman Hunt's.[11]

Since, however, the sexual activity they referred to occurred approximately three months before Talbut conceived it was not even relevant to her pregnancy. Both Talbut and Wood, at that time, were working for Daniel Hovey. The cowyard would have been Wood's territory. It is unlikely, given Wood's assiduous courtship at that time that she would have been petting with Story in that location. Additionally, a distance of fifty to sixty rods, or more than 800 feet, at twilight, would make identification difficult, if not impossible.

A second strategy was to accuse the female defendant of having intercourse with someone who had a reputation for sexual immorality, as Martha Woodie, a probable relative of Wood, did. She claimed that:

> Samuel Bowden said that the night before he had been at Hovey's with Mary Talbut and that he had her maidenhead that night and that if she had had nine more he had taken them all. These very words he used to the best of my remembrance further she the said deponent. . . . had observed the said Bowden to be of very light behavior among maids upon all occasions.[12]

Her testimony provided evidence of an alternative sexual partner at the time that Talbut conceived, so on the surface it was credible. However, Samuel

Bowden did not corroborate her testimony, although, to be fair, it was not in his interest to do so.

The most damaging set of depositions about Talbut was supplied by other women who make it clear that Obadiah Wood's affection for Mary Talbut was commonly known and that Talbut's contempt for Wood was equally well known. They had no compunction about chiding Wood for setting his affections on Talbut, but Wood continued to insist that Talbut behaved affectionately to him when they were in private. Mary Fuller testified that:

> Obadiah Wood came to our house one time and I asked him what the matter was; I heard that he was about to hang himself for Mary Tarball. He asked me who told him that lie. I told him that he was a fool to go about any such thing for she thought she would never have him, which said Obadiah, why. Because she does not love you I think she did not love him. Oh said he it's no matter for she does love me well enough when we are alone together. Obadiah said that he had spoke to Goodman Hunt to forewarn Seth Story of the house and Hunt said he would; Seth will leave [bravely:] Obadiah told me she was as loving to him when Seth was gone as she was to Seth when he was there; and Obadiah and Mary came to my house twice in the evening together and they went away together again.[13]

Fuller's testimony is ambiguous. It is clear that, in public, Talbut did not always treat Wood well, but Wood defended Talbut's actions toward him.

Sarah Healy also testified to Talbut's feelings for Wood:

> Being in company with Mary Talbut and Jonas Grigri being present & we talking concerning Obadiah Wood and Seth Story the aforesaid Talbut said that she did not care a straw for Obadiah Wood but only kept his company to make a fool of him and that she would make a fool of him before she had done: And that Seth Story was worth a hundred of Obadiah Wood & the aforesaid Healy further said that Seth Story and Mary Talbut was very frequently together & I told Seth Story that I wished all ended well & I wished Seth Story to have a care what he did.[14]

Hester Hovey, Talbut's mistress, added:

> I observed by her actions that she never loved Obadiah namely Mary Talbut. She would often threaten Obadiah if he did not what she would have him she would say she would be even with him. This I observed that though she seemed to love Obadiah yet if other young men came in then he was cast off and made a fool of the play.[15]

There is one more deposition attesting to the relationship between Mary Talbut and Obadiah Wood. This deposition is the most credible, because it was supplied by John Dane, Sr., a respected Ipswich resident. Since Wood went to live with Dane when he left the Hoveys, Dane had the opportunity to observe the relationship first hand. However, that Wood was residing with Dane may have colored his testimony. His testimony may have been influenced as well by the fact that sixteen-year-old Mary Dane, his daughter, had been convicted of fornication in 1654.[16] Although the father of Mary Dane's illegitimate child had a local record for promiscuity, Dane received the severer sentence. She was whipped for fornication and required to support her infant by herself.[17] John Dane testified:

> Obadiah Wood boarded at my house when he came from Daniel Hovey's and he carried himself very well and unblameable so far as I could observe though Mary Talbut often sought to allure him he seemed constantly to be averse to her though she used much means to prevail with him in his company. She would seem to show much respect to him and when some other were present then she set light by him. This I speak after he came to my house. Formerly he loved her but she always carried it so at last it so exasperated his spirit as that he could not give her a good word.[18]

However, Dane's testimony, as he admits, is limited to behavior observed after Wood and Talbut had left the Hoveys, by which time Talbut knew she was pregnant and had informed Wood of the fact. It is not surprising, then, that from Dane's point of view, Talbut appeared to be pursuing Wood. She needed a husband to legitimize her baby.

The women's community of Ipswich performed the oversight role theoretically assigned to them by Laurel Ulrich: "Women needed protection, not because they were innocent but because they were not."[19] Three generations of women from Samuel Hunt's family, his mother, seventy-year-old Anne Reading, his wife, thirty-seven-year-old Elizabeth, and his daughter, fourteen-year-old Elizabeth, all warned Wood off. Other women performed the inquisitory function of the midwife, questioning Talbut about the father of her child. Sarah Healy presented a second deposition, no less favorable to Talbut, in which she reported the content of a conversation about the baby's paternity:

> That on the 22nd of September last being at the well, by the riverside near Goodman Hunt's Mary Talbut came to them. Sarah Hely asked her the said Talbut when she thought she should be delivered. She answered she did not know when, but counted it would be sometime this month. Sarah Hely told her that Obadiah Wood said that he did not know anything of these things she accused him with, adding further that she believed the said Wood would not own the child. Mary Talbut replied that he was a

> fool if he did own it, adding that if it were her case, she would not own it herself, laughing much in the time of her speaking, and was as merry. As if she were not in such a condition, as she is judged to be.[20]

Even a thirteen-year-old, Anne Cotton, weighed in with a deposition. She had spoken with Mary Talbut at Samuel Hunt's well in August. She had taunted Talbut, asking her who would support her child, for Obadiah Wood would not. She deposed that Talbut had told her Seth Story would support both her and her child.[21]

In all, 19 neighbors presented depositions in this case. Much of the evidence presented would have been declared inadmissible by today's standards, but Ipswich's citizens, from John Dane, Sr., to thirteen-year-old Anne Cotton, felt it their duty to bear witness where community moral standards had been violated.[22] Obadiah Wood was an Ipswich native, the eldest of ten children of a baker, also named Obadiah Wood. Everyone who deposed knew the Woods and shopped at his father's bakehouse. Talbut was a newcomer to town and had no local family.[23] Talbut balanced the sure affections of Obadiah Wood against the chance of securing a more eligible husband. It is likely that local sympathies rested with Wood. Mary Talbut lacked a reservoir of good feeling to draw upon when she became pregnant, and she had violated the Puritan gender stereotype. While the deponents stated the obvious, that Wood had claimed to be "in love" with Talbut and had courted her publicly, they seemed anxious to exculpate him of paternity.

One important deposition is missing. There is no testimony from the midwife. Nor is there reference to a midwife's testimony in the magistrate's paperwork. In the majority of cases, the midwife's testimony is at the heart of the prosecution, and its lack, in this instance, is puzzling. It is likely that this deposition existed at the time, because Obadiah Wood, although he was not convicted of fornication, was assessed child-support payments by the court.[24]

Mary Talbut's legal problems were just beginning. There is no official record of her conviction for fornication, but in October, 1674, a month after her child's birth, Obadiah Wood was ordered to pay her employer, Samuel Hunt, 40 shillings in corn for Hunt's loss of Talbut's labor during her pregnancy.[25] He was further required to pay Talbut 12 shillings a month toward their child's support. Samuel Hunt was back in court the following April, seeking damages for the "loss he had suffered by his servant Mary Talbut's being with child" beyond the 40 shillings in corn he had been paid by Wood for the loss of Talbut's time. Talbut was ordered to serve a further two years beyond the time her current indenture with Hunt ended.[26] Two years later, in 1677, Talbut sought a clarification of the court's ruling. Apparently Samuel Hunt had sold her indenture to someone else, and Talbut hoped that the extra two years the court had assigned Hunt because of the time lost during her indenture, were not transferable. The court declared otherwise. She had been bound to Samuel Hunt and to "his assigns."[27]

Perhaps the most interesting aspect of this case is the repeated references to love.[28] Obadiah Wood said he was in love with Mary Talbut. Many of his neighbors also used the phrase, "in love." Wood appears, in their descriptions, to be remarkably similar to a twentieth-century adolescent in the throes of a crush. The seventeenth-century onlookers regarded Wood's repeated assertions of love with derision. It was an emotion not to be trusted, and that Wood's "love" was so transient is a salient reminder that twentieth-century conceptualizations of love cannot be reliably used to assess seventeenth-century relationships.

PRISCILLA WILLSON

Priscilla Willson, while younger at her conviction than many fornication defendants, is representative of the single women who appeared in Essex County Quarterly Court between 1640 and 1685 as victims of coerced sexual activity who, because they had conceived or their circumstances did not fit the narrow legal requirements to merit a rape prosecution, were tried for fornication.[29] Willson was a sixteen-year-old orphan under the guardianship of her grandfather when she got pregnant. Her partner, Samuel Appleton, was twenty-nine, married and active in the business and social affairs of Essex County. The character reference supplied by sixteen of Willson's neighbors indicates that they had perceived her to be a virtuous young woman who must have been seduced by Samuel Appleton. They said that they had been:

> the nearest neighbors unto Priscilla Wilson of Lyn, who hath greatly dishonored God and her relations together with her self by committing fornication: yet we make bold to signify to the Honored Court: That it was a matter of great admiration to us to hear of it: because from her childhood she behaved herself so modestly and civilly all her time before this transgression as that none of us ever saw or heard of any immodest or uncivil behavior or wantonness and that we believe she was overcome by some subtle slights and temptations of one that beguiled her to yield to his lust and we are all persuaded that she doth not wrongly accuse him who she doth lay the charge upon: and so much we present to the Honored Court hoping god will return her by repentance and help her to deal truly in the case.[30]

Evidence supplied during the trial, which took place a week after Appleton's first wedding anniversary, indicated that the sexual intercourse, which Appleton denied had occurred, might not have been consensual.

The first two witnesses testified that Appleton had had the opportunity to father Willson's illegitimate baby. Hester Witt, Willson's eighteen-year-old friend said that:

> one night when I the deponent lived at the old Iron Works with my father Stocker, in the room that my father Stocker lived there was a bed on which Priscilla Willson lay down saying she was not well and Mr. Samuel Appleton came into the room and went and lay down upon the bed and drew the curtains and the said Priscilla desired him several times to let her go forth, but he kept her in when she desired to come away and so he hindered her and they tarried there a considerable time.[31]

Naomy Flanders, a twenty-four-year-old servant, presented even more damaging testimony. She claimed to have questioned Appleton about his treatment of Willson and to have been rebuked by him. Her testimony was that:

> Mr. Appleton of Lyn came into the room and went and lay down upon the bed where she was. And the said Priscilla Willson desired him to let her go forth: but he kept her in until Mrs. Purchis came and called for her and then in a little time after he let her go. And a little while after this deponent asked Mr. Appleton why he did so: viz: stop her and keep her at that time: when she was so desirous to go away. And Mr. Appleton told me I was a fool and knew nothing.[32]

More witnesses followed the next day. Both Sarah Hathorne, the midwife who had delivered Willson's baby, and Experience Tarbox, testified that Willson, after much persuasion, had named Appleton during labor as the father. Hathorne deposed that:

> by the Providence of God it was her lot to be midwife to Priscilla Willson of Lynn when the time of her travel came; before I entered upon performance of anything, though her pains came upon her, this deponent said Priscilla deal truly and plainly with me and tell me truly who is the father of the child and do no body any wrong, she the said Priscilla answered no more she would not. In the instant of time her grandfather Purchis came into the room and said to this purpose oh my child, thou hast not god's fear before thee when thou didst this evil but now let the fear of god be upon thee and doe no person any wrong but as thou knowest not but thou mayest dy. I charge thee in god's fear deal truly and declare truly who is the father of ye child and so spake to this purpose-left the room. Immediately her pangs came upon her and still this deponent and the rest present pressed her to tell truly and in her extremity she said she did & Mr. Appleton of Lyn was the father of it and that there was never no other man had to do with her.[33]

Despite character testimony from Willson's neighbors, evidence of coercion, the considerable age disparity, and a childbirth statement, the charges against Appleton were dismissed while Willson was convicted and fined.

Appleton had a special relationship with the judges. One of them was his father; the rest were business and social acquaintances. For this reason, the court issued a compromise decision. While dismissing fornication charges against Appleton, the judges required him to pay one-half of the infant's expenses prior to its death, and one-half of the court costs. This was a tacit admission that the court believed him guilty. Appleton retained his reputation and was accorded a series of honorific titles upon his death in 1725. Willson disappeared from view. Her only appearances in the seventeenth-century record are her birth notice and her fornication conviction.

This case illustrates the disparate penalty paid by male and female fornicators, the imbalance of power that often existed between men and women who engaged in extramarital sexual intercourse, and the coercive nature of much of the sexual activity. This type of sexual behavior will be revisited in chapter eight in a discussion of coerced sexual activity.

SARAH STICKNEY

Sarah Stickey, nee Morse, was married at twenty-two and widowed in 1678 at thirty-seven. Her husband left her a prosperous farm—an estate valued at almost £300 pounds, six sons, one of whom was only nine months old, and two daughters. Little more than a year later she was in court, charged with fornication. She presented herself as a defenseless widow who had suffered repeated sexual assaults at the hands of a sailor, Samuel Lowell. The first time, she deposed, Lowell came with a pint of alcohol and a friend who quickly fell into a drunken stupor. She testified that:

> when she saw she could not be rid of them she went to bed & being fast asleep with four children in bed with her, Samuel Lowell undressed himself & came into her bed, which when she awakened and perceived, she cried out, and would have awakened the sd Stevens who was fast asleep in the chimney corner: and could not awake him but with striving the best she could, he at last went away and said he would come no more.[34]

Stickney claimed that after this she had locked her doors securely at night to no avail. After Lowell had made two more attempts, "breaking open the doors & coming into the bed," frightening both herself and her children in the process, she had gone to her brothers for advice. They advised her to make sure that a man slept in the house each night to "bear witness" to the harassment. At this point she reported an incident so implausible that it raises questions about her veracity:

> One night he came and keeping a noise at the door to come in and one of Rowley being in the house, she called to him, who in rising saw a man run away but could not tell who it was- when he came into the bed she persuaded him and spoke resolutely to him, yet could not prevail to make him cease his attempt, but that with her struggling and striving with him, he made her sick almost to death.[35]

How Lowell got into her bed with "one of Rowley" in the house is not explained. She claimed that Lowell had entered her house, undressed, and climbed in bed with her yet again one night when her brother, Joshua Morse, was on guard duty. While they had been unable to catch Lowell, she deposed, they had one of his shoes as evidence.

It does not seem likely that Sarah Stickney was subjected to repeated sexual assaults from Samuel Lowell. In her version, Lowell was remarkably adept at getting through locked doors and avoiding her protectors. Moreover, there was overwhelming testimony to the contrary. A neighbor testified that Stickney hoped to marry Samuel Lowell, but that he had refused on the grounds that he did not have enough money.[36] Lowell claimed that Stickney had often invited him to visit and to bring friends.[37] Further, the neighborhood apparently believed that Joshua Morse had acted as Lowell's "pimp" rather than in defense of his sister's virtue.[38]

In March, 1681, Stickney was charged with fornication a second time. She named no father, and Lowell presented depositions proving he was at sea when this child was conceived. A year after this fornication conviction, she claimed that John Atkinson, a forty-six-year-old father of nine, was the father of this latest child. Her accusation unleashed a series of bitter and acrimonious court battles. She claimed she had not named him before because he had paid her to remain silent, and one of her sons provided convenient testimony that Atkinson had visited her at night. Atkinson's wife was six month's pregnant at the time Stickney's child was conceived, so he has to be considered as one of the potential fathers. Atkinson was convicted of paternity and required to pay child support. From then on, he and the Widow Stickney were stock figures at the Essex County quarterly court sessions as he sought to have the fornication conviction overturned. At no point was he ready to concede that he had fathered the child, and he fought vigorously to have the child-support payments first reduced and then discontinued. Even Mrs. Atkinson entered the fray, physically attacking Stickney, and petitioning the court to have the payments discontinued because of the hardship it was causing Atkinson's legitimate family. In 1682, this curious court order was entered:

> Court being informed that the clerk of the writs of Newbury had entered the bastard child of Sarah Stickney of Newbury in the record of births as the child of John Atkinson, upon whom she charged it, although he did not own it, it was declared to be an irregularity, and the clerk was ordered to appear at the next Ipswich [unless] he give satisfaction to said Atkinson before that time. The clerk was ordered to erase the entry from the book of records and cause it, if it be returned to the county records, to be altered or erased from those records.[39]

Atkinson had been judged to be the father of Stickney's child, he was paying child-support, and yet he was able to prevent his name from being officially recorded as its father.[40]

It seems clear that Sarah Stickney, in her widowhood, was sexually active with multiple partners and that this was a problem for the Essex County Quarterly Court. Testimony indicates that John Atkinson lost a lottery cynically conducted by Sarah Stickney: "They did draw lots and the lots fell upon John Atkinson to father the child."[41] Further, Stickney had told a neighbor that the father was a "young man of the town that came to my house with a bottle of liquors & I was fasting and I prayed him that he would not abuse me and he said he would not but did."[42] The following year child-support was discontinued and the Widow Stickney married Stephen Ackerman. Ackerman had not been mentioned in any of the depositions relative to Stickney as a possible sexual partner in either of Stickney's fornication prosecutions. He was too poor to have made a desirable marriage partner and I postulate that Stickney's ability to live in peace in Newbury depended upon the mantle of respectability cast by marriage to Ackerman.

Sarah Stickney's sexual activity appears to be alcohol-related. It may be that local men knew that if they brought Stickney alcohol they could get sex in return. That would explain why so many men were potential fathers of her two illegitimate children. It would also explain why Stickney depicted herself as a victim. Her mention that she had been fasting at the time of her second conception may exhibit a sophisticated understanding of the effects of alcohol on an empty stomach. Her claims of abuse could also be predicated on a desire to be perceived as conforming to the Puritan ideal of womanly chastity despite her circumstances. She may have resented the reputation she had gained for sexual availability. Certainly she was cynical of the court's attitude toward sexual malefactors. Upon her return from sentencing for her second presentation she told a neighbor that: "the Court did not regard the Sin so they could get the money."[43]

SARAH KENNEY

The only permissible form of sexual intercourse from the Puritan point of view was heterosexual man-on-top coitus between persons who were married to each other for the purpose of procreation. If, at the same time, this sexual intercourse promoted mutual affection and marital harmony, that was a side benefit. Seventeenth-century sexual taboos reflected the values of a Biblically-oriented agricultural society in which sodomy and bestiality were capital crimes. Women were largely exempt from charges of homosexual activity or bestiality because the legal requirement of penetration defined them as male acts.[44] Father-daughter incest, so heinous to today's sensibilities, was regarded as adultery.[45] The victim was the wife, who had been deprived of her rightful sexual activity, not the daughter who had been abused. In 1688, when Sarah Kenney told the magistrates that her father was the father of her illegitimate child, she was charged with fornication.[46] It was her sexual misbehavior, not her father's, which concerned the court.

The first deposition filed in Sarah Kenney's case is unique because it appears to be the only document related to a fornication case in a question and answer format. In February 1688, sixty-four-year-old Henry Kenney of Salem Village was summoned to appear before Major Bartholomew Gedney and Major William Browne, two members of "His Majesties Honorable Council here" and Justice of the Peace, John Hathorne, in order to tell them the whereabouts of his thirty-year-old, pregnant, unmarried daughter.[47] Rumor had it, they said, that he, Henry Kenney, was her child's father. That three justices were in attendance for a preliminary hearing is in itself extraordinary; proof either that they believed something serious might have happened to her, or that removing a suspected fornicator from their jurisdiction was a serious offense:

> Question: Where is your daughter Sarah Kenney
>
> Answered that there had been many reports he had carried her away.
>
> Q. Where have you carried her?
>
> Ans. To the house of one Thwaites a considerable distance from Dedham, towards Secunk.
>
> Q. Why did you carry her away?

> Ans. She was with child I verily believe & according to her relation near six months gone and there being many reports concerning it I was willing for my own peace & the peace of my family to carry her away.
>
> Q. What reports are there concerning it?
>
> Ans. To tell you the truth I have heard she saieth that I am the father of the child although she has often said that Mrs. Putnams Negro is the father of it & I have good ground to believe it is so.
>
> Q. If there be such reports & you know yourself clear, why have you done so imprudently as to carry her away privately & nobody knew but yourself, which has caused everybody to suspect there is something further in it?
>
> Ans. I am clear of any such thing. & I doubt not but times will clearly manifest it.[48]

The three magistrates ordered Kenney to post a £20 bond to bring a certificate to them within two weeks from the Justice of the Peace where Sarah Kenney was boarding which stated that his daughter was well and being provided for in a manner suitable to her condition. Further, within six weeks to two months of her delivery Sarah Kenney was to appear before them to answer charges of fornication.

Kenney returned two weeks later as ordered with proof that his daughter was living in Henry Thwaite's "public house of entertainment." On July 23, 1688, Sarah Kenney appeared herself before the Justice of the Peace, John Hathorne, accompanied not by her father but by her brother and her brother-in-law who said they had come on Henry Kenney's behalf. Sarah Kenney said that:

> in her travails with the child Mrs. Buxton the midwife examined her who was the father of her said child, unto which She then answered that it was her own father, Henry Kenney that was the father of her child she then was in travail withal.[49]

Sarah Kenney was ordered to post bond of £20 and to appear at the next session of the Essex County Quarterly Court to answer charges of fornication. Henry Kenney was freed of his recognizance at this meeting. He had done all that was required of him by the court. He surfaced next in the court record during the Salem witchcraft trials as a deponent. Unfortunately the docket book containing the final disposition of this case is lost. There is no reason to think, however, from the existing paperwork, that Henry Kenney suffered further repercussions. Probably Sarah Kenney appeared at the next session of the quarterly court, pled guilty to fornication, was fined, and had the remainder of her £20 appearance bond, less court costs, remitted.

The aim of this chapter has been to provide a human dimension to the quantitative data presented in the previous chapters. The numbers provided insight into the incidence of extramarital sexual activity in seventeenth-century Essex County, the limited degree to which unmarried women and men shared prosecution for fornication, and the imbalance in the severity with which men and women were punished. The depositions filed in individual cases clarify the attitudes and behaviors that the numbers indicated existed.

The details of the Mary Talbut/Obadiah Wood fornication trial are replicated again and again in seventeenth-century Essex County depositions. Wood was not the only servant who pursued a fellow servant until he caught her and then used a defense of female promiscuity to try to evade child-support payments. The depositions filed in the Talbut case make clear how critical it was that women marry. Marriage was "basic to survival for many New England women."[50] Their identity, their future standard of living, their status in the community, literally their whole way of life was dependent upon the men they married. Mary Talbut did not have much to offer. She had no dowry, and she had sold her service for an unknown number of years. Obadiah Wood had offered her marriage, and whether she engaged in sexual intercourse because it was his expectation, as some of the depositions indicated, or because she wanted to cement their relationship, she still thought she might be able to do better. Seth Story represented a step up economically and socially, but when she became pregnant her options were foreclosed. Talbut had to make do with Wood, but she found that he did not want a pregnant bride. Talbut had tried without success to manipulate the Puritan marriage system.

Women such as Mary Talbut engaged in sexual intercourse as part of a strategy to marry. Others, like Priscilla Willson, were victimized by sexual predators who were already married or did not plan to marry. Widow Sarah Stickney epitomized the stereotypical lusty widow, but for the consumption of the court she sought to recast herself as a victim. Women in seventeenth-century Massachusetts bore illegitimate children for diverse reasons and under different conditions, but they shared the common experience of bastard-bearing which limited their marriageability, confirmed the traditional understanding of women's innate lustfulness, and earned the contempt of the Puritan community for violating the standard of female chastity.

Men felt the effect of a fornication or paternity conviction differently. It did not affect their marriageability, but it did affect, at least for a time, their standing in the community. The lengths Henry Jaques went to in order to keep his sexual relationship with his servant secret and John Atkinson went to in order to clear his name after a paternity conviction indicate the strength of Puritanism's negative attitude toward extramarital sex. It was not the wrath of their wives or the potential burdens of child support which they feared; it was the public exposure of their extramarital sexual activities. Their standing in the Puritan community depended on the public perception of their characters. The highest aspiration of Puritan men was to be recognized as members of the Elect. Living sainthood in Puritan Massachusetts brought with it the respect of one's neighbors, material well-being, and eternal life. Men (and women) might know in their hearts that they fell short of the ideal, but appearances were important to the maintenance of honor. Fornication convictions and judicial assignments of child support brought public awareness to private sexual behaviors the community considered shameful. Puritans thought of themselves as parts of a larger, Godly, community. The exposure of sexual activity that violated community standards, that was commonly described through the use of terms like "incontinence" and "filthiness" by a society that expected conformance to community values, was a source of great shame and an experience to be avoided by men if at all possible.[51]

Chapter Six

"She Being Presented for Fornication": Pregnant Brides in Seventeenth-Century Essex County

> Margaret Welch appeared in open Court & owned the fact she being presented for fornication. Her husband in all likelihood taken by the French appeared not. The Court considering her case determine that the said Margaret Welch shall pay to the Treasurer of the County of Essex the fine of 40s or be whipt ten stripes & costs of Court & stand committed till all be paid on the next Wednesday after Lecture.[1]

Margaret Batten and her absent husband, Edward Welch, are representative of the one hundred and fifty-one couples who were charged with fornication following the birth of their first child within 32 weeks of marriage in Essex County, Massachusetts, between 1640 and 1685. They engaged in sexual intercourse in late April, 1689, in a tavern garden. Four months later, Batten went to Salem magistrate, John Hathorne, to swear out a complaint against Edward Welch for paternity. Batten claimed they had intercourse only that one time: Welch said he would marry her if she would swear that "no other man had had to do with her"[2] The following July, Welch was gone from New England and his wife was in the Salem prison, perhaps accompanied by their six-month-old child. If she was unable to pay the fine and court costs she would be removed from the jail, displayed to the residents of Salem, perhaps in a cage as in Ipswich, prior to meeting on Wednesday, and then stripped to the waist and whipped after the sermon.[3]

It would appear from the low number of presentments that either not all persons were prosecuted or that few couples engaged in coitus prior to marriage. Clearly, the prosecutorial network was in place. It must be then, that couples eschewed sexual intercourse prior to marriage. It is instructive at this point to look at practices in contemporary England where between 20 and 27 percent of the population never married and that portion of the population that married waited until age twenty-eight for men and twenty-six for women.[4] Although this marriage rate reduced one in four English adults to perpetual virginity or casual sexual relationships, the illegitimacy rate in England was low, too, at between two and four percent.[5] The premarital pregnancy rate, however, was between 20 and 30 percent. This suggests that fully-consummated sexual intercourse was initiated only after marriage seemed certain. Casual extramarital sexual intercourse was not considered criminal behavior in England but neither, in the seventeenth century, was it a common practice.[6] Plymouth Colony fornication legislation presented an intermediate position. There, a betrothal contract became a mitigating factor when assessing punishment. Marriage, however, was a common expectation in Massachusetts Bay Colony.[7] Ninety-eight percent of men and 94 percent of women married at least once and the average marriage age was four years lower than in England. In Essex County, the question was not "would a young woman marry?" but "who?" and "how soon?"

An out-of-wedlock pregnancy precluded the free choice of a marriage partner, the single most important decision young women, assisted by their family and friends, made. Women derived their identity from their husbands; they assumed his status and reputation; they accepted his authority; and they placed confidence in his ability to provide for them and the inevitable clutch of children that would follow. This would make the choice of a mate stressful enough in this life, but in Puritan Massachusetts, women's hopes of heaven might be dependent upon their choice of an earthly partner, for Puritan religious ideology linked marriage and grace. Anne Bradstreet made that link explicit in a poem dedicated, "To my Dear and loving Husband," in which she described marital love as the means of election: "(T)hen while we live, in love lets so persevere, That when we live no more, we may live forever."[8]

The choice of a marriage partner was important to men as well. The ideal was a virgin with a substantial dowry, equivalent or moderately superior socio-economic status, and marketable housewifery skills. If she was part-possessor of resources which would enhance her potential husband's assets, such as a bordering farm or male relatives with similar or complementary business interests, that helped. Marriage was the primary means of transferring land, material goods, and familial influence from parents to children.[9] But for men, the decision when to marry was as important as whom to marry.

Marriage was a significant male rite of passage in early modern England and in New England, representing "autonomy, mastery, responsibility and the prospect of fathering a lineage."[10] It marked men's entries into adulthood through the establishment of an independent household, which provided them a local voice in the community. It could not be undertaken until they could afford the transition from dependent son to patriarch. Their choice, and the conditions under which that choice was made, could influence parental disbursement of property upon their entry into marriage. An attempt was made to balance the contributions of both partners' families. If one family was unable to contribute much because pregnancy had forced an unequal match, or was unwilling to contribute anything because of its anger and shame, it might limit the amount the other family felt obliged to provide. An untimely pregnancy followed by a hasty marriage could have long-term ramifications. Limited parental financial support and a pregnant partner who lacked a dowry, an estate, commercial connections or housewifery skills would materially affect a man's future prosperity and domestic comfort.

Marriage, then, was serious business and New England Puritans enacted legislation to ensure parental control of marriage entry. The most generous reading of Puritan marriage legislation is that it was enacted to protect young persons from the consequences of an ill-considered marriage which, Puritan parents felt, had been all too easy to make in England. In both jurisdictions romantic love and marital companionship were considered less important than a status-appropriate match.[11] Obadiah Wood of Ipswich, for example, testified in 1674 that "contrary to the advice of all his friends, especially his father whose counsel and command he ought to have attended in that matter" he had fallen in love.[12] He had sworn he would marry Mary Talbot or die; until he learned that Talbot was pregnant. Wood made himself an object of contempt in Ipswich not for abandoning a woman whom the court adjudged to have borne his child, but for having loudly proclaimed his enthrallment prior to his disillusionment.

In England prior to the Interregnum, judges accepted as legitimate marriages based on mutual consent. While parents could try to control their children's choice of a marriage partner through inheritance, the English courts honored marriages that had been made without parental consent as long as three conditions had been met. Couples had to have reached puberty; each partner had to have given verbal consent to the marriage; and the marriage had to have been consummated. In Massachusetts, parents asserted legal control over all aspects of their children's lives.[13] Not only did marriage require the written consent of both families or, in cases where no parents were available, that of the local selectmen, courtship required parental consent. Massachusetts gave parents legal control over courtship, with enforceable legal remedies as early as 1647.[14]

For religious and cultural reasons men did not want to marry pregnant women. To yoke themselves to a woman who had been unable to control her sexual appetite meant a possible forfeiture of grace and a certain loss of honor. Marriage represented the admission they had been unable to refrain from "uncleanness," or "filthiness," and while male virginity did not carry the same import as female chastity, having a wife who lacked a good sexual reputation meant a loss in status. There was the fear that if their wives had been incapable of controlling their sexual appetites prior to marriage, even if they had been the temporary beneficiary of that loss of control; they could not be trusted to control themselves with other men after marriage. Margaret Batten had thought it important to incorporate into the written record her statement that she had "lain" with Edward Welch only once. For his part, he sought an oath that he had been her only lover. Chance-met in a tavern, after sexual intercourse that may have been fueled by alcohol, undoubtedly furtive, in the tavern-yard, essentially strangers to each other, they tried to do the right thing. Marriage under these circumstances brought with it an inevitable fornication conviction and certain punishment, a humiliating series of shame rituals in church and court, loss of status, and financial penalties. Margaret Batten experienced all of these. Welch's French captivity precluded his appearance in court where his presence would have deflected some of the opprobrium directed toward her because as a married woman, she would be, legally, a feme covert, and her husband would be required to answer for her.

The consequences of a premarital pregnancy might be supportable if the couple had used that pregnancy to force a marriage. With status-appropriateness a primary criterion for marriage formation, a visible out-of-wedlock pregnancy represented a compelling argument in favor of an unequal match. Differences of rank could be overcome when fond parents were confronted by pregnant daughters and their ineligible suitors. In some instances, men used the knowledge that to some parents any husband might be preferable to a daughter with no husband and an illegitimate child. For example, when Joseph Mayo got two well-born Newbury step-sisters pregnant in 1674, he married the younger, more richly-dowered, one. Her brother, Mr. Henry Short, proved willing to put more cash on the line than Mr. Robert Adams, the father of the elder woman and stepfather of the bride.

Whether the motivating factor behind the pregnancy was an ambitious man willing to trade temporary opprobrium and a fornication conviction for a beneficial alliance or a couple who saw no other way to marry, a bridal pregnancy presented a viable marriage strategy with one caveat. It only worked if it was the woman who possessed superior economic and social status.

A number of questions beg answers. Was impending marriage the cause or the effect of an unplanned pregnancy? Did pregnancy result from an uncontrolled moment of passion between committed persons as their parents or guardians haggled over the financial terms of the proposed union? Did economic downturns force couples who had initiated intercourse in expectation of imminent marriages to part, as has been asserted for early modern England? These questions are inter-related because they presuppose committed partners who expected to marry soon. Was marriage an expected outcome if a woman conceived as a result of casual sexual intercourse between persons where there was no bar to marriage, such as a preexisting marriage, an indenture, apprenticeship or poverty? Did some couples use a pregnancy to force marriage when they knew that parental permission to marry would not be forthcoming? Was there the cultural expectation that men would "do the right thing?" Was community pressure applied to assure that they did? Was the community interested in protecting errant young women in this manner? Or, were these "shotgun" marriages? How great was the incentive for the woman's "friends," her family, employer, and interested neighbors to ensure that marriage occurred? Did the willingness of men to marry change over time? And, a related and even more basic question—did the amount of premarital sexual activity increase relative to the population as the century unfolded?

Another important set of questions concerns the aftermath of premarital fornication prosecutions. What were the procedures couples engaged in to reknit themselves into the social fabric of the Puritan community? Why was the outcome of this type of prosecution more rehabilitative than an illegitimate fornication prosecution? Why were men who married their pregnant partners punished more severely than men who fathered illegitimate children? Is the assumption of reintegration in itself flawed? The answers to these questions combined with comparative data from illegitimate fornication prosecutions will enable us to come closer to some definitive conclusions across the complete range of Puritan sexual attitudes and behaviors.

The judicial course of a premarital fornication case was relatively uncomplicated compared to that of an illegitimate fornication prosecution. No complicated issues of paternity were contested since marriage was a tacit admission of fatherhood. Both husband and wife were summoned to appear at the session of the Essex County Quarterly Court that followed the birth of a child within the first 32 weeks of marriage. For example, Thomas Verry of Salem married Elizabeth Proctor, also of Salem, March 28, 1681. A son, Thomas, jr., was born eight weeks later. The following month, at the June session of the Essex County Quarterly Court meeting in Salem, "Thomas Verry and his wife, for fornication before marriage, were fined."[15] Verry's wife was not named, and the amount of their fine was left unrecorded. From the point of view of conducting a detailed quantitative analysis of premarital fornication cases, the Verrys' experience is all too typical. Most premarital prosecutions were conducted with similar dispatch. Given the uncontested nature of the cases, few depositions were filed and few cases required more than one court appearance.

It is difficult to develop financial and occupational information on couples who were prosecuted for premarital fornication from court records, since the handling of these cases is so matter-of-fact. The amount of genealogical and occupational data available in the Essex County docket books for women and men prosecuted for illegitimate fornication is missing in the cases of couples who were prosecuted for premarital fornication. Bastard-bearers were identified in terms of their relationship to a male in a position of authority over them, a father or an employer. Women who appeared as co-defendants in premarital fornication cases had become femes covert, subsumed in the legal identities of their new husbands. While there is less information on these persons in the court records, the very fact that they could afford to marry meant that they, or their families, had a financial presence in the community and they are easier to locate in genealogies and probate records.

Thirty-two weeks was designated as the cut-off point for prosecution. This provided a seven-week window of opportunity between conception and marriage. It's never as simple, however, as counting back from the birth-date to determine the date of conception. Twenty-three percent of births occur naturally in the eighth month, 66 percent in the ninth month, and nine percent in the tenth month.[16] It is impossible to assess on a quantitative basis how many couples initiated intercourse, as some did in England, a few weeks before their wedding. Certainly Puritans saw the practicality of short betrothals. Once a couple was contracted, Puritans urged that marriage occur within a month. But, the assumption that a contract was a license for sexual experimentation is very far from the mark. Foucault reminds us that sexuality is not static. The existence of certain practices or the expectations of certain levels of sexual activity in the present is no guarantee that equivalent levels of youthful sexual activity existed in the past. I would add that Massachusetts Bay Puritans were very much a self-selected group, that there was an intense degree of community oversight, that young women were indoctrinated in the belief that their virginity was their most important asset, and that, whatever beliefs and practices the few non-Puritans brought to Essex County, this was an intensely hierarchical society in which the sexual ideology of the dominant class was reinforced on a regular basis.

In 1651, John Putnam was fined 40 shillings "for his relations after contract" following the birth of his first child 35 weeks after his marriage to Rebecca Prince in 1651.[17] Their prosecution is the exception that makes the rule, coming as it does in 1651 when the court was particularly intolerant of sexual irregularities as evidenced by its rigorous punishment of bastard-bearers during the same decade. This is one of the few Essex County prosecutions that specifically mentions that coitus had occurred after a marriage contract had been formalized and the only conviction in which the pregnancy went longer than 32 weeks. Plymouth Colony routinely fined couples who engaged in sexual intercourse prior to a marriage contract twice as much as contracted couples. A second Essex County case, tried seven years later, clarified the court's position on the length of time allowable between marriage and birth: "Hanah, wife of Nehemiah Howard, presented for suspiciousness of uncleanness, being delivered of a child about thirty-two weeks after marriage, was discharged."[18]

The nature of the court clerk's recording of the sentences is such that it is difficult to draw hard-and-fast conclusions about sentencing patterns (see Table 6). In some instances there is specific mention of a couple being assigned the same fine: "Georg Samon and his wife were fined £5 each for uncleanness before marriage."[19] The sum assigned was often a combined assessment. For example, in April 1673: "Joseph Chase and Rachell Chase, his now wife, presented for fornication, confessed and were sentenced to be severely whipped tomorrow morning or pay a fine of £6."[20] Some husbands and wives were fined different amounts. In October 1668, Henry True was fined £3: his unidentified wife was fined 40 shillings.[21] There is also no way of telling how many of the couples, given the option of being whipped or fined, chose to be whipped, or had a whipping forced upon them because they lacked the money to pay a fine. In October 1674: "John Heriman and his wife, convicted for fornication and confessing, were ordered to be whipped, he twenty stripes and she fifteen, or pay a fine of £8."[22] The number of lashes assessed by the court in this instance is higher than usual and constituted what the court usually described as a "severe whipping," or a "whipping severely laid on."[23]

Table 6 Sentences Issued by the Essex County Quarterly Court to Married Fornication Defendants, 1640–1685

Sentence	% Defendants Receiving (N=131)[27]
Admonished	1%
Fined	46%
Whipped or Fined	37%
Whipped	2%
Severely Whipped or Fined	11%
Severely Whipped	2%

A couple might be offered a range of alternatives. While the number of cases in which there is a specific mention of a promise by the court to reduce the severity of the sentence if the couple married is limited, marriage had been listed as the first remedy for fornication in the Massachusetts Bay Colony law code issued in 1641.[24] A decision rendered by the court in November, 1669, presents the most complete range of alternatives as well as providing evidence of the seriousness with which the court regarded the crime of fornication since it makes reference to the fact that the couple had been jailed prior to trial:

> William Sanders and Mary Vocah were sentenced for fornication, he to be whipped or pay 41i. And she to be whipped or pay 40s unless they agree to be married, when their sentence was to be abated one half. They were to remain in prison until the payment be made.[25]

Since they were to be imprisoned until their fines were paid, it may be that the common expectation was that a couple would pay to avoid whipping. Sanders and Vocah married that day and received an abatement of half of their fines.

Eighty-three per cent of premarital fornication defendants received the option of paying a fine. This is likely reflective of two factors: class was always a determinant in the decision to fine rather than to assess corporal punishment, and judges viewed couples who legitimated their relationship through marriage more leniently than women who bore illegitimate children. Only 56 percent of bastard bearers were given an equivalent option.[26] Ironically, while women prosecuted for illegitimate fornication received more severe sentences than women who married, men who abided by the letter of the Massachusetts Bay Colony fornication law which enjoined marriage as the first remedy for fornication paid a more severe penalty than their male peers who fathered illegitimate children. The likelihood that a husband would be prosecuted for fornication was 100 percent: a man whose name had been wrested from an unmarried mother by the midwife during labor stood only a 28 percent chance of prosecution. Specific child-support payments of between two and three shillings per week were reported for only 13 of the 99 men who had been named as the fathers of illegitimate children. As it was only necessary to pay child support for two years, men convicted of illegitimate fornication, if they were given the maximum fine of £5 and paid child support of £6 a year for two years, paid a maximum financial penalty of £17.

The median length of time that elapsed between the wedding ceremony and the birth of the first child was sixteen weeks. Seventy percent of couples prosecuted for premarital fornication did not marry until the fifth month of pregnancy or later. A visible pregnancy, then, expedited marriage formation. By a second measure, one half of the women convicted of premarital fornication were six months or more pregnant at the time of their marriage. There are five plausible explanations for this time lapse: (1) the five to six months that elapsed between conception and marriage represented the length of time required for the young woman to realize she was pregnant, for the families to negotiate a marriage settlement, and for the couple to assemble the wherewithal to establish an independent marital household, (2) couples who knew they had conceived a child waited to marry in November or December, the traditional New England marriage months, (3) the five to six month lapse between conception and marriage meant that in many instances the groom had to be persuaded to marry the woman he had impregnated, (4) legal action initiated by a pregnant female, usually in the fifth month of her pregnancy, focused judicial and community pressure on the putative father to marry, and (5) women and men used a premarital pregnancy to force parental permission to an unequal marriage.

It would not require six months for a couple who already had parental permission to court to realize they had a child on the way and to complete their marriage arrangements. An incipient birth lent urgency to marriage negotiations. Given the sentences issued by the Essex County Quarterly Court to women who bore illegitimate children and their diminished opportunities for marriage after a fornication conviction, women's families had an incentive to press for quick marriages. Once the pregnancy was visible, the expectant mother was harassed by neighbors who felt it their civic duty to determine paternity and encourage marriage. Women interrogated other women who appeared to be pregnant. They discussed possible fathers among themselves and they took the moral high ground:

> I told her it was an aggravation to her sin for her to say she did not know the father of it.[28]

The above words are those of thirty-year-old Susannah Osgood, who described her self-important questioning of Elizabeth Gould, "then big with child," as "some discourse." Osgood and her fellow goodwives focused on three prospective fathers. They suspected Gould's employer's married son, Abraham Foster, as well as Ralph Farnum, an eligible local man of marriage age, and John Allen. John Allen's relatives partook in the questioning. They were anxious to hear Gould rule him out. At one point, when Gould suggested defiantly that when the child is born, they'll know his father because of the resemblance, Susannah Osgood informed her that "a child might be like a person, who in no ways was related to it." One gets the impression, that Elizabeth Gould is, for perhaps the first time in her life, the center of attention and that she relished the thought of Deacon Acie bustling around the neighborhood questioning possible, and improbable, partners, and that she derived some excitement from jousting verbally with women who, in the ordinary course of events, would expect deference and obedience from her.

The women's community policed its own. They did not question the local men; that was Deacon Acie's responsibility, and, in most instances of premarital pregnancies the identity of the father would be patently obvious since the couple would be openly courting. Gould's defiance did not serve her well. No man was prosecuted with her; the very breadth of possible suspects, and her coy denials and subsequent accusations had made the prosecution of any single individual impossible.

A comparison of the months in which pregnant and non-pregnant women married will indicate whether the time lapse can be explained in terms of the second posited explanation; adherence to customary marriage patterns. Puritan marriages occurred within a clearly defined curve that followed the agricultural calendar. The months with the lowest percentage of documented marriages were July, August, and September (at five percent each) and October (at six percent). Thirty-nine percent of non-pregnant women married in November (17 percent) and December (22 percent).[29] The months of marriage for pregnant brides do not fit this pattern. The percentage of pregnant women who married in the months of August (10 percent), September (10 percent), and October (12 percent), was twice as high as the non-pregnant cohort for the same months, and higher than the percentage of pregnant women who married in November (nine percent) and December (nine percent).

The first two hypotheses cannot be sustained. Premarital sexual intercourse did not begin after contract and before marriage, nor did couples delay their marriages to adhere to the customary New England marriage pattern.

The conclusion, then, that up to one-half of the men prosecuted for premarital fornication were initially unwilling to marry a woman who could be persuaded to engage in fully-consummated sexual intercourse without marriage is warranted. Whether because of traditional Puritan beliefs about women, because women who conceived out of wedlock had violated the new Puritan standard of womanliness, or because of the disproportionate legal penalty paid by men who married their pregnant partners, it is not surprising that it took time to persuade many of them to marry. The first two factors meant that in some instances there may have been more male loss of honor and status involved in marrying a pregnant woman with a doubtful sexual reputation than in denying paternity to escape a fornication prosecution. Since the median time that elapsed between marriage and birth was a surprisingly short 16 weeks, fewer than half of the couples, then, can be characterized as engaged in a committed relationship before they commenced sexual intercourse.

For some couples, the problem was money. Three men married their partners after the birth of an illegitimate child. They might have been willing to marry sooner, but needed more time to save enough money to make a home. While it has proved difficult to develop financial information on male co-defendants due to the limited number of available seventeenth-century Essex County tax assessment lists and their lack of detailed identifying information, five of the 36 men in the lowest Salem tax bracket (which comprised only seven percent of the taxable male population) were convicted of premarital fornication within ten years of their assessment.

The time elapsed between conception and marriage (see Table 7) varied considerably between the first and final decades of this study. Between 1650 and 1660, which is the first decade in which date of marriage and date of birth information is available for seven of the couples, five of them, (70 percent) married in the first trimester of their pregnancy. It is possible they were married before they realized that the female partner had conceived. In the final decade of the study, 1682–1692, only one of the 21 couples (five percent) for whom date of marriage and date of birth information is available was married in the first trimester. These figures denote significant change over time. Men were no longer willing to marry their pregnant partners, more couples were having sex without being in committed relationships, and community pressure had ceased to be an effective goad.

Table 7 Frequency Distribution: Number of Weeks Elapsed Between Marriage and Birth

Number of Weeks Elapsed	Number of Couples (N=88)[30]	Percent of Couples
1–4	10	11%
5–8	9	10%
9–12	12	16%
13–16	15	17%
17–20	16	18%
21–24	7	8%
24–28	14	16%
28–31	5	6%

Prior to 1660, when the number of individuals prosecuted for sexual offenses was in the single digits annually, if marriage did not follow conception, it was because the father was already married, still indentured, or had left Essex County. Otherwise, community pressure or legal action initiated by the pregnant woman was enough to bring him to marriage. In the period 1682 to 1692, the situation was very different. The population of Essex County had grown to the point where community pressure was no longer sufficient to force men to marry their pregnant partners. Justices no longer advised defendants that if they married before the end of the day their whippings or, more likely, their fines, would be cut in half or commuted, and the religious argument was no longer convincing to many men. Fewer men were willing, in the final decade of this study, to marry their pregnant partner in the first place, and when they did marry them, the marriage no longer occurred in the first trimester of the pregnancy.

Pregnant brides married at twenty-two years of age: their husbands were twenty-five-years-old. Other early American historians have found that couples who married without the unpleasant incentive of an out-of-wedlock pregnancy married at similar ages. Kenneth Lockridge found that women and men in Dedham, Massachusetts, between 1640 and 1690, married at the ages of twenty-three and twenty-five respectively.[31] John Demos documented a slightly different situation in Plymouth Colony. While age at marriage for women was lower than in Dedham, 21.3 between 1650 and 1675, and 22.3 between 1675 and 1700, the mean age at marriage for men was very similar, at 25.4 between 1650 and 1675, and 24.5 between 1675 and 1700.[32] Philip Greven calculated marriage age in Andover, Essex County, and found that second generation women had an average marriage age of 22.8 years and second generation men married at 27.1 years of age.[33]

Greyen's marriage age data for one Essex County community parallels the age data for premarital couples in Essex County as a whole. Clearly, couples who engaged in premarital sexual intercourse were in the same age cohort as their more continent, or fortunate, peers.[34]

There is a strong correlation between male marriage age and economic independence. Men who had inherited their patrimonies were more likely to marry at a younger age. It is clear that the converse was also true and not unexpected. Couples were more likely to engage in sexual intercourse if they were older when they commenced their courtship. Or, having conceived a child together, their relative maturity compared to couples who bore illegitimate children, had enabled them to assemble more financial resources during the period of time that they had been working.

The ages at trial of persons convicted of illegitimate fornication and premarital fornication was also compared (see Table 8).

Eighteen percent of the women who bore illegitimate children were 17 years of age or younger. Only six percent of the female premarital defendants fell into this age category. These data support my conclusion that sexual activity involving women in this age category was opportunistic. Three times as many of these women bore illegitimate children. Three factors limited the ability of women in the 15–17 age category to marry: (1) they were more likely to have had sex with married men, (2) they were not in the age cohort that would have been engaged in serious courtship, and (3) they had not worked a sufficient number of years to make a material contribution to their dowry.

Prior to 1660 the number of couples convicted of premarital fornication and individuals convicted of illegitimate fornication is very low and the conviction rates are comparable (see Table 1). But in each succeeding five-year interval between 1661 and 1685 the number of couples convicted of premarital fornication increased markedly. This group is significantly larger than the number of women convicted of illegitimate fornication. There are two possible explanations. Either these figures confirm the expectation that when a pregnancy occurred during courtship, men married their pregnant partners if possible, or the number of committed couples who believed that premarital sexual intercourse was appropriate when marriage negotiations had commenced increased. As the average time elapsed between marriage and birth remained constant at 15 to 17 weeks for each five-year interval between 1661 and 1685, it is clear that many couples who were prosecuted for premarital sexual intercourse married because of the pregnancy. There is no way to know if they might have married later had the female partner not conceived, but given the premium Puritans placed on female chastity,

Table 8 Comparative Age Distribution of Illegitimate and Premarital Fornication Defendants By Percent in Essex County, 1640–1692[35]

	Women		Men	
Age	Illegitimate (N=66)	Premarital (N=96)	Illegitimate (N=54)	Premarital (N=88)
15–17	18%	6%	2%	0%
18–20	27%	27%	11%	8%
21–23	24%	31%	22%	25%
24–26	14%	20%	20%	25%
27–29	8%	8%	11%	24%
30–32	1%	1%	9%	11%
33+	8%	6%	24%	7%

women who had sex under these conditions were putting their futures at risk. The only factor, and it was a major one, that distinguished them from their peers who had illegitimate children was that their partners married them, even if belatedly, before the births of their children.

The five-year interval 1671–1675 is particularly interesting. The number of couples prosecuted (36) was more than double that of the previous five-year interval (16). The number of couples prosecuted was also double the number of women prosecuted for illegitimate fornication in the same five-year interval. If sexual irregularities are an indicator of deeper societal problems, it appears that the period prior to Metacomet's War was particularly unsettled. The ramifications of Metacomet's War extended into the following five-year interval when the number of couples prosecuted for premarital fornication decreased slightly while the number of women prosecuted for illegitimate fornication rose by 25 percent. A probable explanation is that fewer marriageable men were available as a result of Metacomet's War. If the presumption that men were expected to marry their pregnant partners is correct, women may have used a pregnancy as an attempt to force a marriage.

The numbers of couples charged with premarital fornication rose from three between 1641 and 1645 to 67 between 1681 and 1685 (see Table 9). At issue is whether the increased number of prosecutions for premarital fornication can be explained in terms of population increase or whether the numbers of persons engaged in extramarital sexual activity increased relative to the population. Population data for Essex County is incomplete, but population estimates have been developed for seventeenth-century Massachusetts as a whole.[36] The rates of illegitimate and premarital pregnancies per 10,000

Table 9 Illegitimate and Premarital Fornication Prosecution Rates for Essex County, Massachusetts, 1645–1685

Years	Illegitimate Fornication Rates/10,000 persons	Premarital Fornication Rates/10,000 persons
1645–1655	5.70	4.99
1656–1665	6.47	9.96
1666–1675	9.33	17.67
1676–1685	13.33	18.36

persons were calculated using this population data. The number of illegitimate and premarital fornication prosecutions relative to the population increased with each interval.

Some preliminary conclusions can be drawn from the quantitative data which will be reinforced by a close reading of the depositions presented in the following chapter by the defendants, their parents, and their neighbors. First, it needs to be reiterated that persons who were prosecuted for premarital fornication constituted a tiny portion of Puritan society. The act of engaging in coitus, despite Puritan strictures against extramarital sexual intercourse, set them outside the mainstream. On the other hand, the age range of couples who married following an extramarital conception is within the same range as their more continent peers who waited until after marriage to engage in coitus. The greater license allowed couples in this age group to spend unsupervised time together increased both the opportunities for intimacy and the confidence of the female partner that marriage would be the likely outcome of a pregnancy. That marriage followed is an indicator that many of these couples were better placed financially than their peers who fathered and bore illegitimate children.

While 45 percent of the men who had fathered illegitimate children made no recorded marriage in Essex County, and a further 30 percent of them were already married, nearly half of the women who bore illegitimate children had been from established Essex County families. The limited amount of tax data available for couples suggest that some men and women reached the age at which they could have hoped to be able to marry and enter into a legitimate sexual relationship without the necessary financial resources. Not willing or able to wait on an indefinite future, they engaged in sexual intercourse and after a pregnancy, were forced to scramble to find enough assets with which to marry. The vast majority of Essex County couples could afford to adhere to the dominant ideology that conflated sexual intercourse and marriage because for them there was a straightforward path through courtship to marriage.

The degree of commitment in extramarital relationships prior to the initiation of sexual intercourse changed over time. Prior to 1660, couples married during the first trimester of their pregnancy, an indication they had commenced sexual intercourse at or near the time they had been contracted. By the final decade the character of the sexual intercourse had changed. That most of these couples married in the final trimester indicates that the marriage was probably the outcome of the pregnancy, not, as earlier, that the pregnancy was the outcome of an anticipated marriage.

The number of couples who engaged in premarital sexual activity increased over time while the length of time that elapsed between marriage and birth decreased. This suggests diminishing willingness on the part of the male partner to legitimize the pregnancy. The religious ideals that had militated against premarital sexual intercourse and proved so influential prior to 1660 had waned. At the same time, the social mechanisms that brought pressure to bear on men to marry their pregnant partners lost their effectiveness as communities increased in size and differences in wealth became more pronounced.

Chapter Seven

"Cover Our Faces with Shame": Sociological Aspects of Premarital Pregnancy

> The presentment I own and must to my shame, and hath proved a great grief and trouble to me and my wife: that we should gratify our corrupt nature rather than to attend to our observance and obedience to the law of god and man, and from a deep sense and apprehension of our great folly desire to cover our faces with shame and desire god and the authority of this land would forgive my so great a miscarriage and that your charity may be extended to so poor a worm[1]

Thomas Verry and his wife, Elizabeth Proctor, excused the gratification of their "corrupt natures" by stating that they had the consent of both sets of parents to marriage. This sounds good, but Elizabeth Proctor was just eighteen, and their child was born 8 weeks after their 1681 marriage. The claim that a contract had preceded intercourse was an attempt to salvage some respectability that cannot have fooled many of their neighbors in Salem.[2]

Although a full-term pregnancy requires 270 days, or almost 39 weeks, Puritans established 32 weeks as the cut-off point for premarital fornication prosecutions. They did so not because they accepted that couples would have intercourse between contract and marriage, but because they wanted to allow for prematurity. To convict a married couple of having committed an act of "uncleanness" so vile that it endangered their entire community, threatened successive generations of their progeny, and required ritual humiliation in church and corporal or financial punishment at a quarterly court session was a serious undertaking.[3] Prior to 1655, only eight persons were prosecuted, such was the strength of Puritan religious/sexual ideology.

The testimony of midwives was critical to the outcome of premarital fornication cases. They were the seventeenth-century equivalent of expert witnesses with the requisite medical skills to provide legally acceptable testimony of prematurity. Even midwives, however, disagreed about the length of time that constituted a full-term pregnancy. They knew that a pregnancy customarily lasted 39 weeks but they were accustomed to seeing exceptions in practice. In April 1684, Sarah White testified that she had delivered "a child of a woman that went but two and thirty weeks and the persons were approved persons both for honesty and godliness."[4] She added that she herself, Martha Rowlandson, and Mr. Prince's daughter had each gone 35 weeks. That Martha Rowlandson's pregnancy had occurred 40 years earlier made it no less of a precedent either to White or the court. Memories were long for perceived or actual sexual misdemeanors.

Humphrey Devereaux and his wife, Elizabeth, of Marblehead, were presented for fornication in June 1681. The charges were dismissed upon testimony from the midwife, Wiborough Gatchell, that:

> Elizabeth Devereaux, whom according to the best of my judgment, came before her time occasioned only by the stroke of a cow upon her body when she was a milking, and my self and the women that were assistant there did judge that the child was born before its time.[5]

Gatchell's professional opinion was backed up by that of Dr. Knott, who was called in to attend to the dying infant and agreed that "the child was born before the full time."[6] Humphrey Devereaux died nine years later leaving his "dear wife Elizabeth sole executrix" of a meager estate inventoried at £54 with which to raise five children.

When John Devereaux, her father-in-law, died four years after her husband, he left one-third of his land and a house to his three grandsons and £10 to his two grand-daughters with the proviso that Elizabeth Devereaux "have nothing to do with the house or land or ever live on them at any time."[7] While no direct connection can be drawn between John Devereaux's animosity toward his daughter-in-law and the fact that her marriage had begun with a fornication trial, even though the charges had been dismissed, it had not been an auspicious start.

A midwife's testimony was not always sufficient to secure a dismissal of fornication charges at the quarterly court level. It did not gain an acquittal for John and Elizabeth Garland of Hampton in 1674. A close reading of the depositions provided in their case enables an examination of the factors that Essex County Quarterly Court judges considered before rendering a guilty verdict. John Garland and Elizabeth Robinson were married December 24,

1673; their daughter was born 27 weeks later, "about eleven weeks before the usual time."[8] The midwife, Mary Wall, testified:

> his wife was in strong travail & I asked her if she had her linen ready & she said no for I am not come to my time, for I have received some hurt by a fall upon a log and she was delivered, and the child was a very poor child.[9]

Three more women attested to the baby's condition at birth. Mary Jones testified that she "never saw so little a child in my life and I think it came before the time." Elizabeth Roby and Elizabeth Robinson testified jointly that:

> the child was a very poor child as we saw and was so weakly we were forced to feed it with a feather being the nurse of Elizabeth Garland and it having no nails to our apprehension upon hand nor foot & being a fortnights time before it could take the breast, or a month, and had very little skin upon it when it was born.

These women appeared to have made a good case. Elizabeth Roby thought so, for she created such an uproar after the guilty verdict was rendered and the young couple had been fined £5 each that she was ordered to prison for "contemptuous carriages." The charge was remitted "upon her confession that she was very sorry."[10] Since Elizabeth Roby was John Garland's mother and Elizabeth Robinson, Elizabeth Garland's mother, the Essex County Quarterly Court considered their testimony to be suspect. Even as they were most likely to be present at birth and to share in the nursing of the young mother and baby, their relationship to the young couple and the negative reflection a fornication conviction would present made their testimony questionable.

John Garland appealed to the Court of Assistants in Boston. He was required to post a bond of £150 in order to have the upper court retry the case. The Essex County Quarterly Court hired Henry Dow to represent them. Both prepared lengthy depositions which are abstracted and interposed below. The crux of Garland's argument was that his daughter had been born prematurely. Garland prefaced it by explaining that he was not a litigious man:

> (I)t is not because I would be troublesome or that I delight to go to Court, especially upon such a dishonorable account as this is; I spoke before God and his people, had I and my wife been guilty, I should have submitted and have owned my sin with all readiness of mind, but being clear and innocent I can not take so great a wrong without further seeing Gods mind in appealing to so serious a Court as this is. I never was

> in court before. It sits the more on our spirits knowing that the holy ghost saieth that a good name is a precious ointment therefore we think we are bound to preserve our names.

John Garland was articulating the importance of a good sexual reputation. The size of the bond Garland was required to post to assure an appeal to the Court of Assistants was beyond the reach of most Essex County residents, so we can infer that it was not a frivolous action. Garland listed four causes for appeal: their consciences were clear; they could have married earlier if Robinson had been pregnant; seven-month live births were not unknown; and any woman, if the verdict prevailed, might find herself accused of fornication following a miscarriage.

Essex County's lawyer was prepared with a defense. Garland and Robinson had lived alone deep in the woods, away from community oversight. Who knew what they had been up to? Dow outlined the Biblical precedents upon which thirty-two weeks had been established as the cut-off point for determining prematurity: a citation from Luke, which involved counting the months between the conception and birth of John the Baptist.[11] It serves as a timely reminder that the mentalité of New England Puritans was closer to the Renaissance than to the twentieth-century. Garland had presented some solid grounds of appeal, however, and Dow fell back on the argument that if the verdict were overturned by the Court of Assistants the quarterly courts would be overwhelmed by similar appellants.

Garland prevailed in the Court of Assistants, which reversed the Essex County Quarterly Court conviction. The Garlands won because the Court of Assistants believed the testimony of the midwife and the other women, despite the familial relationship. Mary Wall had applied contemporary medical knowledge to assess prematurity, as did other midwives, and the Court of Assistants considered her testimony credible. That the baby was born 28 weeks after marriage, a full month before the time allowable by law, attests to a degree of ambiguity about what constituted prematurity as well as to the weight assigned by the courts to midwives' testimony. The Court of Assistants accepted the mothers' testimonies because it was customary for close relatives to be present at birth, and they did not feel that this necessary led to biased testimony.

Nevertheless, the Essex County Quarterly Court knew the individuals involved and suspected that there had been a conspiracy to prevent outsiders from viewing the baby after her birth. All three families involved were aware how damaging fornication convictions could be to the reputations of the persons involved and their families. Elizabeth Robinson's brother, Jonathan, had been convicted of premarital fornication in April, 1670.[12] Henry Roby's daughter, Judith, had an illegitimate child in December, 1671.[13] Also, John Garland's step-brother, Joseph Chase, had been convicted of premarital fornication in April, 1673.[14] At the very least, the parents were lax in their supervision. Since all of these individuals lived in Hampton, Garland's and Robinson's fornication conviction may have been more than the families' reputations could handle. Or, having been justly convicted in the other cases, it became a matter of principle, as Garland had suggested in his opening statement, to prevail when they knew themselves to be innocent. That they raised £150 to appeal the case to the Court of Assistants reveals that they felt strongly about the conviction.

Whether John and Elizabeth Garland and their parents engaged in a conspiracy to avoid further tarnishing their families names' or they felt that their families' poor sexual reputations had led to an unjust conviction is impossible to know, but two facts can be stated on behalf of a conspiracy. First, although Garland claimed that he and Robinson had been contracted and could have married earlier had she been pregnant, Garland was nineteen at the time of the baby's conception, not an age at which he would have normally expected to be able to marry. Second, the previous fornication convictions indicate that other family members had not refrained from sexual intercourse prior to marriage. Once one family member has been convicted, the likelihood of a second individual in the same family also facing a fornication prosecution increases. Whether this indicates a propensity within some families to flout the moral precepts of Puritanism, or if one child, having transgressed and survived parental disapproval and a fornication prosecution, other children become less intimidated by the notion of the consequences of premarital sexual activity, or because, as I think most likely, a fornication prosecution impacted the sexual reputation of all the family members and women became more vulnerable to sexual solicitation is unknowable. It is also unimportant here. What matters about this case, besides the information provided about Puritan attitudes to premarital sexual intercourse, is that the Court of Assistants, when faced with two conflicting sets of evidence, chose to accept the midwife, Mary Wall's, assessment of prematurity instead of supporting the legal judgment of the Essex County Quarterly Court.

Despite economic opportunities that limited parental power, Puritan parents had not wrested their children loose from a presumably permissive Anglican society to lose control of them in the New World; they instituted legal controls over courtship and marriage entry that mandated parental permission by 1648.[15] Parents invoked the law against courting without permission when they felt their child was in danger of making an inappropriate match. In 1649, Matthew Stanley was fined £5 "for drawing away the affections of the daughter of John Tarbox his wife without liberty first obtained of her parents."[16] In 1660, Daniel Black was fined £5 for "making love to the daughter of Edmund Bridges, without consent of her parents."[17] Both sets of parents, however, were fighting the inevitable. John Tarbox's step-daughter was already pregnant and she married Stanley. Mr. Edmund Bridges had no control over his daughter, Faith's, activities. She let Black into her parents' house while they slept and met with Black in empty houses to drink with him. Moreover, other persons helped Black to subvert the authority of Bridges' father:

> Having taken William Danforth from his master Pritchetts work to go with him to Rowley, they carried a bottle of wine to the house of Edmund Deere in Ipswich; and being there, he employed the said William as his messenger and instrument to draw the said wench to him at Deere's house, from her father's house, her father and mother being absent from home; that she stayed at Deere's house half an hour, when Deere and his wife were not at home.[18]

Though Faith Bridges married Daniel Black; her marriage was unsuccessful. It might be deduced from this that Roger Thompson is correct to state that parents had little control over their children.[19] Bridges, however, came from an anomalous household. Mr. Edmund Bridges sr., had proven equally incapable of controlling his three sons, Edmund, Jr., Hackaliah, and Obadiah, all of whom were charged with fornication.[20] Moreover, other testimony indicates the common expectation that both sets of parents would be approached for permission to court. In 1665, John Dodge accused John Haskell of "transgressing the law" for courting a young woman before he had secured her "friends" permission. Haskell defended himself by claiming that "he had spoken to his father and he promised to go down to her father."[21]

Parents were not always consulted in the first phase of a courtship, which could lead to problems once a couple's affections were fixed. In 1675, John Hopkinson deposed that:

> divers years ago myself and Hannah Palmer being drawn into society one with another by some of her relations, our affections in time being set upon each other, it was discovered to my mother whose consent I labored to gain but she still remained opposite & the reasons was she said we were childish, and our beginnings was contrary to the ways that gods people went in; but her chief reason was because she would not be so near related to the Acies.[22]

Hopkinson's mother remained opposed to the match and Palmer and Hopkinson did not marry. His mother's opposition was the determining factor. The secret courtship, conducted with the permission of the Palmer family, was advanced; the couple had exchanged tokens of affection, and Hopkinson may have hoped that if he had committed himself too deeply to withdraw honorably before he apprised his mother of it, her consent would be easier to gain. But from Goody Hopkinson's point of view, the young couple's conduct was "contrary to the ways that god's people went in." John Acie, Hannah's uncle, the promoter of the match, forced a reluctant Hannah to return the small gifts Hopkinson had given to her to seal their betrothal, gave her a new coat, and promised her £10 for her dowry to assuage her grief.[23] Hopkinson married another woman when he was twenty-three, but Palmer did not marry. I conjecture that her reputation was damaged by her entry into a courtship that lacked the approval of both families.

Parental consent was also required for marriage. If no parent was available, a magistrate acted as surrogate parent and granted permission.[24] Secret marriages were prohibited; banns had to be posted for three weeks prior to the marriage ceremony. Thomas Rowlandson was fined 10 shillings in 1648 for "marrying without being published three times" and his marriage to sixteen-year-old Martha Bradstreet was annulled.[25] There was, however, resistance to the Puritan assertion of control over marriage formation. Seven years after Bradstreet's marriage to Rowlandson was annulled, Bradstreet married William Beale. Twenty-two years later a neighbor, the wife of Mr. William Hollingsworth, was forced to pay a £5 fine for defaming Beale by calling her an adulterer. That the wife of a gentleman was prosecuted in the first place emphasizes the seriousness with which the court regarded her accusation because, as they said in their judgment, her claim reflected on "civil justice and the church."[26] Hollingsworth had 10 shillings of her fine rebated in return for reading this statement in church:

> Whereas I Eleanor Hollingsworth was convicted to have spoken to the wife of William Beale railingly that she was an adultress & hang you jade, many times repeated, & and that she made the church a cover for her rogery & that she had another husband alive to the dishonor of God, the church and court & to the great reproach of the parties and evil example to others: I do humbly declare I am sorry for the same, and desire all good people that may be offended, to forgive me, & take warning by me of such evil practices.[27]

Later that year, William Beale was threatened by men engaged in a traditional charivari who stood before his house and shouted: "come out, you cuckoldly cur: we are come to beat thee. Thou livest in adultery."[28]

While these actions occurred within the context of an extended neighborhood dispute, more than two decades had elapsed since the annulment. When neighborhood tempers were aroused the circumstances surrounding the Beale marriage could be resurrected and used against them. Fortunately for the Beales, questioning their marriage also meant questioning the right of the civil authorities to make or break marriages, so the court was willing to intervene on their behalf.

Puritans instituted a second legal control over marriage entry. As well as the consent of both sets of parents or a magistrate, banns were required to be publicly posted for three weeks prior to the marriage to ensure that any person who might have reason to object to the marriage knew it was about to occur. At least two magistrates were fined and had their licenses to perform marriages temporarily suspended for performing illegal marriages. In November 1679, Mr. John Woodbridge married John Sandy to Elizabeth Peters after they and their friends who accompanied them said that they had been legally published. Sandy was legally published, as required, but to another woman, Mary Starkweather. Their wedding was scheduled to occur on the day following that on which Woodbridge married Sandy and Peters. Peters was barely seventeen, pregnant, and the daughter of a prominent Andover publican and distiller, Mr. Andrew Peters. Since Woodbridge was a magistrate with a keen sense of his legal responsibilities Peters' father must have been present at the marriage and willing to break with procedure to see his daughter securely married. Mary Starkweather, like Hannah Palmer, having been contracted but not married, had entered into an ambiguous arena, neither married nor single, and found herself unmarriageable.[29] Starkweather was also hampered by the lack of a dowry, however, or family connections which may have contributed to her unmarriageability. Her father had died five years earlier leaving his eight children five shillings each.

A second father tried to intervene to annul an unsuitable marriage, this one contracted by an underage son. When Simon Wainwright, an Ipswich resident persuaded Mr. Edward Woodman of Newbury to marry him to Sarah Gilbert in 1681, a month before his twenty-first birthday, his father, Mr. Francis Wainwright, sued Woodman for performing the marriage without his consent.[30] In this instance, the marriage was allowed to stand; probably because it had been consummated.

These examples show that parents expected to have a say in their child's choice of a marriage partner. Whether their opposition was based on something as serious as the character of the suitor and the unequal assets brought by each partner to the match as in the case of John Tarbox's stepdaughter, or as frivolous as Goody Hopkinson's dislike for Hannah Palmer's uncle, John Acie, parental consent was necessary for marriage formation. And, when parental persuasion was not sufficient to prevent young persons from keeping company, they used the court, with mixed success, to reinforce their authority. Clearly, too, the rules of courtship and marriage were well-known and generally accepted.

I advanced as the first possible explanation for premarital pregnancies the theory that couples engaged in sexual intercourse between contract and marriage. Since Plymouth Colony had established a dual system of fines in which the amount was determined by whether or not the couple had been contracted prior to conception and since intercourse between contract and marriage seemed to be an acceptable practice in early modern England among non-Puritans, it seemed logical to assume, as Mary Beth Norton suggested, that there might be a variance between the expectations of civil authorities and customary practices.[31]

Puritan lawmakers were not simply authoritarian killjoys. They understood the temptation that sexual union represented. For this reason they encouraged couples to marry within a month of being contracted. This prescription, coupled with the low marriage age relative to that of early modern England and the very high percentage of persons who married meant that very different circumstances prevailed in old and New England. Only one presentment, that of John Putnam and Rebecca Prince in 1653, specifically mentions that conception occurred between contract and marriage.[32] Other couples claimed as an exculpatory factor that sexual intercourse had been preceded by a marriage contract. William Randall and his wife, Elizabeth, were fined 40 shillings for "suspicion of uncleanness before marriage," in 1651.[33] The couple had married in mid-October, 1649, and their first child was born five months later. Randall admitted that they had commenced intercourse after contract and "from six or seven weeks before marriage he would own the child to be his" but he swore that "if his wife came before this time of their contraction he would take his oath upon a book that the child was none of his."[34] Whether or not the child was his, the Randalls had admitted to premarital fornication and their fine was commensurate with those of other couples fined during the same time period.

Elizabeth Randall lost her sexual reputation not only because she had been sexually active prior to her marriage but because her husband questioned whether or not the child was his. The following year she was presented for "evil language" after calling Goody Silver a "base lying devil, base lying toad, base lying sow, and a base lying jade."[35] Fortunately for Randall, Goody Silver did not appear in court to testify against her, and she was discharged, but it is probable that the quarrel had arisen because of accusations made by Goody Silver about Randall's sexual reputation. Twenty years later, Randall was still concerned about public opinion. When the Newbury church was reseated in 1669, Randall felt that she had been allocated a less prestigious location. She was admonished for disorderly carriage, "behavior altogether unbecoming her sex," after she tried to force her way into her former pew.[36]

Peter Cheney and his wife, Hannah Noyes, both of Newbury, admitted that they had begun intercourse after they had been contracted but an exculpatory explanation was offered. Cheney appeared at the May session of the Quarterly Court meeting at Ipswich in 1664 and was fined for fornication. His wife, Hannah, did not appear with him. She was sentenced to pay a £3 fine unless she came to court before it adjourned. A petition was presented on her behalf by Thomas Parker and William Gerrish explaining that she was subject to fits which a court appearance would exacerbate and that "having been published according to law, and the time of marriage appointed, [they were] unexpectedly delayed by their parents by reason of extraordinary accidents."[37]

The quantitative evidence indicated that the number of couples who married in the first trimester dropped dramatically between the first and last decades of this study. Few defendants after 1664 used the defense that sexual intercourse had commenced after contract. In 1681 Thomas Verry argued that he had made amends for engaging in sexual intercourse by marrying the woman he had impregnated:

> Let me pray your honors to consider that my wife and I that now are did commit a folly after solemn engagements of marriage and the consent of parents and I have made the parties amends by marrying the party now my wife.[38]

Verry's response is typical of men accused of premarital fornication in the later period of this study. Verry did not feel the same sense of obligation to marry his pregnant partner as was evidenced by men in the first two decades of this study. As to the impact of a fornication prosecution, Verry lamented the financial and emotional cost to himself and his wife. He said that it had proved "a great grief and trouble to me and my wife."[39]

Cases in which couples married less than 16 weeks before the birth of their child are the most difficult to document. The bare facts can be determined through court dockets and vital records, but since there was no exculpatory evidence to be presented and no issues of paternity, few of the cases are supported by depositions. My presumption is that two factors brought the fathers of these children into marriage. The first factor was the community expectation that men would "do the right thing." The second factor was the initiation of formal paternity proceedings initiated by the woman in the fifth or sixth month of her pregnancy.

Lawrence Stone argued that the common expectation in early modern England when a pregnancy occurred during courtship was marriage.[40] Edgar G. McManus stressed the amount of pressure applied to create legitimate families in order to lessen the burdens of public support of illegitimate children and to prevent the perceived social chaos inherent in the presence of incomplete families in a society predicated on the patriarchal household.[41] Respected community elders like Samuel Sewall of Boston were in a position to apply this type of communal pressure. Sewall described an instance in which he tried to use moral suasion on a young man who had impregnated his fellow-servant. He advised twenty-year-old Sam Haugh to marry, that "a father was obliged to look after mother and child. Christ would one day call him to an account and demand of him what was become of the child." Sewall spoke movingly to Haugh of his responsibilities to his child that could only be met through marriage and his continued presence in the life of his child. The limited efficacy of this type of appeal, by the early eighteenth-century when Sewall wrote, is indicated by his wry comment that he "could not discern that any impression was made upon him."[42]

The direct approach was used by Caleb Boynton, a Rowley blacksmith, in March, 1678. He used physical intimidation, if not to force a marriage, to exact revenge for a dishonored sister-in-law. As Samuel Perkins of Ipswich traveled to court, accompanied by a deputy, to answer fornication charges, Boynton attacked him and:

> proceeded to abuse him by laying violent hands upon him, pulling off his hat, taking him by the neckcloth and shoulder, challenging him and calling him vile names.[43]

The following month Perkins married Hannah West, and her father, Twiford West, paid her £3 fine for fornication.

The three cases for which the most documentation survives involve unequal relationships. That these cases generated the greatest amount of paperwork is an indication of the importance Puritans placed on status-appropriate marriages. In the first two instances the relationships were based on sexual attraction in which women resisted parental control in favor of the unsuitable men, both landless servants, to whom they were attracted. The third case, in which a sexually-experienced older man impregnated two step-sisters and eventually married the younger, wealthier woman, is almost a parody. In each instance, parents were torn between their hopes of an equivalent partner for their daughters and the realities of insuring that their daughters not give birth to illegitimate children.

These three cases represent the difficulty of finding common analytical ground because each family reacted differently when faced with the problem of a pregnant, unmarried daughter. In 1664, Robert Cross waffled about whether or not he wanted his pregnant daughter, Martha, to marry her property-less fellow-servant, William Dirkey. His ambivalence created a rift with his daughter and endangered the marriage. William and Beatrice Canterbury allowed their daughter, Rebecca, to marry, but after the marriage Goody Canterbury harassed her new son-in-law so bitterly that the Essex County Quarterly Court was forced to intervene. In the third instance, Henry Short forced his sister's suitor, Joseph Mayo, into marriage, despite the fact that Mayo had also impregnated Short's step-sister. While Short may have salvaged some family honor, it is difficult to imagine that his action promoted the long-term happiness of his sister.

Evidence provided in the premarital fornication case of William Dirkey and Martha Cross indicates the reluctance of prosperous parents to agree to marriage when the suitor lacked equivalent resources. It also demonstrates the role neighbors and employers might play in conciliation. Martha Cross and William Dirkey both worked in the household of Thomas Bishop. Cross was the twenty-year-old daughter of Robert Cross, a substantial Ipswich planter: Dirkey was a thirty-year-old Irish servant who had arrived in the Bishop household via the Barbados. It is unlikely that Robert Cross would have given Dirkey permission to court or marry his daughter, had he been asked but by April 1664 Martha Cross was pregnant. It is possible that the pregnancy was a deliberate attempt to force a marriage. There was a ten-year age difference between Dirkey and Cross, and in terms of experience they were literally worlds apart. That summer, her employer, Thomas Bishop, was deputized to speak to her father to get his permission to marry. Martha Cross told Bishop that: "she would have William Dirkey and no other while she lived."[44] In an undated letter to Bishop, Robert Cross spoke of his and his wife's feelings about the match: "our hearts are sore oppressed: we are as full of sorrow." He assented to the marriage, although he would have no part of it.[45]

The marriage was set for September 18, 1664. However, shortly before September 18, Robert Cross turned up at the Bishops' and demanded his daughter. Martha Cross was in a dilemma. Her father and the traditional "friends" were there not to see her married but to take her home: William Dirkey didn't want her to leave the Bishops. Martha had little option but to leave with her father after chiding a jealous Dirkey. She reminded him that she had trusted him: "why will you not trust me as well as I have trusted you hitherto."[46] Martha Cross had asked a good question. She had placed her trust in Dirkey when she had sex with him. Now it was his turn to trust her. She promised William that "she would not forsake him."[47]

William Dirkey and Robert Cross both turned to the court. Dirkey sued Cross for withholding his daughter from him after Cross had given his reluctant consent to the marriage. Cross countersued Dirkey for abusing his daughter. The court, in a verdict worthy of Solomon, found in favor of both parties. Martha Cross was nine months pregnant by this point. Her father, a formidable man, having removed Martha from the Bishops, now threw her out of the family house because she refused to give Dirkey up. She found refuge with a married sister, Elizabeth Nelson, who seized gratefully upon the offer of a neighbor, Goodman Story, to serve as an intermediary. Goodman Story described his efforts:

> Martha being in sore distress of mind in the consideration as she confessed she had been cast out of her father's favor & family; was so harried and distressed in mind that her sister Nelson came down to me much affected lamentation with tears that much affected my heart to hear her. Woe she said I thought my sister would have died tonight: but she thought she could not live another in that condition: I being much affected with their condition: said why do you not go to your father & make your condition known to him: to which she answered Oh I dare not go to speak a word on her behalf. Then I said will you go if I go down with you, then Goody Nelson said I, with all my heart. So we went down to Goodman Cross & then we found them in a very sad and sorrowful condition, very much harried in their spirit not knowing which way to turn and what to say: and as my apprehension then led me: did treat with them about the suffering them to marry, the which he did & that was the way then that we thought to be the best.[48]

Story's deposition is a poignant reminder of familial affection, the power of a young woman's love, and the timeless dilemma created when parents and children differ in fundamental ways. Then, now that Robert Cross had consented to the marriage, William Dirkey had second thoughts:

> He wished he had never spoke as he had done in owning of the child to be his and he had eighteen meals in a week but he would spare six of them to keep the child.[49]

He agreed to marry Cross, saying: he had rather keep the child than keep her," but: "if he kept one he would keep the other." Cross responded to his ungracious offer with an assurance of her continued affection. Their son, John Dirkey, was born four days after the wedding.

Martha Cross was the loser in all this. While working away from home as a servant, she had been vulnerable to the sexual advances of a fellow-servant ten years her elder who had no assets beyond the food his employer was obliged to give him. She opposed the will of a formidable parent. Even her married sister, Elizabeth Nelson, was reluctant to approach Robert Cross on Martha's behalf without the support of Goodman Story. Cross alienated her parents and found herself the object of efforts by the court, her sisters and their husbands, and their neighbors to ensure her marriage prior to the birth of her child. Then, having finally secured parental consent, she discovered that Dirkey was wavering. Dirkey lamented he had ever "owned" the child. If he had denied paternity, as so many of his peers did, he could have escaped prosecution. Martha Cross' dilemma illustrates how much more a woman who entered into an extramarital sexual relationship had to lose than her male partner. If she had not conceived, her father's status meant that she could have found a more status-appropriate husband than Dirkey.

The 1660 premarital fornication prosecution of Rebecca Canterbury and Benjamin Woodrow illustrates the bitterness that could result when an untimely pregnancy led to an unequal marriage. Benjamin Woodrow, a servant, was not the husband William and Beatrice Canterbury would have chosen for their daughter. Not only did Woodrow possess neither money nor prospects, he had already angered his future mother-in-law three years earlier by testifying against her and the Canterbury's only son, John, following a neighborhood quarrel in which John and Beatrice Canterbury had beaten Woodrow's employer's wife, Goody Rowden. As a result of this altercation, Beatrice and John Canterbury and Goody Rowden were fined, and Woodrow was placed in the stocks for perjury.[50] The following year Woodrow and a second indentured servant had conspired to run away from their masters.

Faced with a pregnant daughter over twenty-one, the Canterburys were unable, had they wished, to prevent the marriage. Rebecca, her father, and Benjamin Woodrow appeared together before Magistrate William Hathorne, February 6, 1660.[51] She admitted she was pregnant; Woodrow that he was the father. By the time they appeared at the next session of the Essex County Quarterly Court to be sentenced, they were married. The Canterburys did not, however, provide Rebecca with a dowry or pay her share of the fornication fine as many parents did.

Woodrow was sentenced to pay two 40 shilling fines for himself and his wife. His employer, John Rowden, advanced the money for one of the 40 shilling fines, and Woodrow promised to pay the second fine within a year. When payment of his wife's fine was due the following summer, Woodrow pled extreme poverty. He had, he argued, "a wife, two small children, and nothing wherewith to relieve them but my daily labor."[52]

It is clear that the Woodrow's financial situation was desperate, even as Rebecca tried with difficulty to maintain a relationship with her parents. At the following court session in December 1661, Beatrice Canterbury was fined "for wicked and reviling speeches toward her son-in-law."[53] Canterbury had called Woodrow:

> a thief for that he had stolen the best flower in her garden, & a rogue because he had brought her body to shame.[54]

When her daughter remonstrated with her, she added that the "devil should pick his bones before she would own him to be her son."[55] Neighbors testified to the frequency and vehemence of Canterbury's criticisms of her son-in-law and the effect they had on Rebecca Woodrow who "wept bitterly and begged her mother to forbear."

While Beatrice Canterbury maintained a running feud with Benjamin Woodrow, William Canterbury, in a will drawn up in April 1661, left equal amounts of money to his daughter, Rebecca, and her children and to his daughter, Ruth. Ruth was to receive a farm as well, and to pay Rebecca a further £30. William Canterbury died June 1, 1663. Rebecca Woodrow did not benefit from her inheritance because she died herself the following day at the age of twenty-four, after three years of marriage. Had she made a status-equivalent marriage, she would have been spared the economic privation and the stress that her mother's dislike of her husband engendered and which may have precipitated her death.

Evidence indicates that after Rebecca's death, Woodrow turned their son and daughter over to his mother-in-law, Beatrice Canterbury, to raise. Canterbury received her husband's entire estate, valued at £470, and married two more times. When Canterbury died intestate 20 years later, Rebecca's sister, Ruth, and her husband claimed the entire estate.[56] Rebecca Woodrow's children, Joseph and Mary, asked for half of William and Beatrice Canterbury's estate. While Ruth and her husband were willing to share a portion of the estate with Rebecca's daughter, they refused to give anything to her son, Joseph Woodrow. The court ordered the estate to be split into half, with Joseph Woodrow and his sister, Mary, each receiving a quarter.[57] So finally, after 25 years and extended litigation, the Woodrow children received their mother's inheritance.

The third case provides the clearest evidence of a "shotgun" marriage. As in the case of Rebecca Canterbury, marriage was precipitated by the appearance of the pregnant woman, Sarah Short, and her brother, Mr. Henry

Short, before a magistrate to lay a charge of paternity. Again, the man involved, was not a desirable marriage partner. Short and Mayo had met while Mayo visited Short's stepsister, Hannah Adams who was herself carrying Mayo's child and hoping to marry him. Sarah Short was only nineteen and a considerable heiress when she conceived; her father had left an estate of £1842 to Sarah and her brother, Henry, six years earlier. Mayo was twenty-nine, not a native of Essex County, and the possessor of a poor sexual reputation. Again, he was not the husband that Henry Short would have sought for his sister, but once she became pregnant, it was imperative that she marry him. Even Joseph Mayo was better than no husband at all. Mayo received Short's dowry of £150 and used it to establish himself in Newbury.[58]

Martha Cross, Rebecca Canterbury, and Sarah Short all had sex with men who would not make status-appropriate husbands. Two of the men were servants, the third a visiting sailor with a poor sexual reputation. Sarah Short left no depositions but both Martha Cross and Rebecca Canterbury attested that they had been in love and both remained steadfast in their choices. There is the possibility that Cross and Canterbury used their pregnancies to force parental approval, but this cannot be proved. What can be stated, is that daughters did not always follow their parents' dictates and that all of Massachusetts's laws to control courtship and marriage could not prevent a few deviant couples from meeting clandestinely and engaging in sexual intercourse. In these three instances, the men involved could have hoped to benefit materially from their marriages. Parents, when their only options were a daughter with an illegitimate child and limited opportunity to marry, or an unsuitable husband, chose the unsuitable husband.

Some men were persuaded to marry through the initiation of formal court proceedings against them for paternity. Margaret Batten of Salem, whom we met earlier, used this method to bring Edward Welch to marriage. She went to the Salem magistrate, John Hathorne, accompanied by her mother, Joanna Batten and a second witness to swear that Welch had admitted paternity and agreed to marry her. Welch, however, had not honored his grudging agreement to marry and his failure had brought Batten to Hathorne who immediately issued a warrant for Welch's appearance.

Welch could not be found for two months, but when Batten's baby was born 12 weeks later, she and Welch were married. However, when the couple was summoned for their fornication prosecution, Welch was gone again. This time his failure to appear was involuntary: he had been captured by the French. The Salem magistrates had cooperated with Margaret Batten to forcibly encourage Welch to marry her but her plight following her husband's capture in no way mitigated the court's intention to punish her for fornication. She was ordered to pay 40 shillings or to be whipped 10 stripes.

At the opposite end of the economic spectrum were those for whom help in marriage formation was not what the defendants sought. They wanted to avoid the shame of an appearance for fornication, and they could afford to forfeit their bonds. In 1682, the court was forced to resummon "Mr. Eben Gardner, Mr. Packer's wife, Mr. Duncan's daughter."[59] Each of these parties had been presented for fornication; none of them appeared in court. While the men provided no excuses, Mr. Ebenezer Gardner's wife, Sarah Bartholomew, sent her sister to court to say she was too sick to attend.[60] Bartholomew died three months later.

In the majority of premarital fornication cases, where depositions are lacking, quantitative evidence is the only measure of marriage formation processes. The willingness of men to marry their pregnant partners declined over time. While five of the seven couples convicted of premarital fornication between 1650 and 1660 married in the first trimester, of the 49 couples whose marriage date and date of birth of their first child can be established between 1676 and 1692, only three of them married in the first trimester of the pregnancy. Since parents appeared anxious to see their daughter married, and women had a vested interest in marrying as quickly as possible, it must be have been the men who were dragging their feet.

A combination of factors may account for this male reluctance. First, the religious fervor of the first generation of settlers which impelled most of them to refrain from sexual intercourse prior to marriage was impossible to sustain. The sense of communal mission that impelled the usage of terms such as "brother" and "sister," promoted "godly watchfulness," and mandated intense supervision of unrelated men and women dissipated. The amendment to the fornication law in 1668 that absolved men from fornication prosecutions and emphasized the collection of child support-payments from them is an indication that extramarital sexual activity had become a gendered issue. Women, not men became the blameworthy sex. It was their responsibility to maintain their sexual integrity. It is also indicative of the fact that extramarital sex, while still an issue of public morality, had become a pocketbook issue. Second, the population of Essex County was no longer homogeneous as status differences became more pronounced. Puritans had always insisted on the importance of status-equivalent marriages. While they were willing to bend the rules to marry a daughter off, parents of sons, and those sons themselves, must have seen child-support payments as a viable alternative to marrying a woman who had been willing to have sex without marriage and who might lack financial resources. A third factor was that the pool of marriageable men had been depleted by losses in Metacomet's War and by out-migration from Essex County communities to the frontier. Competition to secure a husband might have led a few women to engage in sexual intercourse in the hopes of cementing a relationship. These factors combined meant that time and considerable pressure was required in many instances to seal a marriage once a woman had conceived.

Once couples legitimized their sexual activity and rectified the aberrant behavior that placed them temporarily outside the Puritan fold, they were ready to be reintegrated into the community. Ritual shame punishments and expressions of penitence were required. The couple, if they were church members, was excommunicated until they had appeared before the congregation garbed in white sheets, whereupon the husband read a penitent statement. This statement served a double duty. It was also read to the court and a few examples remain in the court files. These statements are similar in content to those filed by the mothers of illegitimate children with one striking difference: two of the three surviving penitent statements present exculpatory defenses. Men needed to retain a snatch of honor in the midst of a generally degrading experience.

In 1674, William Barber, a fisherman, and his wife, Elizabeth Ruck, were sentenced to be fined or whipped following the birth of their child 24 weeks after their marriage. While expressing all the correct sentiments, Barber also flattered the court by comparing them to the "kings of Israel of ancient time," used his youth as an excuse, "I am a young beginner in the world," and then fell back on a legalism, questioning the right of the court to charge him since more than a year had elapsed since his marriage.[61] While Barber's wife appeared in court with him, he made no mention of her in his petition which was written entirely in the first person. Three years later Barber was dead. He left his wife a meager estate valued at £17. While the sums paid in fines by premarital fornicators between 1674 and 1677 are not recorded, couples usually paid a minimum of 40 shillings each. This £4 would have represented a substantial portion (25 percent) of Barber's resources. It is understandable that Barber was anxious to placate the court, especially when he had been given reason to think he and his wife might escape conviction given that a year elapsed between the marriage and the prosecution.

Isaac Bailey was twenty-nine, his wife, Sarah Emery, twenty-three, when they married in 1684. Their child was born 26 weeks later. Both came from established Essex County families, all four of their parents were living, and they were in the age cohort that would be expected to have the resources with which to marry. Their statement presents the expected mix of sentiments. They had committed "folly," sinned against God, the community, and their own souls, "to the great grief of our aged parents."[62]

Bailey and Emery, both of Newbury, are representative of the majority of couples who were convicted of premarital fornication. Isaac Bailey was the fifth of seven surviving children of a Newbury weaver and husbandman. With three older brothers and an elder sister already married and established, Bailey had reached the age of twenty-nine unmarried. Sarah Emery was the fifth of twelve children of John and Mary Emery. While her father had more children to establish than Bailey, he also appears to have had more resources. John Emery held the rank of sergeant in the local militia and was a church member. There were no financial impediments to marriage and nothing in the record indicates that either Bailey or Emery had been in any trouble before this time. Like the majority of fornication defendants they did not engage in any aberrant behavior after marriage that brought them back into court again. Isaac Bailey was identified as a yeoman and in the ten years prior to Sarah's death they had five children together.[63]

Most couples, like the Verrys and the Baileys survived their premarital fornication prosecutions without apparent long-lasting repercussions. Their fornication prosecution represented their only brush with the law. Those who began their marriages with few resources remained poor. Rebecca Gault was a twenty-year-old servant when she married John Bly of Salem in November 1663. Gault's father had died in 1659, his widow had remarried and the house the family lived in was sold to pay his debts. John Bly was not better circumstanced. He was in Salem by 1653 at the age of fourteen, and identified as a laborer at the time of marriage, but he does not seem to have been accompanied by parents who could assist him materially. Seven weeks after their marriage their child was stillborn. The circumstances surrounding the baby's birth are questionable. The Blys may have been trying to abort the baby as midwives were called in the day after the birth to examine its body at the request of the magistrate, William Hathorne. They reported that the baby's thigh bones had been broken and that the child had been six weeks premature at most.[64] The Blys were prosecuted for fornication only, though, not because of the child's injuries but because an examination of its body indicated that sexual intercourse had preceded marriage. They were fined £4 for fornication. He and Rebecca had at least seven more children between 1665 and 1676 when Bly was identified as a brickmaker. In 1673, the selectmen of Salem threatened to remove the Bly children from the household and place them with other families unless their parents looked to their education and disciplined them. In 1683, when John Bly's name appeared on a Salem tax list, his tax rate placed him in the bottom seven percent of Salem ratepayers.[65] Their daughter, Mary, while working as a servant in a Salem household, was convicted of fornication following the birth of an illegitimate child in 1690.

Middling daughters who married because they were pregnant shared the financial fate of their husbands. Ann Devorix was the daughter of a prosperous Marblehead fisherman when she married Walter Boaston. He was sentenced to be severely whipped or fined £4. Devorix did not appear with him and was ordered to attend the next Salem session of the quarterly court. There is no record that she appeared, and her father may have posted her bond and allowed her to default to save her the shame of a court appearance. Six years later, Boaston was dead, and his inventory indicates the dire poverty in which they were living[66] His estate was valued at £11. Almost every item in the inventory is prefixed with the word, "old." The family possessions included "one canvas bed filled with cattails, three old chairs, and one cradle." There is no mention of a house or land in Boaston's inventory, however, so her father, John Devorix, may have been supporting the couple to the extent of providing them with housing.

Middling sons and daughters, while they may not have shared equally in the material status of their siblings if they made an unequal marriage, usually received inheritances equivalent with their continent siblings. Although Ruth Hewes had been convicted of premarital fornication in 1683, she and her two sisters each received £20 in her father's will probated seven years later.[67] Hewes was twenty when she was prosecuted, her husband, John Browne, only eighteen, so the impetus for their marriage was undoubtedly the pregnancy, yet her father did not penalize her for it when he drew up his will.

Marriages that began with an unplanned pregnancy were, then as now, not always successful. One of the bitterest was that of Samuel Perkins and Hannah West. Perkins had been attacked by his erstwhile brother-in-law on his way under guard to court for his trial in 1678 and nine years and at least four children later the acrimony was open. While Samuel and Hannah Perkins each blamed the other for the failure of their marriage, it is clear that Samuel Perkins' honor was threatened by his inability to control his wife. It was important to him that his wife deferred to him, at least in public. Perkins sued his wife for abusive carriages, claiming that she refused to do housework, hindered him in his employment as a shop-keeper, and made excessive demands upon him for material goods. During a quarrel in the shop where Perkins worked, Hannah told him that "she had lived twenty years a maid and then her mother had married her to a fool."[68]

Two days after this incident, Hannah Perkins had returned to her widowed mother's house and Samuel Perkins had gone to the Essex County

Quarterly Court to force his wife to return to him and to treat him respectfully. Part of the dispute revolved around their bed. The mattress-ticking was torn and needed to be refilled. Hannah Perkins refused to mend it, saying that she needed to sell her feathers for food. If the duty of each partner to a marriage was to engage in sexual intercourse, then Hannah Perkins was making a statement about her willingness to engage in sexual intercourse by not fixing the marriage bed, saying "You may fill the bed yourself . . . if you had a bed yourself you would not trouble me . . . I had as lives lie on the ground as any where.[69] Apparently the court was able to force some kind of reconciliation, and perhaps compel Hannah Perkins to stuff and repair their mattress, as they had a fifth child in 1692.

Thomas Hobbs went to court to force his son-in-law to return to his daughter. Martha Hobbs and Richard Prior had been convicted of fornication in 1666. In 1672, Prior was presented for living apart from his wife for four years. He was jailed, and an order was issued prohibiting anyone from providing him with food, lodging, or employment. Thus the Massachusetts Bay Colony ensured that the family unit remained intact, the basic building block of Puritan society. In this instance the family unit may not have remained intact for long. Although the records are unclear, and Thomas Hobbs had launched the suit requiring Prior to return to his wife, Hobbs had told others that "Richard Prior should not come within his doors nor come near his daughter and that there should be no more of the breed of them"[70]

For the majority of couples, however, who married following an unplanned pregnancy and who received enough money from both sets of parents to establish themselves respectably in the community, rehabilitation was possible. Henry True of Salisbury and his wife, Jane Bradbury, both aged twenty-three, were fined £3 and £2 respectively for fornication in 1668 when their first daughter was born 10 weeks after their marriage. Subsequently, however, Henry True was elected to the rank of captain in the militia, an office his father-in-law also held, and became a deacon of the Salisbury church. Nothing in the court records indicate why it took them so long to marry, but the conviction did not impede True's promotion. Rehabilitation was possible because Henry True was an eldest son who had already inherited his father's estate and his wife, Jane Bradbury, was the daughter of a gentleman.

The diverse nature and the limited depositional data available in premarital fornication cases make definitive conclusions difficult. The court established 32 weeks as the cut-off point for a premarital fornication prosecution, allowing eight weeks leeway between marriage and birth, not because sexual intercourse was customarily initiated between contract and marriage, but because a premarital fornication conviction had such serious personal and financial ramifications. It was not a charge to be levied lightly.

Three conclusions, nevertheless, can be stated with a degree of certainty. First, most Puritan couples waited until their wedding nights to initiate sexual intercourse. Only 151 couples were convicted of premarital fornication between 1640 and 1685, the period for which Essex County Quarterly Court docket books survive. This illustrates the strength of Puritan hostility to sexual activity between unmarried persons and the degree to which the majority of Puritans adhered to community sexual mores. Second, the length of time elapsed between marriage and birth indicates that men were reluctant to marry women who were willing to give up their virginity prior to marriage, even if it had been to them. This indicates that the ideology about women that was applied to women who bore illegitimate children applied to women who conceived prior to their marriage. What saved them from the same ignominious fate as bastard-bearers was their ability to force an often reluctant partner to marry. Third, couples convicted of premarital fornication fall into three categories. In the first category are the couples who planned to marry and were prevented, for some reason, from marrying when they had planned. This is the smallest category because couples whose marriage was actively being planned by their parents or guardians were socialized to wait for their wedding night, which was expected to occur within a month of the contract, to initiate sexual activity. These couples were able to marry within the first trimester of the pregnancy and some may have remained undetected. The second category comprises uncommitted couples who engaged in sexual activity on the spur of the moment, whether it was fueled by alcohol, by sex play that went too far, or the willingness of the man to engage in coercion. Marriage formation in these cases was possible because the women's families were able, through financial inducements and community pressure, to persuade their partners to "do the right thing." The third category of premarital sexual offenders took the longest time to marry. Having reached the age when they could normally expect to marry and engage in legitimate sexual activity, they were precluded by poverty from engaging in the formal processes through which they could have hoped to enter marriage. Sexual restraint was more difficult to maintain if marriage could not be plausibly hoped for in the near future. These couples engaged in sexual intercourse and hoped for the best. When the worst happened, they scraped together enough money to marry, but it took time, and most of these couples spent their entire married life in the same impoverished state in which they had entered it.

For women, marriage was a rehabilitative event. Their feme covert status deflected the worst of the humiliating rehabilitative rituals. Marriage established potential bastard-bearers and their children within a family unit with a temporarily weakened patriarchal head. For men, the punishment was more severe, having married their pregnant partner, than it would have been if they had abandoned them because they linked their fate with that of women who had lost their sexual reputations. These men could be legitimately prosecuted for fornication because marriage was an admission of paternity. There was no question but that they had engaged in sexual intercourse without the sanctifying balm of marriage. There was no permanent loss of male status and authority involved, however. Men could be shamed through presentation in church and court because they had redeemed themselves through marriage. As the heads of their own little family, they assumed the status of Puritan householder. Thus, the couple who fornicated and then married could be used as an example of retribution and rehabilitation to the community without permanently impairing the position of men in general in a society based on the belief that men were better equipped intellectually and physically to control their sexual appetites.

Chapter Eight

"Playing the Rogue": Rape and Issues of Consent in Seventeenth-Century Massachusetts[1]

> I stood still and heard one say, you french cur, let me alone. Soon after I went toward the place I heard the voices and I saw Peter Croy brushing off his cuff with his hand and Sarah Lambert was rising from the ground and went away homeward. When I came to Peter I said to him you have been playing the rogue with Pod's girl.[2]

Sarah Lambert was thirteen-years-old when she was raped by Peter Croy in 1673. Her case met all the criteria for a capital conviction. She called out, there were two witnesses, her sister and the youth who provided the account above; and a committee of goodwives deposed, after a physical examination, that she had been penetrated. Yet Peter Croy was not convicted of rape. After an equivocal verdict, he was sentenced to wear a noose. Nor was any other unmarried Puritan man convicted of the rape of a single woman in seventeenth-century Massachusetts Bay.

There are constants in the female experience of rape. The typical rape victim in the seventeenth-century, as today, was unmarried, employed, knew her attacker, and was unlikely to report the assault. Her assailant, in the unlikely event of prosecution, offered a defense as effective in the early modern world as today: The sexual activity had been consensual; there had been no struggle; and, he would assert, her sexual reputation was such that no reasonable man could have expected to meet with a refusal.

These constants, however, mask significant differences. The physical and psychological effects of rape were exacerbated by the Puritan conflation of chastity and femininity. Public knowledge of loss of virginity materially affected her marriageability. Shame, too, was a powerful incentive to silence.

In addition, the Puritan belief in predestination meant that as women who successfully resisted rapists credited God for their salvation, those who failed felt the full weight of God's abandonment. These women had little to gain and much to lose by reporting a sexual assault.

Rape victims faced additional difficulties. First, the seventeenth-century belief in female inferiority and the concomitant application of a sexual double standard led to conflicting notions about the seriousness of the crime of rape. Grand jurymen had the power to ignore a complaint, or they could lay a charge along a continuum of criminality from fornication, which penalized the victim too, through assault, or lewd or lascivious behavior, to attempted rape or rape. Grand jurymen were influenced by the class, the age, the marital status and the reputation of the female victim and the man she accused. Second, the ideological construction of women as lustful daughters of Eve imbued everyday female behavior with sexual meaning. A smile while mutually engaged in field work could be construed as an invitation. Third, the language of sexuality, the discourse of intercourse, privileged male aggressiveness over female submission. In consensual sexual intercourse, women 'submitted,' or 'suffered' men to 'use' or 'occupy' their bodies for the purpose of 'begetting children upon' them.[3] Fourth, rape was difficult to prove. Two witnesses and an outcry were required. Even in cases where the rules of evidence appear to have been satisfied, a guilty verdict was not certain. Fifth was the narrow legal definition of rape. The judges of the Massachusetts Bay Court of Assistants relied on an English jurisprudence manual, Michael Dalton's, *The Countrey Justice* to assist them in their interpretation of rape law in 1641 and again in 1648. Dalton defined rape as violent nonconsensual sexual intercourse. The issue of consent was paramount to Dalton. If a woman had consented after the fact, or if she had consented to intercourse out of fear for her life, her attacker was to be charged with rape. Dalton believed, though, and Puritan judges and juries agreed with him, that:

> [if] a woman at the time of the supposed rape do conceive with child by the Ravisher, this is no rape, for a woman cannot conceive with child, except she doth consent.[4]

This presumption of consent upon conception made a world of legal difference to young women in seventeenth-century Massachusetts. All of these factors meant that a decision to lay a rape charge was never cut and dried nor a guilty conviction a foregone conclusion.

Rape was a capital offense, but men were reluctant to hang other men for engaging in heterosexual sexual activity including rape. Only fourteen men were tried for rape and three men for attempted rape by the Massachusetts Court of Assistants between 1630 and 1692.[5] One might conclude then that sexual violence against women was limited, but in this chapter, I will argue that these low numbers are not evidence that sexual violence was rare in seventeenth-century Massachusetts. Rather, women were reluctant to report incidents, and those responsible for administering criminal justice, from the grand jurymen of the local quarterly courts to the justices of the Massachusetts Court of Assistants were predisposed to see the use of force as an extreme, but not necessarily illegal, expression of normal male sexual activity. Men charged with attempted rape by local grand juries were not consistently sent for trial to the Court of Assistants which had jurisdiction over crimes involving life, limb, or banishment.[6] Only those cases in which the victim was married, where the issue of consent could be bypassed, or cases in which the victim was 10 years of age or less and incapable of consent, resulted in guilty verdicts from Puritan juries.[7]

A close reading of depositions presented in Essex County Quarterly Court prosecutions indicates a pervasive pattern of hidden and unpunished sexual violence against women. It is most commonly found in illegitimate fornication case depositions in which the female defendant described coerced sexual activity. These incidents did not fit the legal definition of rape because conception had occurred and Puritans did not believe that conception was possible unless a woman was a willing participant to sexual intercourse and had "reached pleasure." A second source for descriptions of coerced sexual activity is slander suits launched by men anxious to reclaim their honor in the face of neighborhood disapprobation following the discovery of an illegitimate pregnancy. A third source is women's depositions in support of a lesser charge such as lascivious conduct or assault which report incidents of a sexually threatening nature.

The depositions filed in the fornication prosecution of Elizabeth Emerson of Haverhill in 1686 open a door into the past that allows us to listen to a disparate group of seventeenth-century women discussing sexual violence and their understanding of the conditions necessary to conception. The discussion is heated: it is during the course of an argument that the diverse viewpoints are presented. The participants are twenty-one year old Elizabeth Emerson, who is in labor, her mother, Hannah Emerson, her sister, Hannah Dustin, the midwife, Johanah Corliss, and at least three neighbors, Liddia Ladd, Mary Neff, and Johanah Hasletine.[8] The quarrel began when Corliss assumed her legal role and asked Emerson to name the baby's father. The required paternity statement had taken on increased significance because when Emerson and her father had gone to the magistrate during her pregnancy to lay formal charges against the father, she had claimed that Timothy Swan, a neighbor's son, had raped her in her parent's new bedchamber, which Swan had asked her to show to him.[9] The neighbors greeted this claim with skepticism. Goodwife Corliss wanted to know why she hadn't scratched or kicked him. Goodwife Haseltine asserted she would have made "the town ring of it before the morning."[10]

The four Puritan matrons, Corliss, Haseltine, Neff, and Ladd espoused an assertive response. A reading of this deposition alone suggests that they were giving Emerson good advice and that there was a community expectation that rape victims should struggle vigorously and call out. However, a cumulative reading of depositions describing similar incidents indicates that most young women lacked the necessary confidence in the system to test the strength of the neighborhood belief in their chastity by making a charge. Emerson had already violated the Puritan ideal of femininity as a teenager when some unspecified act on her part had provoked her father to beat her so severely that he had been prosecuted by the quarterly court for assault.

Depositions in this case provide evidence of the Puritan expectation that conception would occur only if the intercourse was consensual, and that it would not happen if the young woman had been a virgin before intercourse. Goodwife Haseltine stated that "it was impossible or very unlikely for a maid to be with child at the first, being forced." These women were not informed solely by some simple folk belief about the origin of babies. Early modern English medical texts advised that a female orgasm, which involved a "mutual exchange of fluids," promoted conception. It is hardly surprising they, like Puritan juries composed of men, believed that conception would not occur as the outcome of rape.

The depositions in the Emerson case also confirm that claims of rape might be met with disbelief if the claimant had a damaged reputation and a weak story. She had failed to cry out, she had not made a timely accusation of rape, and her mother had contradicted details of her story. Swan was not charged with rape, although he was required to pay child supports for Emerson's daughter, whom she named Dorothie after Swan's sister. Six years later, in 1691, Emerson committed infanticide after giving birth secretly to illegitimate twin daughters rather than face a second inquisition.[11] She was hanged in June, 1693.

Puritans looked not to traditional English common law, in which heterosexual rape was a capital crime, but to the Bible when they drew up their first law code for Massachusetts Bay. Mosaic law was the more complex of the two systems, the penalties for rape differed according to the marital status of the victim. The Bible prescribed death by stoning for rape in cases where the victim of rape or attempted rape was either married or engaged. The rationale for making the rape of a married or engaged woman a capital offense was rooted not in the egregious nature of the act but in the fact that if a woman was married or engaged, sexual intercourse with her was an injury to her husband and threatened the integrity of the patriarchal family. Further justification for the death penalty for the rape of a married or engaged woman was rooted in adultery law. This was a convenient way of getting around issues of consent. Whether coitus had been consensual or not, the penalty was death for both parties.

Mosaic law enjoined marriage between the victim and her rapist in cases where the young woman had no prior attachment.[12] The Puritans, to their credit, given their devotion to the idea of establishing a Commonwealth governed by Biblical precepts, did not think that marrying a rape victim to her rapist was an appropriate or fair remedy. Nor did they think that capital punishment was appropriate in the case of the rape of a single woman because of the issue of consent. They were caught between Mosaic Law, which was inadequate in this instance, and English common law, which was too secular for their religious Commonwealth. Further, there was no Mosaic precedent to follow in cases of the sexual abuse of a child or statutory rape.[13]

The first rape case tried in New England reflects this judicial uncertainty. In 1636, an indentured servant, Edward Woodley, broke into a neighboring house and assaulted a female servant. He was charged with "attempted rape, swearing, and breaking into a house," and sentenced "to be whipped 30 stripes, a year's imprisonment at hard labor with coarse diet, and to wear a collar of iron."[14] Four months later, the Court ordered him released to his master who required his labor, if the woman he had assaulted would declare herself to be free of fear from him. There is no suggestion in the court record that marriage was considered as an alternative to the court-ordered punishment.

The Court was forced to include a law specifically addressing the issue of rape in 1641 when they issued their first formal law code because they wanted to execute three men accused of sexually abusing two young girls, Dorcas and Sarah Humfrey. They discovered that nothing in the colony's current law code prohibited either consensual or nonconsensual sexual activity between adults and children.[15] The Court of Assistants moved swiftly to close this loophole. They revised the rape statute in 1642 to make the rape of a child less than ten years of age or consensual intercourse with a child less than ten years of age capital crimes. The rape of an engaged or married woman was also a capital crime, but the punishment for raping a single woman was left to the discretion of the judges. It could be capital punishment, but "some other grievous punishment" could be levied, depending on the circumstances.[16]

The Court rationalized its decision to levy the death penalty in cases where the victim was less than ten years of age in two ways. Mosaic Law ordered the death penalty for sodomy and bestiality. As with sexual intercourse between men, or with animals, intercourse with children under the age of ten could not possibly be fruitful and was therefore unnatural. John Winthrop articulated their reasoning, saying:

> it should be death for a man to have carnal copulation with a girl so young, as there can be no possibility of generation, for it is against nature as well as sodomy and buggery."[17]

This logic cut two ways. Dorcas also accused two of her brothers, but since neither of them had reached puberty, they were not charged. The second rationale was that children under the age of ten were incapable of giving informed consent. But the Court was not comfortable with this line of reasoning because, if a child could not give informed consent to sexual intercourse, neither could the child make an informed refusal. When a new law code was issued in 1648, *The Laws and Liberties of Massachusetts,* the only rape law that remained in force involved married and single women over the age of ten.

This law sufficed until 1669, when Patrick Jeannison raped eight-year old Grace Roberts. The judges wanted to hang Jeannison, but they found that there was no provision in the law to execute Jeannison since his victim was under ten years of age. They referred the case to the General Court which decided that since the rape of a child was a more heinous crime than the rape of a single woman, the judges could infer that capital punishment was legal in this case and in other similar cases involving children.[18]

Colonial historians have often assumed that once an accusation of rape was laid against an individual the case proceeded swiftly to trial. Lyle Koehler states that "(r)ape was considered so serious that a woman could not lie about it," and that charges were inevitably brought when a woman complained to the authorities.[19] The assumption is also made that once the rules of evidence had been satisfied, a guilty verdict would be invariably rendered. "Throughout New England the victim's testimony sufficed to convict a man of attempted rape."[20] However, these conclusions are not borne out by the evidence.

Sarah Smith lived in the frontier settlement of Deerfield in 1693.

Recently married to a widower, Martin Smith, who had been captured and taken to Montreal by the French and Indians, and a relative newcomer to Deerfield, she lacked her husband's protection and financial support. Smith claimed that a local man had attempted to rape her and she lodged an official complaint with the Justices of the Peace in Hatfield. John Evans, she said, had come to her house near the palisade ostensibly to chat before he went on guard duty. Finding her alone, he had thrown her to the floor and attempted to rape her. She had resisted him physically and had screamed, whereupon two young men who were on guard duty, deposed to hearing Smith and seeing the attack, the door of the house being ajar, but being so: "surprised with fear and from trembling at such actions that we darest not go into the house to the woman's assistance."[21]

John Evans was not charged with attempted rape. It is possible that since Sarah Smith was a relative newcomer to Deerfield and lacked the protection of a male relative in the community, there was no one to pursue a case on her behalf. Perhaps the lack of action in her case is due additionally to the fact that her community was engrossed in defending itself against French and Native American attack. But according to the letter of the law, we might have expected Evans to be charged with attempted rape, especially as Smith was a married woman. We can only speculate about the number of similar depositions that were never acted upon and did not become part of the public record. This affidavit survives due to the personal notoriety Smith achieved a few years later when she committed infanticide and became the first woman to be executed in Western Massachusetts.

Sarah Smith had gone to the Justices of the Peace immediately, but to no avail. The experience of Susanna Reade in 1669 has parallels. She, too, had no senior male relative to speak for her, for her father, Captain Thomas Reade of Salem, had died the previous year.[22] She, too, was unable to sustain a charge of attempted rape. Instead she found herself convicted of slander. On February 2, 1669, seventeen-year-old Reade told a Salem magistrate, William Hathorne, that Ephraim Herrick, who had contracted for her labor for a month the previous autumn, had attempted to rape her three times. His first attempt had occurred on her second day of employment while his wife was absent. His second attempt came four days later as they worked in a field together gathering corn. She claimed that there had been a third attempt:

> [A]fter this his wife was gone to Salem and there was none but he and I at home and he came to me and took up my coats and pulled out his member and would have forced me and many other words he used to persuade me to yield to him his desires that is not fit to be spoke.

Her conscience troubled, but understandably reluctant to make these incidents public, Reade had complained privately to a committee from Herrick's church. They advised her to go to the magistrates. She delayed until the beginning of February. The severity of the winter weather had prevented her, she said, from going to Hathorne earlier. More likely she was constrained by embarrassment and reluctance to make the matter public.

Hathorne must have gone to Herrick immediately to learn his side of the story, for the following day Herrick filed a slander suit against Reade. Six days after Reade's official complaint, John Hill, the Beverley constable arrived at her door with a summons to answer Ephraim Herrick's suit for slander and required her to post a £20 bond. The following week Hathorne filed charges of uncleanness against both Reade and Herrick.

Both parties appeared in court. Reade presented evidence that Herrick's behavior was part of a pattern. Two more women testified that Herrick had acted improperly with them. One of them, Elizabeth Whiteheare, claimed that when she was riding horseback with Herrick to his house to help his wife with her laundry, Herrick had pulled up her skirts and speculated about her thighs and who had been between them. In response Herrick produced brothers, sisters, and sisters-in-law who described a labor dispute, with Reade determined on revenge because Herrick would not give her food and tobacco.[23]

Herrick won his lawsuit. Since he had "proved" that Reade was lying and the incidents she described had never occurred, the charges of uncleanness against both of them were dropped. There was a considerable status differential between the married Herrick whose extended family lived locally and his orphaned servant. The most likely explanation for Reade's failure to get the court to believe her story was that she had not quit her job and charged Herrick immediately after the first incident. Herrick's behavior, while regrettable, was within the parameters of expected male behavior. Reade, however, needed her job, she was only seventeen, and she didn't have a male advocate to accompany her to a magistrate and speak for her. She may have hoped that the members of Herrick's church would act for her.

Fourteen men were prosecuted for rape and three men were prosecuted for attempted rape between 1636 and 1692 in the Massachusetts Bay Court of Assistants. The prosecutions occurred in two clusters. The first cluster occurred between 1636 and 1642 when three men were tried for rape and two more for attempted rape. The second cluster occurred after a 25-year interval which saw no recorded prosecutions for rape or attempted rape in the Court of Assistants. Twelve of the 17 cases tried by the Court of Assistants between 1636 and 1692, or 70 percent, occurred in a 15-year period between

1667 and 1683. During the 25-year hiatus between the two clusters of Court of Assistants rape and attempted rape prosecutions only eight men were tried for attempted rape in the Essex County Quarterly Court.

In the first cluster of rape prosecutions, between 1636 and 1642, all the assailants and four of their victims were unmarried young persons. Four of the men were indentured servants; the age of the fifth (17) suggests he was too. Four of the women they assaulted were female servants. The fifth, Mary Greenfield was a seven-year-old girl who lived with her family. The punishments levied by the court during this period were consistent. Two attempted rapes in 1636 and 1639 were punished by a whipping and a short prison term. In the 1639 case the attempted rapist was ordered to compensate his female victim. In 1641, Mary Greenfield's rapist, Jonathan Thing, was whipped and ordered to pay her father £20 within three years.

In 1642, the Court of Assistants tried two more indentured servants, Robert Wyar and John Garland, for rape. The verdict clearly illustrates the reluctance of Puritan judges and juries to punish young men who engaged in coitus with single women with the death penalty and their propensity to treat coerced sexual intercourse as consentual coitus. There had been enough evidence to initiate a prosecution; the will to convict was lacking.

> Robert Wyar and John Garland being indicted for ravishing two young girls, the fact confessed by the girls & the girls upon search both found to be deflowered & filthy dalliance confessed by the boys; the Jury found them not guilty with reference to the capital law. The Court judged the boys to be openly whipped at Boston, the next market day and again to be whipped at Cambridge on the Lecture day & each of them to pay £5 a piece to their master in service. It was also judged that the two girls Sarah Wythes & Ursula Odle, being both guilty of that wickedness, shall be severely whipped at Cambridge in the presence of the Secretary.[24]

This initial cluster of rapes and attempted rapes, while it presents only five cases, provides the first opportunity to assess the attitudes of the elected representatives to the Court of Assistants to sexual violence. All five of the men were whipped, but so were two of the women who reported rapes. Compensatory payments were made on four of the five occasions, but in only one case was the payment made to the victim. None of the rapists or attempted rapists suffered a penalty more severe than that paid by a man who fathered an illegitimate child during consensual coitus.

There had always been a dissonance between Puritan religious ideology that ascribed chastity as the defining female characteristic and popular cultural beliefs about women. The early modern ideology of women as the instigators of sexual activity was more powerful. Under both belief systems, however, women bore the responsibility to protect themselves from aggressive male sexual behavior. As Massachusetts was increasingly drawn into the Atlantic community, early modern English economic and social values competed with the Puritan ideal. The adoption of the Halfway Covenant in 1662 to make church membership more inclusive was symptomatic of a general decline in religious fervor. Fornication prosecutions increased in number, due not to any intensification of already strenuous efforts to control sexuality in the face of a changing moral climate, but to the fact that greater numbers of couples were engaging in extramarital sexual activity despite the social controls long in place in the Puritan community. Prosecutions for rape at the superior court level also resumed.

The second cluster of rape and attempted rape cases occurred after a 25-year interval with no recorded prosecutions at the superior court level, which had jurisdiction. Twelve of the 17 cases tried by the Massachusetts Court of Assistants between 1636 and 1692, or seventy per cent, occurred in the 15-year period between 1667 and 1683. The five men who were hanged for rape were executed during this 15-year period. In one quarter of the cases, the female victim was also declared culpable, and these cases were referred back to the Quarterly Courts and tried as fornication cases. There were no further rape or attempted rape prosecutions prior to 1692 by which time the population of New England had reached 90,000.[25]

Four of the defendants in this second cluster were non-white. Three of them, Tom Indian, Twenty Rod, and Samuel Indian were tried in the four-year period prior to King Philip's War. All were convicted. Twenty Rod brutally raped a nine- year-old native American child while drunk. He was ordered deported to the Caribbean and sold. Tom Indian raped a married Native American woman and was hanged. Samuel Indian was found guilty of the attempted rape of a 52-year-old Puritan woman, Mary Bacon. His fate is unrecorded. The fourth was an African American, Basto Negro, who raped his master's three-year-old daughter in 1676. His master, Robert Cox, petitioned the court to have Basto, who had been sentenced to hang, released to him.[26] In each of these cases, the victim was either a child or a married woman so the cases clearly came under the jurisdiction of the Court of Assistants where they were tried.

No young man, whether white, African American, or Native American, was ever executed for raping an unmarried woman, although jail terms, fines, and, in Peter Croy's case, the wearing of a symbolic noose, were imposed as punishments. The law allowed judges discretion in sentencing unless the victim was either married or under the age of ten and the judges exercised this option. The judges, whatever the depositions stated, assumed that the victim had consented, had provoked her rape through seductive behavior or that coitus had resulted from consensual petting that got out of control. Such rationalizations were not possible in the case of the last man to be convicted of rape prior to 1692, William Cheney, a middle-aged, married and prosperous Dorchester planter. He was convicted and executed for the rape of his unmarried maidservant in 1681.

The sample is too small to draw definitive conclusions about the prevalence of sexual violence in seventeenth-century Massachusetts but some inferences can be drawn. First, the very fact that the sample is so small indicates that the likelihood a woman who was raped would report it to the authorities was low. We can infer that the consequences of a public admission of loss of virginity were severe. Only three of the ten girls or young women who were unmarried at the time of their rape can be definitively proved to have married.[27] One of them, Ursula Odle was fourteen when she was raped in 1642. Grace Roberts had been eight at the time of her assault, so in both these instances, considerable time elapsed between their rapes and their marriages. A third woman, Elizabeth Holbrook, who was nineteen when she was raped, did not marry until she was thirty-two. A loss of chastity, however involuntary, apparently represented an obstacle to future marriage.

Second, there was a risk to accusing a man of rape. Six of the eight single women of marriageable age found that when they made a charge of rape or attempted rape that was prosecuted in the Court of Assistants they were subsequently charged with fornication themselves. For example, Elizabeth Pierce's rapist, Benjamin Simonds, was tried for rape and convicted of attempted rape by the Court of Assistants. Despite this verdict, Simonds was retried three months later for "wanton dallying with Elizabeth Pierce tending to uncleanness" by the Middlesex Quarterly Court. The timing of the trials suggests that after the attempted rape conviction in the Court of Assistants, it was discovered that Pierce was pregnant. As a result of this, Pierce and Simonds were convicted of fornication and each fined two pounds.

Efforts were also made to intimidate witnesses. A twenty-seven-year-old married woman, Mary Ash, was harassed by her rapist and his brother. In an attempt to frighten her and confuse her about which brother had been the actual rapist, Samuel Guild and his brother, John, appeared repeatedly before her at her house wearing identical clothes. This behavior did not help Samuel. He was hanged because the woman he had raped was married. There were no issues of consent to muddy the waters: Guild was guilty of adultery, also a capital offense.

Third, the justices followed the letter of the rape law in all but two instances. A married tinker, Thomas Waters, was charged with raping nineteen-year-old Bethiah Johnson. Although Waters was acquitted, he was ordered to leave Massachusetts within 10 days.[28] He had been prosecuted previously for lying, cheating, theft, and swearing."[29] The authorities may have welcomed an excuse to expel him. William Cheney, as mentioned above, was hanged, but he had compounded the rape with an escape attempt and his age and status precluded returning him to the community unpunished. All of the defendants that were executed, with the exception of Cheney, had raped either a child or a married woman. Cheney and Waters were also the only rape defendants who were married.

The 1673 trial of Peter Croy, a twenty-year-old French servant, demonstrates the difficulty of securing a conviction given the rules of evidence and the reluctance of the Court of Assistants to punish youthful male defendants to the full extent of the law despite a preponderance of evidence and the youth of the victim. She was a thirteen-year-old servant, Sarah Lambert, who, with her fifteen-year-old sister, had gone at nightfall to collect cattle owned by Mistress Pod, their employer, from Ipswich's day pasture. Croy was searching for his master's cattle in the same darkening field. Her assailant, Peter Croy, was searching for his master's cows in the same darkening field.

Lambert provided a graphic description of sexual violence. She testified:

> Peter Croy came to her and took her by the middle and threw her on the ground and took up her coats and lay upon her belly. She cried out to her sister that was not far off and he stopped her breath with his hand on her throat. He lay upon her a long time and she felt his member in her body which did hurt her and afterward she felt wet upon her shift and that her privy parts did burn.[30]

Her sister, Mary, added that she had seen "his naked privities and the agitation and thrashing of his body upon my sister."[31] An additional witness, John Divan, Croy's thirteen-year-old companion, reported that he had heard Sarah cry out, "you french cur, let me alone," that he had accused Croy of "playing the rogue with Pods girl," and that Croy had enjoined his silence.[32] The testimony of Mary Lambert and John Divan met an important Puritan evidentiary requirement. Both could attest that Sarah Lambert had cried out. Only Mary Lambert, however, could provide direct eyewitness testimony because Divan had arrived as Croy straightened his clothes. The testimony of two eyewitnesses or a confession was required to convict in capital cases.

The sequence of events over the next few days can be learned from Peter Croy's testimony. Sarah and Mary Lambert did not tell their employer, Mistress Pod, about the rape until the following morning. This was not the timely disclosure hoped for by the court. Mistress Pod waited a further four days before informing a magistrate. Whether she was inhibited by the harm that public awareness might cause Lambert's sexual reputation, or by fear that the news might place her household in a negative light is unknowable. Croy claimed that Mistress Pod had gone to the magistrate: "for fear that she should prove with child and then she should be undone forever." Whether Croy meant that Lambert would suffer social and economic repercussions, or, as I think, Mistress Pod feared for her own reputation as the head of a household that lacked sexual discipline is unclear. What is quite clear is that all involved understood that an out-of-wedlock pregnancy had long-term ramifications.

Two panels were assembled eleven days after the supposed rape. Lambert's body was examined by a committee of women who determined that she had been penetrated by "this or some other man." Croy and the other witnesses were questioned by a grand jury. Croy provided a statement which allows a unique insight into his actions. He pled not guilty and requested a jury trial. He admitted that his intent was to have sexual intercourse with Sarah Lambert:

> I confess I would have been naught with wench whether she would or no but was hindered from carnal knowledge of her body by reasons John did come and called to me which made me rise up before I could commit the act. Nor could it be conceived that I could easily in that time commit the act
>
> 1. Because of my clothes were all up and I was not naked with her nor did I fully enter her body.
>
> 2. Her sister might easily have hindered.
>
> 3. There were no signs of her being deflowered that were seen or observed.
>
> 4. If I had committed the act I humbly conceive I could not legally be charged with it by Sarah or her Dame Pod
>
> 1. Because Sarah never spake of it either to John Divan when he came to us or any else.
>
> 2. Nor did she speak of it to her Dame until next morning & her Dame did not complain to any officer until 4 days after and that was only for fear she should prove with child & then she should be undone for ever as she said.[33]

This statement was sufficient to bind Peter Croy over to the Massachusetts Court of Assistants on a charge of rape.

Croy recanted this statement at his trial. The requirements for conviction in a capital crime were strict and they had not been met. Lambert was no longer a virgin, but there was only one direct eyewitness, reporting had been delayed, and Croy refused to confess. No official verdict survives but since Croy was charged with not wearing his noose around his neck at the Essex County Quarterly Court in Ipswich in 1674, it appears he was convicted of rape, but given only symbolic capital punishment. Wearing a noose served the dual function of shame punishment for Croy and warning for the community that there was a convicted rapist in their midst.

Seven years later, on a cold, moonlit January evening in 1680, the same young woman, now nineteen, was accosted by John Hunkins as she crossed Mr. Nathaniel Roger's pasture. He "overcame her by persuasion that he would do her no hurt and there lay with her."[34] It is impossible to measure the degree of coercion implied in this statement. The "no hurt" may have referred to a shared assumption that intercourse without affection or a mutual orgasm would be necessarily sterile.[35] The phrase may have represented a physical threat or a promise to withdraw before ejaculation. Despite Hunkin's assurances, Lambert became pregnant. She was convicted of fornication and given the option of paying a fine or being whipped. John Hunkins denied being in Mr. Roger's pasture that night, let alone having sex with Sarah Lambert. Since he was already supporting one illegitimate child, the judges did not find him credible and bound him to pay 2s. 6d. per week in corn to Goodwife Pod, still Lambert's employer, who was given charge of Sarah Lambert's child.

Sarah Lambert aptly illustrates the dilemma faced by victims of sexual violence in seventeenth-century Massachusetts. As a girl of thirteen, she was raped undisputedly but was unable to secure a meaningful conviction against her attacker who was returned to her community. She was victimized again in 1680 by John Hunkins, a sexual predator who had already impregnated another young woman, Hannah Hayward, three years earlier. Because she conceived on this occasion, she was charged and convicted of fornication.

A rape victim was perceived not merely as a woman who had been deprived of her virginity by force, but as a woman who had had her sexual appetite aroused in an untimely manner and who could not be trusted to act in a chaste fashion in the future. Extrapolating from modern psychological research it seems likely that Sarah Lambert, in common with up to 80 percent of rape victims today, suffered from depression and low self-esteem.[36] The justices of the Essex County Quarterly Court were not surprised by

Lambert's later sexual behavior. They had no way of comprehending its link to psychological trauma; their understanding was linked to their heartfelt belief that women were innately carnal, a belief shared by John Hunkins.

A number of depositions filed by women in illegitimate fornication cases in the Essex County Quarterly Court indicate that violence played a role in the sexual activity.[37] Sixty-three per cent of the women who describe the circumstances under which they conceived were between the ages of 15 and 20 and worked away from home. Their situation made them vulnerable. In an economic system where production occurred in a patriarchal household containing a husband and wife, sons, daughters, apprentices and servants, both male and female, and every person worked, ate, worshiped and slept (often in the same room) as part of a family unit, the potential for physical and sexual abuse existed.

When an unmarried woman conceived, no matter how vile the physical assault had been, how virtuous the young woman had been perceived to be in the past, or how many witnesses there were to attest to the fact that she had been forced, there was no possibility of a rape prosecution. As Dalton had stated, and popular opinion believed, conception, to the Puritans, "proved" that a victim had consented to her rape.

Anne Chase, the twenty-two-year-old daughter of a well-established carpenter, was working in at least her third household.[38] At the time she became pregnant, she was a servant in the household of her uncle, Henry Wheeler, and his wife, Abigail. They had seven children ranging in age from ten years old to eight months old, including two-year-old twins.[39] Chase's labor would have been essential to the maintenance of a household that included so many young children. In 1669, Mrs. Wheeler's brother, John Allen, came to stay. During Allen's stay, Chase moved from Wheeler's house. It is impossible to know if she left the household each night because there was no room for her to sleep in, or if Abigail Wheeler's twenty-one-year-old brother was harassing her. On a March evening, she left John Allen sitting in the Wheeler household to walk from the Wheelers' to the Hubbard household:

> She knew nothing of his coming from hence until he met her by the way as she was going to her lodging and suddenly laid hands on her; and she told him he would wrong her: his answer was he would right her again: she said that she would cry out, he told her that he would stop her mouth, and he forced her against the Rails, and she being in a sore fright was not able to cry out.

Anne Chase was prosecuted for fornication in May 1670, and sentenced to be whipped or to pay a fine. She had borne an illegitimate child, whom she named John Allen for his father, in late December. The midwife, Elignor Baily, testified:

> (t)his she constantly affirmed, being in labor and extremity about six days, and in appearance at the point of death I often told her that her pains continued the longer because she had not spoken the truth; her constant answer was, that if she died for it she had spoken the truth and nothing else.[40]

Chase was not a stranger to Baily. She had worked for Elignor Baily previously for two years. Baily testified that: "she never saw any light or unseemly carriage all that time."[41] Still, Baily did not believe Chase's version of the circumstances under which she had conceived. Nor did the court. Allen was not charged with fornication, nor was he required to pay child support.[42] This indicates how thoroughly the seventeenth-century residents of Massachusetts had inculcated the notion that conception was impossible unless the victim had consented to, and received pleasure from, that particular act of intercourse. Chase had also worked for John and Mary Brown who attested that:

> Anne Chase lived with us for a year and for our parts we never saw any light carriages by her but she kept the house and did not go out at nights but carried herself very honestly as far as we could perceive: nor never perceived any wanton carriages by her, but carried herself very severely and honestly as far as we saw.[43]

Chase's story is most illustrative because it not only describes a rape in explicit terms, but it notes the midwife's skepticism of Chase's account. The dissonance between the conditions under which many young women charged with fornication had conceived and their expectations of what was necessary for conception must have been considerable. The legal assumption that conception implied consent deprived Chase and other young women of the traditional support of the women's community during labor. The midwife arrived as inquisitor, not comforter.

The number of rape and attempted rape prosecutions in the Massachusetts Bay Colony Court of Assistants does not reflect the true incidence of sexual violence in seventeenth-century Massachusetts. There was no incentive for single women to report incidents of sexual violence. The cultural expectation of female chastity enjoined silence. Moreover, the practical considerations were considerable. The loss of sexual reputation and concomitant marriageability and the knowledge that an accusation of rape might result in a mutual fornication prosecution, precluded making a rape public. Sarah Lambert belatedly reported her rape to the authorities. Would she have done so without the prompting of Mistress Pod? It is not surprising that seven of the seventeen prosecuted cases involved children or married women.

While rapes and attempted rapes were not prosecuted with vigor, there is no indication that sexual violence against women was pervasive. This was a society that monitored young people closely and socialized them to view sexual intercourse as the province of married persons. The low numbers of persons convicted of fornication indicates that extramarital sexual activity was not widespread, and it can be inferred that levels of coerced sexual intercourse were correspondingly low. Nor do the circumstances surrounding the reported rapes fit common theoretical assumptions about rape. These rapes were not the enforcement arm of patriarchy under threat. The patriarchal order was firmly entrenched and unquestioned. Neither were they an expression of generalized hatred of women as the depositions do not record extensive physical injuries beyond the genital area. Certainly Puritan men indicated from the bench and the jury box that they believed rape to be a sexual offense.

Grand juries were reluctant to characterize acts of coerced sexual intercourse as capital crimes. They proved this every time they prosecuted rapes or attempted rapes at the quarterly court level where corporal punishment or a fine was the only punitive remedy. The juries of the Court of Assistants were equally reluctant to draw fine distinctions between coerced and consensual intercourse when both the defendant and the victim were unmarried and the maximum penalty was capital punishment. Four of the 14 rape cases were reduced to fornication and the women were prosecuted as well. Four more cases involved children, which would be considered aberrant sexual activity in any century, and two more involved married women. Of the four remaining cases, three defendants were whipped, fined, or both. The one remaining defendant, William Cheney, gained the unenviable fate of being the only man in seventeenth-century Massachusetts to be hanged for the rape of an unmarried woman. He had compounded his original crime by stabbing the constable who came to arrest him and attempting to escape on the constable's horse.

The penalties assigned to two sets of defendants at the September 1681 Essex County Quarterly Court session meeting in Ipswich illustrates the relative value the justices placed on male sexual violence and consensual sexual intercourse between unmarried persons. Twenty-one-year-old William Nelson was tried for the attempted rape of Mehitabel Avis, a child younger than ten. There was a witness to the attack, the testimony of

Mehitabel Avis, and an admission of guilt from Nelson. Additionally, one of Nelson's friends told the court that Nelson had "buggered a cow." One might have expected a grand jury to send this case on to the Court of Assistants for adjudication rather than trying it locally.[44] Nelson, however, was sentenced to be severely whipped. The defendants in the previous case, John Ring and Martha Lamson, were also sentenced to be severely whipped. Their crime was fornication.[45]

Chapter Nine

Conclusion

Puritans had moral, structural and economic reasons for prohibiting extramarital sexual intercourse. First, sex between single women and single or married men was explicitly prohibited in the Bible, which was foundational to Puritan jurisprudence. Intercourse unsanctioned by marriage was a sin and as such, Puritans believed, it exposed not just the persons involved, but the entire Puritan Commonwealth to the wrath of God. Massachusetts was a corporate society in which the pursuit of individual interests, in this instance the satisfaction of sexual desire, had to be subordinated to the common good; it was essential that personal behavior be in conformance with community norms. Thus, there was a strong moral imperative against extramarital sexual activity in general and extramarital sexual intercourse in particular.

There were, however, practical reasons as well for restricting sexual intercourse to married persons. The household served not only as the basic structure of society but also as the primary unit of economic production. Puritans were required by law to live in patriarchally-structured households. Married men who immigrated to Massachusetts without their families were expected to bring them over as quickly as possible. If they did not do this, they could be ordered to return to England themselves rather than be allowed to remain in Massachusetts with an ambiguous marital status. Single men were required to live in households as well. There was no way for a single woman (even if she had the financial resources) and her illegitimate child to be incorporated as an independent family unit into a social structure that required single persons to live under the guidance of a parent, husband, or employer.[1]

The economic imperative for prohibiting extramarital sexual intercourse was considerable, as evidenced by the 1668 amendment that privileged the collection of child support over the punishment of male fornicators. Bastards represented a potential drain on town resources.

Moreover, there were economic costs to employers in the form of lost or more limited production from pregnant female servants. In the initial two decades of settlement, when the demand for labor was high and the supply low, this loss represented an economic cost not only to the individual employer, but to the developing society as a whole.

A different type of economic cost was borne by couples, who married within 32 weeks of the birth of their child, their parents, and siblings. An untimely pregnancy could be used to force the premature disbursement of family resources at the expense of more continent brothers and sisters. It limited the length of time women had in which to amass the capital required to contribute their portion to the establishment of a separate household. And, while married women made undeniably important economic contributions to the economic well-being of their marital households, wages saved by female servants prior to their marriages served as important stimulants to the nascent colonial economy.

The basic structural and economic imperatives for restricting extramarital sexual intercourse did not deviate significantly from other English jurisdictions, but the moral impetus behind Massachusetts sex prosecutions that seemed to be a primary consideration prior to the 1660s was distinctive. The stakes were high for the first generation of Massachusetts settlers. Extramarital sexuality was a sin of such import that it threatened the existence of the Colony. Puritans believed they had signed a Covenant with God in which He had promised them prosperity and in return Massachusetts Bay Colony had promised to live as perfectly as possible. Moreover, the Colony had positioned itself as a moral exemplar to Europe. It believed itself to be the cynosure of European eyes, and its destruction, for moral lapses, would damage the Puritan movement irreparably. For reasons as practical, then, as fear of losing the daily labor of a female servant in an Ipswich household or as ideological as apprehension for the future of Puritanism, it was necessary to limit expressions of sexuality to marriage.

The low numbers of persons prosecuted for transgressing Puritan sex laws demonstrate that few Puritans were willing to engage in sexual behaviors their neighbors deemed "unclean." Puritans successfully repressed extramarital sexual intercourse using a combination of criminal prosecutions and cultural conditioning. Ministers and magistrates, working in combination from pulpits and benches, exhorted their parishioners to refrain from sin and administered humiliating public punishments to those who failed.

It was illegal for single women to have sex in seventeenth-century Massachusetts. In fact, for much of the eighteenth-century as well, the potential for criminal prosecution for consensual sexual intercourse remained for women who bore bastards. While prosecutions of couples who married following the conception of their first child were discontinued early in the eighteenth century, the selective prosecution of women who bore bastards continued until after the American Revolution. A pregnancy provided irrefutable evidence that a woman had engaged in coitus. Men who had engaged in sexual intercourse could not be identified so readily. Unless there was a voluntary confession, or a tacit admission of paternity through marriage with a pregnant woman, men could not be convicted of fornication.

Fornication prosecutions alone would not have deterred single Puritans from sexual intercourse. Cultural constraints and behavioral expectations are powerful determinants of sexual behaviors and Puritans successfully used them to limit most sexual expression to marriage and to influence the conduct of sexuality within marriage. The most important were religious and cultural imperatives that promoted male and female chastity prior to the wedding night. Sexual intercourse was the province of married persons for the primary purpose of procreation. That it also provided pleasure and cemented the marital bond was a positive benefit. Nevertheless, for every positive affirmation of the benefits of marital sexuality to be found in the ministerial and advice literature, there is an admonition lest sexual pleasure divert Puritan couples from their religion.

Love was supposed to develop between husband and wife as an outcome of marriage, not as a precursor to it. Sexual intercourse promoted love, eased the transition to marriage, and served as a mutual comfort to husband and wife, but Puritans were very clear about the right order of events. Couples married, began a mutually-exclusive sexual relationship, and sexual attraction, personal compatibility, and status-equivalence, all qualities deemed necessary to successful marriage formation, evolved into marital love. Puritans drew a clear distinction between marital sexual intercourse which was a "comfort" and a "delight," and extramarital coitus which was "filthiness," "incontinence," "uncleanness," "wickedness," and "wanton dalliance."

There were other factors that militated against extramarital sexual intercourse. The homosocial structure of youth networks, the relatively low marriage age, and the ability of most young persons to marry limited the number of persons who were unable to wait for marriage or who were forced to seek sexual partners outside of marriage. There were practical problems as well. Houses were small, supervision constant, and privacy limited. At the same time, however, women commonly worked as servants, beginning in adolescence and continuing until marriage. Even women whose families possessed sufficient resources to provide dowries lived in other people's households for extended periods during adolescence learning housewifery skills. Parents would not have sent their daughters into service if they had believed that they were placing them in a sexually-charged environment or if they did not believe their daughters had been sufficiently socialized to understand the value of remaining chaste prior to marriage and to resist sexual overtures.

If only prosecutions of couples who married subsequent to conception are considered, Puritans appear to have rejected the sexual double standard and prosecuted men and women equally for sex crimes. This presumption is negated by an analysis of fornication trials involving single women and single or married men. For every three couples who married following an out-of-wedlock conception, two women bore illegitimate children. In these instances women paid a higher price than men for violating (or being forced to violate) laws prohibiting sexual intercourse.

Women were prosecuted more frequently; 104 single women and 35 single or married men were convicted of fornication and punished more severely. In 75 percent of cases, although the class of the male and female defendants was often equivalent, women received more rigorous sentences. Moreover, the act of engaging in sexual intercourse had life-defining implications for a single woman. Fewer than 25 percent of convicted women married subsequently. Women who did not marry were essentially debarred from full participation in the community of women because they were not wives and mothers, the adult life-cycle role of Puritan women. These women were victims of a sexual system that simultaneously restricted sexual intercourse to marriage, used a sexual vocabulary that stressed female passivity, and accepted a sexual double standard.

For men, the overt consequences of being named as the father of an illegitimate child in terms of corporal punishment or the payment of a fine were relatively minor. Fifty-five percent of men named as the fathers of illegitimate children were either married at the time of their trial or married subsequently. The most significant consequence, and one most men sought to avoid by refusing to confess, was the loss of honor. While their honor was temporarily impacted by the community perception that they had violated Puritan sexual mores, however, the ownership of a small farm or the possession of a viable trade combined with the belief that women were responsible for protecting their chastity ensured that men could reestablish themselves following a conviction with less difficulty than their partners.

For every three women convicted of fornication and sentenced to be whipped or fined following the birth of an illegitimate child, only one man was convicted. Three-quarters of the time, he received a lesser sentence than his female partner. This indicates the existence of a sexual double standard in seventeenth-century Massachusetts. It was mitigated, however, by the strict Puritan regimen of punishing fornicators who could be clearly identified such as pregnant women and men who married pregnant women. Also, in societies with a traditional sexual double standard, since the negative consequences of male sexual activity are limited, the illegitimacy and premarital pregnancy rates are high. This was not the case in Massachusetts. While men were privileged by the court, the rate of extramarital sexual intercourse remained low.

Many of the women who were prosecuted for breaking laws against extramarital sexual intercourse were forced to do so by rape. Sadly, contemporary understanding of the mechanics of conception meant that women who conceived as a result of a rape were prosecuted for fornication because it was believed that conception was impossible unless both partners had reached orgasm. The Court of Assistants prosecuted only seventeen rape cases between 1630 and 1692 and while rape was a capital crime if the victim was married or contracted at the time of the assault, no young man was convicted and executed for the rape of a single woman in seventeenth-century Massachusetts. Women were victimized by a legal system that privileged aggressive male sexual behaviors, had a mistaken notion of conception, and was predisposed to treat women who experienced out-of-wedlock pregnancies with contempt.

The Puritan sexual regimen can be divided into two separate and distinct phases. The year, 1668, in which an amendment was passed that placed the collection of child support above the prosecution of men for fornication, makes a convenient demarcation line although the amendment itself was a pragmatic recognition that conditions had already changed. Prior to the 1660s, less than one woman per year bore an illegitimate child. She and her male partner were presented, prosecuted, convicted, and usually whipped. The number of couples charged with premarital fornication was equivalently low and most couples married in the first trimester of the pregnancy. In the decade of the sixties the number of prosecutions for both illegitimate and premarital fornication increased while the incidences of corporal punishment declined. Fines, even for those of lower social status, became the preferred alternative. After 1668, women became the sole focus of punishment and the number of female defendants increased from seven in the first decade of this study (1641–1650) to 124 in the final decade of this study (1676–1685).

The 1660s were a transitional decade. Native-born Puritans lacked the religious fervor that had impelled their parents and grandparents across the Atlantic. The Restoration meant the end of supportive Puritan government in England and the beginning of efforts to incorporate New England into the broader British Atlantic legal and economic systems. The ability of some Essex County Puritans to capitalize on the developing triangle trade between England and the Caribbean created greater wealth differentials in Massachusetts. As a few Puritans became wealthier and as others became less religious, the population lost the homogeneity that had enabled them to call each other "brother" and "sister." The sense of corporate identity that had enabled the repression of individualistic behaviors lessened. While extramarital sexual intercourse remained relatively low throughout the seventeenth-century, the extreme sexual discipline that characterized the period 1630–1660 was impossible to replicate as Puritans became increasingly drawn, economically, culturally, and legally into the broader British Atlantic community.

The stories of women who were prosecuted for fornication in Essex County, Massachusetts, during the seventeenth century, when placed in a broader context, are more than moving, or funny, or sad explications of individual lives. They provide unparalleled opportunities for examining the sexual mentalités of early modern women and men and they explain why, although a modified sexual double standard existed in Puritan Massachusetts, the rates of illegitimate and premarital births remained so low. Women's motives for engaging in coitus were varied, and often pathetic. Susanna Bowden engaged in sexual intercourse "in the upper end of the pasture where her father dwells" in return for an unfulfilled promise of marriage. Mary Sheffield engaged in coitus with her employer, Isaiah Wood, in his barn, during his wife's pregnancy. Sheffield's prior fornication conviction evidenced to Wood she was sexually available at a time when his own wife was not. Anne Chase was raped by her employer's brother, but even people who knew her well refused to believe her account of the circumstances she had conceived because they deemed it impossible. Hannah Souter, however, was boldly unrepentant when discovered in bed with her employer, Mr. Philip Parsons, by the Marblehead selectmen.

A specific social mechanism underlaid the demonstrated low rate of Puritan extramarital sexual intercourse. The Puritans who arrived in New England in the 1630s were the vanguard of Protestant intellectualism. They wanted to create a spiritualized family headed by a new type of Protestant patriarch, whose thoughts and behaviors were controlled not by a priest-confessor who mediated between the individual and God, but through direct communication with God and the development of a conscience. This upgraded image of men required that women be reconfigured from the traditional view that posited them as sexually uncontrollable into suitable helpmeets. As a result, chastity was declared to be the defining characteristic of femininity. Once chastity and womanhood were linked, premarital sexual intercourse was construed as a social evil. To this end, all consensual sexual intercourse between single women and single or married men that resulted in a pregnancy, whether illegitimate or premarital, was prosecuted in the quarterly county courts of Massachusetts as fornication. Coerced sexual activity that resulted in conception was also prosecuted as fornication. The conflation of chastity and womanhood and the concurrent elevation of women's status within marriage both motivated and inspired most women to refrain from premarital sexual intercourse. The stringent sex discipline evidenced by fornication trials and the consequent shunning of women who did not meet the new Puritan standard of femininity intimidated other women from satisfying sexual urges through intercourse.

The most opprobrious epithets women cast at other women related to sexual reputation. To be called a "baud" or a "whore" almost inevitably led to a slander suit with expensive repercussions. The fact that women resorted so immediately and so frequently to the courts if their sexual reputation had been impugned is a sign both of the tenuous hold the new ideology commanded and the potential power of the imagery of the virtuous woman. One of the themes that resounded throughout the seventeenth-century, and, I would argue, resonated until the American Revolution and the articulation of republican motherhood is the tension created by the existence of two competing ideologies about women's natures. On the one hand, there was the old, implicit ideology depicting women as the lustful daughters of Eve. It was so imbedded in the mentalité of seventeenth- and eighteenth-century men and women that it did not need to be openly articulated. On the other hand, there was the new ideology that Puritans sought to promote. The notion of virtuous wives promoted not only the status of married women but also the institution of marriage, and made possible the elevation of men to patriarchs. Its newness, however, required constant, explicit reinforcement.

Marriage was the only possible option for adult women in Massachusetts since household service was structured for women between adolescence and marriage age. The Puritan ideological conception of marriage that accorded wives increased status within their marriages and within the Puritan community was worth protecting. It was necessary to ensure that marriage entry was limited to women whose sexual behaviors reinforced the association between femininity and chastity. In the Chesapeake and the Caribbean, the limited number of women and the traditional view of women as incapable of sexual control created an ideological climate in which it was possible to bear an illegitimate child and marry subsequently or to marry when pregnant without the concomitant fornication trial. In Massachusetts, a good sexual reputation increased marriage opportunity; a poor sexual reputation severely limited it.

Both married and single women had a vested interest in policing the sexual behaviors of other women who evidenced, through their sexual behaviors, that they were not representative of the new, improved, sexually continent version of Puritan womanhood.

With Puritan women socialized to see chastity as the essence of femininity, Puritan men found the number of women prepared to engage in consensual premarital sexual intercourse was limited. Moreover, when it came to marriage, men wanted a woman with a reputation for chastity because it enhanced their status. But these men were required to demonstrate virtue as well, so sexual intercourse with a willing third partner was not an option for them. The public exposure inherent in a paternity suit would limit their access to women who might have enhanced their status through their reputation for virtue or their possession of a large dowry. Puritan men were constrained from premarital sexual activity for three reasons: 1) willing female partners were limited, 2) men did not want to marry a woman who was pregnant, 3) eligible women did not want to marry fornicators.

Puritan women would not have articulated the notion that they were withholding sex as part of a broader strategy to elevate the image of wives, which, in turn, enhanced the status of their husbands and the patriarchal family. Women were motivated to remain chaste not only because a reputation for virtue enhanced their marriageability but also because they genuinely feared that they would go to Hell if they did not. Women were predisposed to believe that they had a greater propensity to sin than men despite what the new ideology told them. Even in the final decade of the seventeenth-century, when women composed the majority of church members in Massachusetts, the Salem witchcraft trials exposed that large numbers of the population still assumed women capable of carnal intercourse with the Devil.

The 104 women who bore illegitimate children in Essex County between 1640 and 1685 were punished with greater comprehensiveness and more severity than their male partners because they confirmed traditional fears about women while failing to meet the new standard of Puritan womanhood. Puritan women and men expected that young women who had been educated to Puritan precepts and socialized to Puritan values would navigate the shoals of service in other households and the reefs of sexual desire during courtship to the safe harbor of marriage. Most women conformed to the new moral code and managed the transition to adulthood and marriage with success. Puritans scorned the daughters of Eve, those women, few in number, who failed and paid for their human weaknesses through exclusion from the community of women and the loss of their hoped-for role as goodwife and mother.

Notes

NOTES TO PREFACE

1. From the records of the Suffolk County Quarterly Court, 1662, property of the Supreme Judicial Court, Division of Archives and Records Preservation. The spelling in the court documents has been modernized to make them more accessible.
2. Suffolk County Quarterly Court, 1662, 874.
3. Socio-economic data, occupational status, age data, marriage data, and the date of birth of first child were gathered for an additional 62 women and 29 men who were presented for fornication between 1686 and 1692. Their trial data is not included in quantitative portion of this study because the Essex County docket books for 1686 to 1692 no longer exist.
4. Bradford added, "for the churches look narrowly to their members, and the magistrates over all, more strictly than in other places." Samuel Eliot Morrison, *Of Plymouth Plantation, 1620–1647 by William Bradford, Sometime Governor Thereof,* (New York: Alfred A. Knopf, 1952), 317. Also, John Winthrop, the first governor of Massachusetts Bay Colony, wrote in his diary in 1640, "as people increased, so sin abounded, and especially the sin of uncleanness, and still the providence of God found them out." Dunn, James Savage, and Laetitia Yeandle, eds., *The Journal of John Winthrop, 1630–1649,* (Cambridge: Harvard University Press, 1996), 370.
5. *The Old Families of Salisbury and Amesbury* was checked for references to children born to unmarried women and to marriages in which the birth of the first child occurred before 32 weeks. Sixteen couples between 1640 and 1692 fit this category. Fifteen were prosecuted; the sixteenth couple had a seventh month child for whom there may have been convincing evidence of prematurity. Eight local women appeared in the same genealogy as bastard-bearers. All were prosecuted. A second local history *A Sketch of the History of Newbury, Newburyport, and West Newbury* revealed the same pattern. There were no single mothers, but 11 couples had children within 32 weeks of their marriage. Ten of these couples were prosecuted.
6. Edmund S. Morgan, "The Puritans and Sex," *The New England Quarterly,* December, 1942, 596. David H. Flaherty, "Law and the Enforcement of Morals in Early America," in Donald Flemming and Bernand Baylin, eds. *Perspectives in Early American History,* V, (Cambridge: Harvard University

Press, 1971), 225. Richard Godbeer, *Sexual Revolution in Early America,* (Baltimore: Johns Hopkins University Press, 2002), 102.

7. Chris Wilson, "The Proximate Determinants of Marital Fertility in England 1600–1799," in Lloyd Bonfield, Richard M. Smith, and Keith Wrightson, eds., *The World We Have Gained: Histories of Population and Social Structure,* (Oxford: Basil Blackwell, 1986), 206.
8. While an egg has a life span of only 15 to 24 hours, sperm remain alive for five days in the cervix.
9. Roger Thompson, *Sex in Middlesex: Popular Mores in a Massachusetts County, 1649–1699,* (Amherst: University of Massachusetts Press, 1986), 19.
10. Angus McLaren, *Reproductive Rituals: The Perception of Fertility in England from the Sixteenth Century to the Nineteenth Century,* (London: Methuen, 1984), 21.
11. John R. Gillis, *For Better, For Worse: British Marriages, 1600 to the Present,* (New York: Oxford University Press, 1985) V.
12. *Records and Files of the Quarterly Courts of Essex County, Massachusetts,* Volume V, (Salem: The Essex Institute, 1916), 290.

NOTES TO CHAPTER ONE

1. From the records of the Essex County Quarterly Court, 1670, property of the Supreme Judicial Court, Division of Archives and Records Preservation, on deposit at the Phillips Library at the Peabody Essex Museum, Salem, Massachusetts, 31–18–1, hereafter referred to as *Essex County.*
2. Virginia DeJohn Anderson, *New England's Generation: The Great Migration and the Formation of Society and Culture in the Seventeenth Century,* (Cambridge: Cambridge University Press, 1991), 44.
3. David Godbeer, *Sexual Revolution in Early America,* 11.
4. Amanda Porterfield, *Female Piety in Puritan New England: The Emergence of Religious Humanism,* (New York: Oxford University Press, 1992), 36.
5. Charles E. Hambrick-Stowe, ed., *Early New England Meditative Poetry,* (New York: Paulist Press, 1988), 251.
6. Samuel Willard, quoted in Edmund Morgan, *The Puritans and Sex, 592.*
7. Ibid.
8. Ibid.
9. Kathleen Verduin, "Our Cursed Natures," Sexuality and the Puritan Conscience, *The New England Quarterly,* Volume LVI, Number 2, (June 1983), 223.
10. Richard S. Dunn and Laetitia Yeandle, eds., *The Journal of John Winthrop, 1630–1649,* abridged edition, (Cambridge: The Belknap Press of Harvard University Press, 1966), 142.
11. Cotton Mather, *Warnings from the Dead. Or Solemn Admonitions unto all People, but especially unto Young Persons to Beware of such Evils as would bring them to the Dead,* (Boston, 1693), 42.
12. Charles Hambrick-Stowe, *Early New England Meditative Poetry,* 46.
13. Ibid., 135.

14. The closeness of the genitalia to organs of elimination was often cited as proof of the carnality of sex. Margaret Hunt, personal communication.
15. Michael Zuckerman, "Pilgrims in the Wilderness: Community, Modernity, and the Maypole at Merry Mount," *The New England Quarterly,* 50 (1977), 265, warns that the fact that marital sexual activity was acceptable does not warrant the conclusion that Puritans "countenance(d) carnal pleasure."
16. *Essex County,* 1682, 38–15–1.
17. I have been unable to trace a later marriage for Catherine Ellinwood in Essex County. Her maiden name, as given in the court records, is Duarce, and I have checked all the permutations of that name that I could think of.
18. Puritans believed that persons who had the best interests of the community at heart would not cross established sexual boundaries.
19. *Essex County,* 1682, 38–15–3.
20. Ibid., 1682, 38–16–3.
21. Thomas A. Foster, "Deficient Husbands: Manhood, Sexual Incapacity, and Male Marital Sexuality in Seventeenth-Century New England," *William and Mary Quarterly,* 3d Series. Volume LVI, Number 4, October 1999, 724.
22. Edmund Leites, *The Puritan Conscience and Modern Sexuality,* (New Haven: Yale University Press, 1986), 3.
23. Laura Gowing, "Language, Power, and the Law: Women's Slander Litigation in Early Modern London," in Jenny Kermode and Garthine Walker, eds., *Women, Crime, and the Courts in Early Modern England,* (Chapel Hill: The University of North Carolina Press, 1994), 27.
24. Fortunately for the 19 married men (20%) who were identified during childbirth as the fathers of illegitimate children in Essex County between 1640 and 1685, the Massachusetts Bay legal code defined adultery as sexual intercourse with a married woman. Property rights, not moral considerations, were paramount. As long as married men restricted themselves to extramarital sexual intercourse with single women they faced a probable fornication conviction and neighborhood opprobrium, not the capital punishment that could legally be imposed following intercourse with other men's wives.
25. George Francis Dow, ed., *Records and Files of the Quarterly Court of Essex County, Massachusetts,* Volume II, (Salem: The Essex Institute, 1912), 372 hereafter referred to as *Records and Files.*
26. Laura Gowing, *Domestic Dangers: Women, Words and Sex in Early Modern London,* (Oxford: Clarendon Press, 1996), 2.
27. Quoted by Lonna M. Malmsheimer, "Daughters of Zion: New England Roots of American Feminism," *The New England Quarterly,* 484.
28. Elizabeth Reis, *Damned Women: Sinners and Witches in Puritan New England,* (Ithaca: Cornell University Press, 1997), 1.
29. Amanda Porterfield, *Female Piety in Puritan New England,* (Oxford: Oxford University Press, 1992), 9.
30. My quantitative data indicate that between 1686 and 1692, illegitimate fornication prosecutions (46) exceeded premarital fornication prosecutions (30) for the first time. In the previous six-year interval, 1679–1685, premarital fornication convictions (54) had exceeded illegitimate fornication prosecutions (42) as they did in all previous six-year intervals. One-third of all illegitimate

fornication convictions between 1640 and 1692 occurred in the final six years of the study. Only 16 percent of all of the premarital convictions came in the same time period. This would appear to illustrate an increased male unwillingness to marry their pregnant partners, perhaps because they no longer feared damnation (or because greater economic disparities had created a larger number of exploitative sexual relationships). Much as I would like to use these figures in support of Porterfield's argument, they are not reliable. I have not included cases after 1685 in my formal quantitative analysis because the court records are not complete. While I can count grand jury presentments and the married couples who appear on them, I can't be sure, since these cases were so routine that they could not be dealt with by a Justice of the Peace in private session.

31. Margaret R. Sommerville, *Sex and Subjection: Attitudes to Women in Early Modern Society,* (London: Arnold, 1995), 25.
32. Ibid., 27.
33. Lonna M. Malmsheimer, "Daughters of Zion: New England Roots of American Feminism," *New England Quarterly,* LXIV (1997), 485–504.
34. Richard S. Dunn & Laetitia Yeandle, *The Journal of John Winthrop 1630–1649,* abridged edition,(Cambridge: Harvard University Press, 1996), 10.
35. Perry Miller, *The New England Mind: The Seventeenth Century,* (Cambridge: Harvard University Press, 1939),477–8.
36. Kai T. Erikson, *Wayward Puritans: A Study in the Sociology of Deviance,* (New York: John Wiley & Sons, Inc., 1966), 40.
37. Flaherty, "Law and the Enforcement of Morals in Early America," 208–9.
38. Martin Ingram, *Church Courts, Sex and Marriage in England, 1570–1640,* (New York: Cambridge University Press, 1987), 152.
39. Ibid., 261–267.
40. Lois G. Carr and Lorena S. Walsh, "The Planter's Wife: The Experience of Women in Seventeenth-Century Maryland," in Stanley N. Katz and John M. Murrin, eds., *Colonial America: Essays in Political and Social Development,* (New York: Alfred A. Knopf, Inc., 1983), 97.
41. Mary Beth Norton, *Founding Mothers and Fathers: Gendered Power and the Forming of American Society,* (New York: Alfred A. Knopf, 1996), 336.
42. Norton, 337.
43. Carr and Walsh, "The Planter's Wife," 73.
44. Norton, 346.
45. Carr and Walsh, 101.
46. Carr and Walsh, 102. This was nearly twice the premarital pregnancy rate found in English parishes at that time.

NOTES TO CHAPTER TWO

1. *Essex County,* 1653, 2–154–3.
2. *Records and Files,* Volume I, 380.

3. Lawrence Stone, *The Family, Sex and Marriage in England, 1500–1800,* documented an illegitimacy rate in seventeenth-century New England of 0.5 percent or one in two hundred births.
4. There is a bias in this sample of cases. Ages were determined, in most instances, from births registered in the vital statistics. Secondary sources of age data were court records which sometimes recorded the age of a deponent and immigration records. While the age of an indentured servant might be gained from these sources, the age sample is skewed toward women born in Essex County of established parents.
5. Thirty women were identified as being twenty years of age or less. The age of their male partner is known in 11 cases. Three of their partners were older by 10 years or more. An additional three of the men were between five and nine years older. In only one instance where both ages are known was the woman older. She was a twenty-year-old servant who engaged in sexual intercourse with the eighteen-year-old son of her employer.
6. Data are available on the length of time that elapsed between trial and marriage for the 32 women who were not married at the time of their trial and did not marry their partners. Eighteen percent married within a year, 12 percent married in the second year, 21 percent married in each of the third and fourth years after their trials, 9 percent in the fifth year, and a further 21 percent between six and 14 years after their trial. However, age at marriage is available for only 24 of the women, which renders this data, while calculable, inconsequential.
7. Ironically, both women died in childbirth. Rebecca Tarbox died after the birth of her sixth child in ten years while her husband was absent during Metacomet's War. Mary Chandler died giving birth to her eleventh child in the twenty-first year of her marriage.
8. Whippings were conducted in public, with the victim stripped to the waist and tied to a post, usually located in front of the meeting house. A whipping was ten stripes, a severe whipping, fifteen stripes.
9. *Records and Files,* IX, 451.
10. Sidney Perley, *The History of Salem, Massachusetts, Volume III,* (Salem: S. Perley, 1926), 140.
11. At the time Chase conceived, under circumstances she described as coerced, she was working in the household of her uncle, Henry Wheeler. Her assailant, John Allen, was her uncle's wife's brother who was living with the Wheeler's.
12. Married women who engaged in sexual intercourse outside of marriage were charged with adultery, a capital crime, not fornication, the charge married men faced.
13. Keith Thomas, The Double Standard, *History of Ideas,* XX(1959), 203.
14. Plymouth Colony jurists applied a more complex set of fornication laws. They drew a distinction between couples who were formally contracted prior to the inception of sexual activity and those who had not made a formal declaration of their intention to marry.
15. I was able to establish the ages of 54 of the 99 men charged with paternity. I am assuming that this is a representative sample, but the nature of the record keeping is that it is skewed toward the more settled community members and may not adequately represented younger, transient men

who appeared in the colony only long enough to father a child or who remained but did not accumulate property.

16. Roger Almond Torrey, *New England Marriages Prior to 1700,* (Baltimore: Genealogical Publishing Company, Inc., 1985). I also checked the Essex County Vital Statistics for evidence of marriage.
17. John D. Cushing, *The Laws and Liberties of Massachusetts, 1641–1691,* Volume II, (Wilmington: Scholarly Resources, Inc., 1976), 55.
18. Those women and men who were not whipped after their fornication conviction were fined.
19. Karlsen, *Devil in the Shape of a Woman,* 195. In Plymouth Colony, I found that while women were charged with fornication along with their husbands, they received a lesser sentence during this first phase.
20. Noble, John, *Records of the Court of Assistants of the Colony of Massachusetts Bay, 1630–1692,* Volume II, 87.
21. *Records of the Court of Assistants,* II, 91. The woman's name was not entered into the court records.
22. *Records of the Court of Assistants,* II, 30.
23. *Records of the Court of Assistants,* II, 79.
24. *Records and Files,* I, 44.
25. Flint was prosecuted the previous year for not living with his wife. He testified that her mother had not been willing to see her come to New England. He brought at least two children with him. *Records and Files,* I, 50.
26. *Records of the Court of Assistants,* II, 137.
27. At some point, Flint was granted a divorce from his wife in England and he married Williams. Williams died in 1700. Flint died in 1673, leaving an estate of £911.15s. Alice and the Flint children were still arguing about the validity of Flint's will and the disposition of the estate in 1694.
28. Richard S. Dunn, Savage, James, and Laetitia Yeandle, eds., *The Journal of John Winthrop, 1630–1649,* 370.
29. *Journal of John Winthrop,* 370. This, and similar quotes by William Bradford, a governor of Plymouth Colony, have been used to indicate official condemnation of sexually uncontrollable colonists. Winthrop's triumphant insistence, however, that all had been found out and punished is the meat of this quotation.
30. *Journal of John Winthrop,* 374.
31. *The Laws and Liberties of Massachusetts, 1641–1691, Volume II,* 280.
32. Karlsen, 195.
33. The two cases where men were punished more severely than their partners were exceptional. In one, a married man impregnated his servant- she was whipped, he was severely whipped. In the other, the young man involved bragged to his friends about his sexual exploits and then lied to the Court. He was sentenced to be whipped; his female partner was sentenced to watch his whipping. I think he was whipped not so much for his sexual activity but for engaging in lascivious talk with his friends and trying to persuade them to join him in perjury.
34. Her father, John Dane, was one of the moral exemplars of the town of Ipswich.

35. In 1650, when Sknelling had been bound to good behavior for suspicion of filthiness, his partner, Elizabeth Symonds, had been whipped. Symonds did not marry. Dane married her stepmother's son, William Chandler.

NOTES TO CHAPTER THREE

1. *Records and Files,* Volume VIII, 64.
2. *Records and Files,* IV, 38.
3. *Records and Files,* I, 280.
4. *Records and Files,* 355.
5. The Salem town records detail annual payments made to specific householders who contracted with the town to raise illegitimate children in cases where no father had been named or the father had fled and the mother's situation did not allow her to raise the child herself. The contract, usually for seven pounds, was awarded to the lowest bidder, who, in some cases, returned to town meeting to ask for an increased sum to meet additional expenses.
6. Normally the child-support payment did not exceed three shillings per week, payable by the father in cash or produce, usually corn, but child support was adjusted up or down in reference to the financial resources of the father.
7. *Records and Files,* VIII, 531.
8. Women who were designated as servants in the court records, had no apparent family in Essex County, or were presented more than once for fornication, were assigned to the category of servant.
9. Her name was Mary Duell; his master Richard Dole. Duell may be an alternate spelling for Dole.
10. *Records and Files,* VI, 338–9.
11. *Records and Files,* VIII, 103.
12. Needham was fined for fornication in 1681. No partner was named in this instance, so either she committed fornication with another gentleman who was not presented or the court caught up with her for her 1679 offense. Parsons had a business relationship with Needham's father. He was also named a second time as the father of an illegitimate child.
13. Conviction data is not recorded with enough regularity between 1686 and 1692 to be used for quantitative purposes.
14. *Essex County,* 1682, 37–76–4.
15. This figure is skewed. Three of the ten fathers paying court-ordered child support were ordered to pay only charges incurred between the birth and the death of their baby. The court knew when it was levying the child-support requirement that the costs would be minimal. If they were eliminated, the court-ordered child support would be reduced to 30 percent.
16. Gloria L. Main, "Gender, Work, and Wages in Colonial New England," *The William and Mary Quarterly,* 3d Series, Volume LI, (January 1994), 48.
17. Roger Thompson, *Sex in Middlesex,* argues for the existence of a New England society in which parents were unable to control their children, teenagers gathered in barns to read sex manuals and men and women bantered openly about sexual activity, but over the fifty year period of his study, there were only 161 prosecuted Middlesex county cases of illegitimate and

premarital pregnancy combined. As well, *Sex in Middlesex* predates much of the recent very good work on gender ideology in early modern England which allows for a more nuanced interpretation of male-female relationships in seventeenth-century New England.

18. Fischer, *Albion's Seed,* 91.
19. Morgan, "The Puritans and Sex," 594.
20. The customary support payment was 2 shillings and 6 pence. Mayo paid more, perhaps because the Court took into consideration the higher standard of living in the Adams household.
21. *Records and Files,* IX, 612.
22. *Records and Files,* I, 80.
23. In the 1630s, two indentured servants, one in Boston, the other in Plymouth Colony became pregnant. When their employers tried to turn the pregnant women off, the courts in both colonies ordered them to retain the women in their households.
24. *Records and Files,* V, 103.
25. *Records and Files,* VI, 20.
26. *Records and Files,* IX, 601.
27. *Records and Files,* IV, 439.
28. *Records and Files,* II, 60.
29. The future of one of these infants can be traced through a series of entries in the Essex County Quarterly court records. Mehitabel Brabrooke was born in 1652. Her father, Richard Brabrooke, was married; her mother was Brabrooke's servant. The court ordered that Mehitabel be raised in her father's household. By the age of 16, she had been declared incorrigible by her stepmother, convicted of arson when her employer's house burned (she claimed the fire was accidental; caused by ashes from her pipe), severely whipped, and fined £40. That same year her father dowered her with half of his farm in order to marry her off to John Downing, 12 years her senior, with his own reputation for disorder. Mehitabel Downing was convicted subsequently of public drunkenness. It is probable that other illegitimate children faced similar emotional problems. Most were supported by their local community and moved annually into whichever household agreed to provide room and board for the least amount of money. This cannot have been conducive to their well-being, either physical or emotional.
30. *Records and Files,* IV, 39. Reeves deposition is illustrative for what it says about the mother/child bond in seventeenth-century Massachusetts. It suggests that Puritans believed in the strength and immediacy of the mother/child bond, and that legal restraints were necessary to keep Durin away from her child.
31. *Essex County,* 1682, 38–81–3.
32. Ibid., 1682, 38–81–1.
33. Ibid., 1678, 30–18–2.
34. *Records and Files,* IV, 424.
35. *Records and* Files, V, 38.

36. *Records and Files,* V, 157. Warr was convicted a second time of fornication in March, 1676. This time, however, the father of her child, Henry Gould, married her.
37. *Records and Files,* VI, 206.
38. *Records and Files,* II, 384.
39. *Letter Book of Samuel Sewall,* 270.
40. *Records and Files,* VIII, 279. Sarah Stickney had a local reputation for promiscuity. It was rumored that Stickney had drawn lots to decide whom to name as her child's father. Atkinson's name had been chosen. However, Atkinson's wife had been seven months pregnant when Stickney conceived, so it is not impossible that Atkinson had gone to her for sexual intercourse.
41. *Essex County,* 1682, 38–85–2.
42. *Records and Files,* IX, 433.
43. *Records and Files,* I, 237.
44. The admonition to "be fruitful and multiply" meant, however, that sexual intercourse with pregnant women was proscribed. A number of married men in this study turned to other women when their wives were pregnant.
45. David Cressy, *Birth, Marriage, and Death: Ritual, Religion, and the Life-Cycle in Tudor and Stuart England,* (Oxford: Oxford University Press, 1997), 277.

NOTES TO CHAPTER FOUR

1. Ibid., 1682, 37–101–1.
2. David Levine and Keith Wrightson, "The Social Context of Illegitimacy in Early Modern England, in Peter Laslett, Karla Oosterveen and Richard M. Smith, *Bastardy and Its Comparative History,* (Cambridge: Harvard University Press, 1980), 169.
3. Fischer, *Albion's Seed,* 77.
4. In chapter two I disputed the notion that a sexually charged atmosphere existed in seventeenth-century Massachusetts. If a sexually charged atmosphere is characterized by open sexual byplay, provocative dress and behavior, and sexual innuendo, then this assertion is correct. However, if a sexually charged atmosphere is defined by the general expectation of marriage and positive rhetoric about the joys of marital sexual intercourse, the presence of courting couples, and evidence of marital fertility, Essex County possessed a sexually charged atmosphere.
5. Of 99 couples presented for fornication, two had more than one child together, and four married after the birth of their child.
6. Lawrence Stone. *Uncertain Unions: Marriage in England 1660–1753,* (Oxford: Oxford University Press, 1992), 11.
7. I was able to determine the date of birth for 130 Essex County children who were conceived outside of marriage between 1640 and 1642. From this, I calculated the approximate date on which these children were conceived. Additionally, I was able to determine from the Newbury, Massachusetts Vital Records, the dates of birth for 1616 legitimate children conceived between 1640 and 1685. Their dates of conception were graphed

and compared to the dates of conception for the children who were conceived outside of marriage.

8. Marital conceptions in Newbury fit the rhythmic pattern observed by James A. Henretta for colonial America as a whole. James A. Henretta, *The Evolution of American Society,* 1700–1815, (Lexington,: D. C. Heath and Company, 1973), 33.
9. David Cressy, "The Seasonality of Marriage in Old and New England," *Journal of Interdisciplinary History,* XVI:I (Summer, 1985), 12.
10. Flaherty, "Law and the Enforcement of Morals in Early America," 225.
11. Chris Wilson, "The Proximate Determinants of Marital Fertility in England 1600–1799," in Lloyd Bonfield, Richard M. Smith, and Keith Wrightson, eds. *The World We Have Gained: Histories of Population and Social Structure.* (Oxford: Basil Blackwell, 1986), 206.
12. While an egg has a life span of only 15 to 24 hours, sperm remain viable for five days in the cervix.
13. *Essex County,* 1669, 15–128–1.
14. Ibid., 1680, 34–8–3.
15. Ibid., 1690, 49–63–3.
16. Ibid., 1686, 47–4–1.
17. Ibid., 1688, 47–135–1.
18. Ibid., 1674, 20–96–1.
19. Clement Coldham spent a lot of time watching the Stanwood family. In November, 1673 Coldham testified that he had seen Stanwood's son, John, kissing Christian Marshman after Marshman had claimed that she was pregnant by John Stanwood. Marshman was whipped immediately; Stanwood was put in prison until he could raise a £50 bond. It was later determined that Marshman was not and never had been pregnant. *Records and Files,* V, 250. Coldham testified against the Stanwood family again in 1674 when he reported that Stanwood's daughter, Jane, had a child eighteen weeks after she had married Timothy Somes. *Records and Files,* V, 258. When another Stanwood daughter, Naomi, was presented for premarital fornication in 1681, Coldham was not involved in the presentation.
20. *Essex County,* 1679, 46–11–1.
21. Ibid., 1683, 39–140–2.
22. Ibid., 1674, 22–67–2.
23. Ibid., 1676, 25–50–3. Salmon was convicted of fornication three times. She and her husband, George Salmon were fined £5 each in 1664. In 1676 she was whipped for fornication with Thomas Greene. Salmon was charged with fornication again in 1679. In this instance, her partner, Philip Veren fled, and the town of Salem was concerned that Salmon and her child would be "a burden to the town." *Records and Files,* VII, 318.
24. *Essex County,* 1687. 47–53–1.
25. Hannah Gray was convicted of lascivious behavior in March, 1674, for "laughing and giggling at the boys bed which was in the same room." *Records and Files,* V, 290.
26. *Records and Files,* IV, 39.

27. That Durin had only one other room or an upper chamber to escape to, is evidence of the close quarters in which unrelated servants worked and lived and seems to be the standard two rooms downstairs with an unpartitioned chamber or loft above.
28. *Records and Files,* 1, 388.
29. *Essex County,* 1654, 37–106–1.
30. Ibid., 1682, 37–114–1.
31. Ibid., 1682, 33–117–3.
32. These depositions raise some interesting issues. I haven't seen the originals. Probably none of these women could write, so my first question is whether or not they were written by the same person, and how much input into the wording the person had who prepared the documents for them. My second question is related to their survival. I could only find four penitent statements in the court records. Since there is copious documentation for cases involving land transactions and business disputes, I think that archivists in the 18th and 19th centuries, who undervalued women's documents and likely found the subject matter distasteful, did not retain them. As an archivist myself, I understand issues of storage space, preservation, and the systematic culling of documents deemed less important. Church records were edited periodically to remove material descendants considered damaging or the church fathers deemed unseemly, and it is possible that the court records were subjected to a similar editing process. It seems entirely possible that these three documents were overlooked when the remainder was removed from the collection. Documents continue to disappear from the court records. Some of the depositions excerpted in the printed volumes of the Essex County Records and Files published in the 1910s were no longer available when the W.P.A. prepared their transcriptions in the 1930s.
33. These penitent statements make no mention that these women considered the characteristics they attributed to themselves to be gender-specific. I am inferring that they believed this was too self-evident to mention, but to be fair, penitent statements filed by men on behalf of themselves and their wives express similar sentiments.
34. *Essex County,* 1691, 50–120–4.
35. Ibid., 1674, 22–70–5.
36. Ibid., 1690, 49–62–1.
37. Ibid., 1690, 49–62–3.
38. Ibid., 1681, 46–9–4.
39. Ibid., 1678, 38–88–2.
40. Ibid.
41. Neither man led a charmed life. Edmund Bridges died about 1682. His widow, nee Sarah Towne, was accused of witchcraft in Salem, 1692, as Sarah Cloyse, along with her sister Mary Easty, and her sister, Rebecca Nurse, who was hanged. Hackaliah Bridges, still unmarried, was lost at sea in 1671.
42. Hackaliah Bridges was sentenced to be fined or whipped for lying and stealing a pair of gloves in April, 1657, *Records and Files,* Volume II, 41. Sarah French named him as the father of her illegitimate child, but a

Scottish indentured servant, John Fargason, was convicted in his stead. *Records and Files,* II, 2.

43. *Essex County,* 1657, 3–137–1.
44. Ibid., 1657, 3–319–3.
45. Ibid., 1657, 3–140–2.
46. None of the youths who provided depositions or who were mentioned in the depositions figure in any contemporary fornication trials. However, John Allen was acquitted in a fornication case in 1669. The acquittal was based on the unwillingness of the court to accept the word of the female defendant, Anne Chase, because the circumstances under which she claimed that she had conceived were coerced and the court thought she lied, *Records and Files,* IV, 244. Allen and his wife, Mary Andrews, were convicted of fornication in 1674, *Records and Files,* V, 408. Thomas Gittins and his wife were convicted of fornication in 1678, *Records and Files,* VI, 424.
47. I have not been able to identify Mary Browne or to determine her date of birth. Quilter married a widower, Michael Cressie, in 1660.
48. *Records and Files,* II, 54.
49. *Records and Files,* II, 52.
50. *Records and Files,* I, 347.
51. Records and Files, I, 347.
52. Thompson, *Sex in Middlesex,* 104, 105.
53. I suspect that the apparent differences between Middlesex County and Essex County in terms of evidence of a viable appositive youth culture lie in the interpretative biases of the researchers. Thompson wants to conclude that there were few patriarchal curbs on adolescent sexual activity: I want to prove the opposite.
54. A third son, Obadiah, was convicted of fornication in 1669.
55. *Essex County,* 1666, 11–95–3.
56. Ibid., 1666, 11–95–3.
57. Ibid., 1666, 11–95–4.
58. Ibid., 1678, 37–49–4. Atkinson and Jaques had significant commonalities. Both were in their forties, they had been married for seventeen and twenty years respectively, and both had wives who were in the final stages of pregnancy when their husbands became involved sexually with other women.
59. M. Halsey Thomas, *The Diary of Samuel Sewall,* Volume I, 155.
60. Kenneth Silverman, *The Life and Times of Cotton Mather,* (New York: Columbia University Press, 1985), 308.
61. *Essex County,* 1674, 22–68–3.
62. *Records and Files,* IX, 64.

NOTES TO CHAPTER FIVE

1. *Essex County,* 1674, 22–68–6.
2. Ibid., 1674, 22–67–2.
3. Ibid., 1674, 22–68–2.
4. Ibid., 1674, 22–69–1.
5. Ibid., 1674, 22–68–3.

6. Ibid., 1674, 22–68–4.
7. Ibid. 1674, 22–68–4.
8. Ibid., 1674, 32–69–2.
9. Ibid., 1674, 22–67–1.
10. Ibid., 1674, 22–67–1.
11. *Essex County,* 1674, 22–69–3.
12. Ibid., 1674, 22–70–6.
13. Ibid., 1674, 22–68–2.
14. Ibid., 1674, 22–70–2.
15. Ibid., 1674, 22–70–6.
16. John Dane was the author of John Dane's Narrative, *New England Historical and Genealogical Register,* Volume 8, April 1854.
17. *Records and Files,* I, 337.
18. Essex County, 1674, 22–70–3.
19. Ulrich, *Goodwives,* 97.
20. Essex County, 1674, 22–70–5.
21. Ibid., 1674, 22–70–1.
22. Nineteen witnesses was not an unusual number. In the adultery case involving John Leigh and Sarah Roe, thirty-five people presented evidence against them. Fischer, *Albion's Seed,* 88.
23. The name, Talbut, is alternately rendered as Talbot, Tarbell, Tarbull, Tarbox and Cabbutt. I have been unable to connect her to any Essex County families or find evidence that she married after her fornication trial and the completion of her extended indenture.
24. Obadiah Wood later moved to Hartford, Connecticut where he married.
25. *Records and Files,* V, 356.
26. *Records and Files,* VI, 20.
27. *Records and Files,* 278.
28. I will consider Puritan ideology about love at greater length in the following chapter on pregnant brides.
29. See also, Else L. Hambleton, "The Regulation of Sex in Seventeenth-Century Massachusetts: The Quarterly Court of Essex County vs. Priscilla Willson and Mr. Samuel Appleton," in Smith, Merril D., ed., *Sex and Sexuality in Early America,* (New York: New York University Press, 1998), 89–115.
30. *Essex County,* 1683, 39–139–1.
31. Ibid., 1683, 39–140–2.
32. Ibid., 1683, 39–139–3.
33. Ibid., 1683, 39–140–3.
34. Ibid., 1678, 46–11–1.
35. Ibid.
36. Ibid., 1681, 37–91–3.
37. *Records and Files,* VII, 317.
38. *Records and Files,* 317.
39. *Records and Files,* VIII, 43.
40. Long after Atkinson stopped making child-support payments, he was still active in court trying to clear his name. He and Stickney and her husband

Stephen Acreman engaged in extensive litigation which included multiple physical assaults and a disputed miscarriage.

41. *Essex County,* 1681, 46–10–1.
42. Ibid., 46–9–1.
43. Ibid., 1681, 46–9–4.
44. John M. Murrin, "'Things Fearful to Name': Bestiality in Colonial America," *Pennsylvania History: A Journal of Mid-Atlantic Studies,* Special Supplemental Issue, Vol. 65 (1998), 9. Only two cases, both in New England, which involved women in cases of sexual play, were tried as lewd and lascivious behavior.
45. Ann Taves, *Religion and Domestic Violence in Early New England,* (Bloomington: Indiana University Press, 1989), 43.
46. I found one incest case in Salem in 1682. Nicholas Manning and his sisters were charged with incest. Manning fled before trial, his sisters were sentenced to be whipped but had their fines remitted by the payment of £5. The penalty for incest was the same as that for fornication. *Records and Files,* Volume VIII, 88–89.
47. *Essex County,* 1688, 47–147–1.
48. Ibid., 1688, 47–147–1.
49. Ibid., 1688, 47–148–1.
50. Koehler, *A Search for Power.* 113.

NOTES TO CHAPTER SIX

1. *Essex County,* 1689, 49–122–1.
2. *Essex County,* 1689, 49–65–1.
3. The lack of biographical detail on Welch and Batten presented in the court records is all too typical of premarital fornication defendants. None of the depositions provide their ages and neither Welch nor Batten appears in the Essex County Vital Records. Margaret Batten's parents, William and Joan Batten, were refugees from Native American warfare in Saco, Maine, which was under siege at the time Batten conceived. It is likely that Margaret Batten had recently arrived in Salem with her parents. Edward Welch may be the son of Philip Welch, an "Irish youth" who had been transported to New England and sold by order of the English government in 1651. The following summer, Margaret's sister, Elizabeth Batten, would also be charged with fornication. However, the father of her child was the eighteen-year-old son of her employer. Age and economic disparity ensured that her baby would be illegitimate.
4. E. A. Wrigley and R. S. Schofield, *The Population History of England, 1541–1871,* (Cambridge: Mass. 1981), 255, 423–4.
5. David Cressy, *Birth, Marriage, and Death,* 277.
6. If they failed to marry, the woman would be charged with bastardy in selected cases, usually when it appeared likely that her child would become a charge on the local community. Her partner, if he could be identified, might be pursued through the system for child support. The criminal act was bearing a bastard, not having extramarital sexual intercourse.

7. Fischer, 77. Cressy, 285, placed the number of English persons in seventeenth-century England who did not marry at 20 percent.
8. Joseph R. McElrath, Jr., and Allan P. Robb, eds., *The Complete Works of Anne Bradstreet,* (Boston: Twayne Publishers, 1981), 180.
9. Gloria L. Main, *Peoples of a Spacious Land: Families and Cultures in Colonial New England,* (Cambridge: Harvard University Press, 2001), 77.
10. Cressy, 287.
11. Holly Brewer, *Constructing Consent: How Children's Status in Political Theory Shaped Public Policy in Virginia, Pennsylvania, and Massachusetts before and after the American Revolution,* Ph.D. dissertation, UCLA, 1994, 192.
12. *Essex County,* 1674, 22–67–1.
13. Ibid., 206.
14. Massachusetts Statutes and Laws, *The Charter and General Laws of the Colony and Province of Massachusetts Bay,* (Boston, 1814), 151.
15. *Records and Files,* Volume VIII, 146.
16. Chris Wilson, "The Determinants of Marital Fertility," in *The World We Have Gained,* 214.
17. *Records and Files,* Volume I, 286.
18. Ibid., Volume II, 101.
19. Ibid., Volume III, 221. Remember Salmon was widowed in 1673. She was convicted of fornication twice more, in 1676 and 1679 following the births of illegitimate children.
20. Ibid., Volume V, 152. A second couple who was presented for a 32 week pregnancy in 1675 was also discharged.
21. Ibid., Volume IV, 64. Henry True's wife, Jane Bradbury, was fined two-thirds of the sum her husband paid.
22. Ibid., 409.
23. Heriman was killed the following year at Bloody Brook, September 18, 1675 while serving in the militia during Metacomet's War. I have been unable to locate any reference to a will or an inventory which would allow a financial analysis. His father, Leonard Heriman, was prosperous enough to be appointed to Essex County grand juries twice during this decade.
24. John D. Cushing, *The Laws and Liberties of Massachusetts, 1641–1691,* Volume II, 280.
25. *Records and Files,* Volume IV, 200.
26. Only 46 percent of the men who fathered illegitimate children were given the option to pay a fine. The 35 men who were convicted of fornication, however, were prosecuted prior to 1660 when penalties were generally severe or represented the most egregious offenses.
27. Seven couples, all after 1679, forfeited their bonds when they did not appear. In the remainder of the cases, the verdict is unknown.
28. *Essex County,* 1682, 38–81–3.
29. One hundred Ipswich and Salisbury marriages were selected at random from the vital statistics in order to arrive at a sample that represented both urban and agricultural Essex County. The established pattern matches that developed for New England by David Cressy, "The Seasonality of Marriage in Old and New England," *Journal of Interdisciplinary History,* XVI:I (Summer, 1985), 5.

30. I did not include the 35 week prosecution of John Putnam and Rebecca Prince in this tally because it was anomalous.
31. Kenneth A. Lockridge, *A New England Town; The First Hundred Years, Dedham, Massachusetts, 1636–1736,* (New York: W. W. Norton & Company, 1970), 66.
32. John Demos, *A Little Commonwealth: Family Life in Plymouth Colony,* (London: Oxford University Press, 1979), 193.
33. Philip J. Greven, Jr., "Family Structure in Seventeenth-Century Andover, Massachusetts in Stanley N. Katz, John M. Murrin, Douglas Greenburg, eds., *Colonial America: Essays in Politics and Social Development,* (New York: McGraw-Hill, Inc., 1993), 138–139.
34. I did not break my age data down into monthly intervals because I think there is too much uncertainty as to whether the dates of birth given in the published Vital Records represented birth or baptism although baptism usually occurred on the Sunday following birth if the parents were church members.
35. There is a bias in this sample of cases. Ages were determined, in most instances, from births registered in the vital statistics. Secondary sources of age data were court records which sometimes recorded the age of a deponent and immigration records. While the age of an indentured servant might be gained from these sources, the age sample is skewed toward women born in Essex County of established parents.
36. *Historical Statistics of the United States,* (U.S.: GPO, 1960, 756.

NOTES TO CHAPTER SEVEN

1. *Essex County,* 1681, 36–11–1.
2. There is a link between sexual misdemeanors and witchcraft accusations. During genealogical research for the thesis that precedes this book, I realized that a fornication prosecution in the family increased the likelihood that one would be named as a witch. Elizabeth Proctor's father, John Proctor was executed in 1692. His new wife, Elizabeth Bassett Proctor was also convicted of witchcraft but saved from hanging because she was pregnant. By the time she had given birth, the witchcraft hysteria had diminished. Proctor and Bassett had recently been prosecuted for fornication. Thomas Verry's sister, Elizabeth, married, in 1678, John Nurse, Rebecca Nurse's son. John Nurse and Elizabeth Verry were prosecuted for fornication, and Rebecca Nurse was hanged along with John Proctor. I expect to explore the link between fornication prosecutions and witchcraft accusations in future work. I think that a family reputation for sexual misdemeanors was one of the factors when it came to deciding whom to accuse as of witchcraft.
3. These persons had been born in England and formed the Great Migration vanguard or had inculcated through church, community, and family, the sense of mission, of partaking in the formation of a Protestant exemplar to the world. They also understood that they had formed a covenant with God which would ensure the success of the Puritan venture in return for conformance with His rules.

4. *Essex County*, April 1684, 36–10–1.
5. Ibid.
6. Ibid.
7. Robert Charles Anderson, *The Great Migration Begins: Immigrants to New England, 162–1633*, Volume 1, (Boston: New England Historic Genealogical Society, 1995), 532.
8. *Records and Files*, Volume VI, 23.
9. The depositions in the Garland appeal are taken from the Suffolk County Court Records, #1413, 7 papers, numbered 103 to 109.
10. *Records and Files*, Volume V, 410. This had been a difficult day in court for Elizabeth Roby. In an earlier case that day, her husband had successfully sued the father of Elizabeth's stepdaughter's illegitimate child for back child-support payments.
11. 36. And behold, Elizabeth thy kinswoman also has conceived a son in her old age, and she who was called barren is now in her sixth month; 37. For nothing shall be impossible with God." 38. But Mary said, "Behold, the handmaiden of the Lord; be it done to me according to thy word." And the angel departed from her. 39. Now in those days Mary arose, and went with haste into the hill country, to a town of Juda. 40. And she entered into the house of Zachary and saluted Elizabeth. 56. And Mary remained with her about three months and returned to her own house. 57. Now Elizabeth's time was fulfilled that she should be delivered, and she brought forth a son.
12. *Records and Files*, Volume IV, 236.
13. Judith Roby, like other women who bore illegitimate children, had a difficult time finding a husband. She married a widower, Samuel Healey, when she was 43.
14. *Records and Files*, Volume V, 152.
15. Brewer, *Constructing Consent*, 206.
16. *Records and Files*, Volume I, 180.
17. Ibid., Volume II, 242.
18. Ibid.
19. Thompson, *Sex in Middlesex*, 53.
20. Obadiah Bridges' widow, Elizabeth, was charged with fornication herself following her second marriage to Joseph Parker in 1681. *Records and Files*, Volume VIII, 100.
21. Ibid., Volume III, 235.
22. Ibid., Volume VI, 15.
23. Unfortunately, the depositions concerning this secret betrothal were given as part of a slander suit against John Acie in 1675, and they provide no information about the ages of Hopkinson and Palmer at the time. It is impossible to know if either or both parties were over 21 at the time they courted.
24. McManus, *Law and Liberty*, 40.
25. Ibid., 142.
26. *Records and Files*, Volume IV, 269.
27. Ibid., 269.
28. Ibid., 282.

29. In rape cases, women who had been contracted had the same legal status as already married women.
30. Ibid., Volume VIII, 216.
31. Norton, *Founding Mothers,* 66.
32. Ibid., Volume I, 286.
33. Ibid., Volume I, 220.
34. *Essex County,* 1650, 2–5–1.
35. *Records and Files,* Volume I, 251.
36. Ibid., Volume IV, 136.
37. Ibid., Volume III, 151–2.
38. *Essex County, 1681,* 16–11–1.
39. Ibid.
40. In John R. Gillis, *For Better, For Worse,* V.
41. Edgar J. McManus, *Law and Liberty in Early New England,* 53.
42. M. Halsey Thomas, *The Diary of Samuel Sewall,* Volume I, 346.
43. *Records and Files,* Volume VI, 425.
44. *Essex* County, 1664, 10–31–2.
45. Ibid., 10–31–3.
46. Ibid., 10–31–4.
47. Ibid., 10–31–5.
48. Ibid., 10–32–2
49. Ibid., 1664, 10–32–2
50. *Records and Files,* Volume II, 11.
51. *Essex County,* 1660, 5–116–1.
52. Ibid., 305.
53. Ibid., 340.
54. *Essex County,* 1661.
55. Ibid.
56. Since Beatrice Canterbury left no will, it is impossible to know if she would have left part of her estate to her Woodrow grandchildren. She was involved in their lives as in 1676 her then husband, Edward Berry witnessed the will of Christopher Waller in which Christopher Waller left £10 to Joseph Woodrow to receive at the age of 21 if he continued to live with Waller's wife until then. This makes it clear that Woodrow, aged 16, was not living with his father and had not been for some time. Neither Joseph Woodrow nor his sister, Mary, despite their eventual inheritance, is recorded as marrying or having children in Essex County.
57. *Records and Files,* Volume IX, 300–1.
58. Hannah Adams conceived a second child out-of-wedlock in 1682. This time the father, William Warham, married her. Family gatherings must have been fraught. Robert Adams, Hannah's father and Sarah's stepsister died on the fourth birthday of Hannah's daughter by Joseph Mayo.
59. *Records and Files,* Volume 8, 437.
60. Ibid., Volume VIII, 372.
61. *Records and Files,* Volume V, 376.
62. *Records and Files,* Volume IX, 202.

63. The timing of Sarah Bailey's death suggests that she may have died during her sixth childbirth.
64. Ibid., Volume III, 118.
65. Perley, *History of Salem,* Volume III, 420. There are 36 men in this tax category. Five of them were convicted of premarital fornication. A sixth married man in this group fathered an illegitimate child.
66. *The Probate Records of Essex County,* Volume II, 421.
67. *Essex County,* 1690, 49–99–1.
68. *Essex County,* 1687, 47–50–4.
69. *Essex County,* 1687, 47–49–1.
70. *Essex County,* 1672, 18–139–3.

NOTES TO CHAPTER EIGHT

1. For the purposes of this chapter, rape is defined as heterosexual sexual intercourse by force or by threat of bodily injury.
2. Suffolk County Court, 1673, # 1254.
3. Garthine Walker, 'Rereading Rape and Sexual Violence in Early Modern England,' *Gender & History,* 10 (1998), 6.
4. Michael Dalton, *The Countrey Justice,* (London: Company of Stationers, 1618). Dalton wrote his manual for English Justices of the Peace with no formal legal training. Dalton's definition of rape was predicated on contemporary scientific understanding of the mechanics of conception: a mutual orgasm was required.
5. Catharine Baker, "Sexual Assault in Seventeenth-Century Massachusetts" (unpublished seminar paper, Brandeis University, 1974) also counted fourteen rape prosecutions in the Massachusetts Bay Colony Court of Assistants.
6. *Records and Files,* Volume I, v.
7. Men who raped married women could be prosecuted for adultery, also a capital crime.
8. Eleven years later, Hannah Dustin became 'the most famous woman in New England.' She and Mary Neff were taken captive during a Native American raid on Haverhill in 1697. Despite the fact that she had given birth five days earlier and been marched a hundred miles into the wilderness, Dustin, with the assistance of Neff and a young boy, killed ten of her captors and returned with their scalps to Boston. Laurel Ulrich, *Goodwives,* (New York: Oxford University Press, 1983), 167.
9. *Records and Files, Volume IX,* 306.
10. *Essex County,* 1686, 46–131–1.
11. She named Liddia Ladd's husband, Samuel, as the father of her child. Liddia Ladd had been one of the women in attendance when she had accused Timothy Swann of rape. Given the likelihood of Liddia Ladd's presence again this time, it would have been awkward, at the least, to name Samuel Ladd as her lover. There would have been economic, as well as social and emotional ramifications for the Ladd family since Samuel Ladd, like Swann before him, would have been required to make child-support payments.

12. Deuteronomy 22, 29–30. If a man find a damsel that is a virgin, which is not betrothed, and lay hold on her, and lie with her, and they be found; Then the man that lay with her shall give unto the damsel's father fifty shekels of silver, and she shall be his wife; because he hath humbled her, he may not put her away all his days. *The Holy Bible Containing the Old and New Testaments* (Oxford: Oxford University Press, 1900), 224.
13. Under English common law, both coerced and consensual intercourse between adult males and under-aged females was rape. McManus, Edgar J. *Law and Liberty in Early New England: Criminal Justice and Due Process, 1620–1692*. (Amherst: University of Massachusetts Press, 1993), 31.
14. John Noble, *Records of the Court of Assistants of the Colony of Massachusetts Bay* (Boston: Suffolk County, 1904), 64–65. It is instructive that swearing ranked as a more serious crime than housebreaking.
15. The abuse began when the elder, Dorcas, was six and ended when she was nine and told a recently married sister about it. Her father, Mr. John Humfrey, a prominent member of the Court of Assistants, had frequently left his children in the care of servants. They became even more vulnerable when he left Massachusetts Bay Colony. The Court punished the offenders as best they could within the constraints of the existing law. One of them was severely whipped and had one nostril slit and seared at Boston. This process was repeated at Salem and then he was restricted to one neighborhood, upon pain of death if he left it, and required to wear a noose around his neck. Winthrop makes specific reference to the fact that this man had a "lusty young wife" and I infer that his punishment may have been greater not only because he had been the one who had initiated the abuse but because he had a legitimate sexual outlet in his wife. This inference is strengthened by Winthrop's mention that of the other two defendants who received lesser sentences, one was unmarried and the other had a wife whose pregnancy constrained coitus. Dorcas Humfrey was also punished. Richard S. Dunn and Laetitia Yeandle, eds., *The Journal of John Winthrop, 1630–1641,* abridged version, (Cambridge: Harvard University Press, 1996), 193–197.
16. Ibid., 21.
17. Koehler, 95.
18. *Records of the Court of Assistants of the Massachusetts Bay,* 200.
19. Koehler, 96. Barbara S. Lindemann cites Koehler as her authority for the same statement in her paper, "To Ravish and Carnally Know: Rape in Eighteenth-Century Massachusetts," *Signs* (1984)1:63–82.
20. Koehler, 96, Lindemann, 66.
21. Original deposition at the Pocumtuck Valley Historical Society, Deerfield, Massachusetts. That the boys were so frightened by what they had witnessed that they ran away is a testament to the psychological prohibitions that the Puritans placed on extramarital sexual activity. However, it could be too that they were afraid of John Evans.
22. When Reade died intestate June 25, 1667, he left an estate valued at approximately £75 and a wife and seven children between the ages of 1½ and 19. Susanna Reade, at seventeen, was the eldest girl. The family's financial situation made it imperative that Reade hire herself out to Herrick. Reade had

only a nineteen-year-old brother, Aaron, who was killed in a shooting accident the following summer, to speak for her.

23. This part may have been true, but Herrick may have been motivated to withhold food and tobacco by Reade's resistance to his advances, rather than by displeasure over the quality of her work.
24. *Records of the Court of Assistants,* Volume II, 121. Wythes was 17, Odle 14. Odle is the only woman in this initial cluster whose married can be traced.
25. Bernard Bailyn, *The Peopling of British North America,* 18.
26. There is no record of Basto's fate.
27. Clarence Almon Torrey, *New England Marriages Prior to 1700,* (Baltimore: Genealogical Publishing Company., Inc., 1985). The 30 percent marriage rate is comparable to that of women who were convicted of illegitimate fornication. Ninety-four percent of Essex County women married.
28. *Records of the Court of Assistants,* Volume I, 158.
29. Ibid., 80, 81.
30. Suffolk County Court record #1254.
31. Ibid.
32. Ibid.
33. Ibid.
34. *Records and Files,* Volume VIII, 12.
35. Statement in Chase deposition, Emerson case.
36. Kathy Doherty and Irina Anderson, "Talking about rape," *The Psychologist,* Volume II (12), December 1998, 583.
37. This could indicate that the depositions that survive were selected for retention by archivists who recognized that they represented a departure from the norm.
38. It was not poverty that drove Chase out of the household. When her father died the following year, he left an estate valued at 336 li. 14s. 3d. Chase was the second of eleven children.
39. David W. Hoyt, *The Old Families of Salisbury and Amesbury, Massachusetts* (Baltimore: Genealogical Publishing Company, Inc., 1982), 354.
40. *Essex County,* 1670.
41. Ibid.
42. Allen and his wife Mary (Pike) Andrews were charged with fornication in October 1674. *Records and Files, Volume V,* 408.
43. Ibid.
44. Nelson had powerful local connections in Ipswich. His maternal grandfather was Robert Cross and three of his uncles, all married to his mother's sisters paid one-half of his 50^ fine. Avis was an orphan who lived with relatives in Chebacco Parish a newly-settled part of Ipswich. Her relatives were leaders in a successful struggle against the local power structure in an effort to establish a church in Chebacco rather than making the long trip to Ipswich twice a week.
45. *Records and Files, Volume VIII,* 15. They were, however, given the option of paying a fine. The fine was to be reduced if they married, and Martha Lamson's sexuality contained. They did not marry.

NOTES TO CHAPTER NINE

1. The young widow, Sarah Stickney, for example, while possessing the resources to live independently, bore two illegitimate children prior to marrying, or being married to, Stephen Ackerman. The general perception of Stickney in Newbury, where she and her family lived, was that she was sexually available. Stickney portrayed herself as a victim. Whichever perception is correct, Stickney needed marriage for sexual protection because her marital status meant potential harassers, and Stickney herself, would be charged with adultery.

Bibliography

Adair, Richard. *Courtship, Illegitimacy and Marriage in Early Modern England.* Manchester: Manchester University Press, 1996.

Anderson, Robert Charles. *The Great Migration Begins: Immigrants to New England, 1620–1633, Volume 1.* Boston: New England Historic Genealogical Society, 1995.

Anderson, Virginia DeJohn. *New England's Generation: The Great Migration and the Formation of Society and Culture in the Seventeenth Century.* Cambridge: Cambridge University Press, 1991.

Bailyn, Bernard. *The Peopling of British North America: An Introduction.* New York: Alfred A. Knopf, Inc., 1986.

Baker, Catharine. "Sexual Assault in Seventeenth-Century Massachusetts." Unpublished seminar paper, Brandeis University, 1974.

Bremer, Francis J. *The Puritan Experiment: New England Society from Bradford to Edwards.* New York: St. Martin's Press, 1976.

Brewer, Holly. *Constructing Consent: How Children's Status in Political Theory Shaped Public Policy in Virginia, Pennsylvania, and Massachusetts before and after the American Revolution.* PhD. Dissertation, UCLA, 1994.

Carr, Lois G. and Walsh, Lorena S. "The Planter's Wife: The Experience of Women in Seventeenth-Century Maryland." In Katz, Stanley N. and Murrin, John M., eds., *Colonial America: Essays in Political and Social Development.* New York: Alfred A. Knopf, Inc., 1983.

Coffin, Joshua. *A Sketch of the History of Newbury, Newburyport and West Newbury from 1635 to 1845.* Boston: S. G. Drake, 1845.

Cressy, David. *Birth, Marriage & Death: Ritual, Religion, and the Life-Cycle in Tudor and Stuart England.* Oxford: Oxford University Press, 1997.

Cressy, David. "The Seasonality of Marriage in Old and New England." *Journal of Interdisciplinary History,* XVI:I (Summer, 1985), 1–21.

Cushing, John D. *The Laws and Liberties of Massachusetts, 1641–1691, Volume II.* Wilmington: Scholarly Resources, Inc., 1976.

Dalton, Michael. *The Countrey Justice.* London: Company of Stationers, 1618.

Davison, William I. "Essex County Price Trends: Money and Markets in 17th Century Massachusetts." *Essex Institute Historical Collections,* 145–185.

Dayton, Cornelia Hughes. *Women Before the Bar: Gender, Law, & Society in Connecticut, 1639–1789.* Chapel Hill: University of North Carolina Press, 1995.

Demos, John. *A Little Commonwealth: Family Life in Plymouth Colony.* New York: Oxford University Press, 1970.

Doherty, Kathy and Anderson, Irina. "Talking About Rape." *The Psychologist,* II(12), 1998, 583–537.

Dow, George Francis, ed. *Records and Files of the Quarterly Court of Essex County, Massachusetts, Volume I, 1636–1656.* Salem: The Essex Institute, 1911.

Dow, George Francis, ed. *Records and Files of the Quarterly Court of Essex County, Massachusetts, Volume II, 1656–1662.* Salem: The Essex Institute, 1912.

Dow, George Francis, ed. *Records and Files of the Quarterly Court of Essex County, Massachusetts, Volume III, 1662–1667.* Salem: The Essex Institute, 1913.

Dow, George Francis, ed. *Records and Files of the Quarterly Court of Essex County, Massachusetts, Volume IV, 1667–1671.* Salem: The Essex Institute, 1914.

Dow, George Francis, ed. *Records and Files of the Quarterly Court of Essex County, Massachusetts, Volume V, 1672–1674.* Salem: The Essex Institute, 1916.

Dow, George Francis, ed. *Records and Files of the Quarterly Court of Essex County, Massachusetts, Volume VI, 1675–1678.* Salem: The Essex Institute, 1918.

Dow, George Francis, ed. *Records and Files of the Quarterly Court of Essex County, Massachusetts, Volume VII, 1678–1680.* Salem: The Essex Institute, 1919.

Dow, George Francis. *Records and Files of the Quarterly Court of Essex County, Massachusetts, Volume VIII, 1680–1683.* Salem: The Essex Institute, 1921.

Dunn, Richard S., Savage, James, and Yeandle, Laetitia, eds. *The Journal of John Winthrop, 1630–1649.* Cambridge: Harvard University Press, 1996.

Erikson, Kai. *Wayward Puritans: A Study in the Sociology of Deviance.* New York: John Wiley & Sons, Inc., 1966.

Essex Institute, The. *The Probate Records of Essex County Massachusetts, Volume I, 1635–1664.* Salem: Author, 1916.

Essex Institute, The. *The Probate Records of Essex County Massachusetts, Volume II, 1665–1674.* Salem: Author, 1917.

Essex Institute, The. *The Probate Records of Essex County Massachusetts, Volume III, 1675–1681.* Salem: Author, 1920.

Fischer, David Hackett. *Albion's Seed: Four British Folkways in America.* New York: Oxford University Press, 1989.

Flaherty, David H. "Law and the Enforcement of Morals in Early America." In *Perspectives in Early American History,* edited by Donald Flemming and Bernard Baylin, vol. 5, 203–253. Cambridge: Harvard University Press for Charles Warren Center for Studies in American History, 1971.

Flaherty, David H. *Privacy in Colonial New England.* Charlottesville: University Press of Virginia, 1967.

Foster, Thomas A. "Deficient Husbands: Manhood, Sexual Incapacity, and Male Marital Sexuality in Seventeenth-Century New England." *William and Mary Quarterly,* 3rd Ser., LVI (1999), 723–744.

Gillis, John R. *For Better: For Worse: British Marriages 1600 to the Present.* New York: Oxford University Press, 1985.

Godbeer, Richard. *Sexual Revolution in Early America.* Baltimore: The Johns Hopkins University Press, 2002.

Gowing, Laura. *Domestic Dangers: Women, Words, and Sex in Early Modern London.* Oxford: Clarendon Press, 1996.

Greven, Philip J., Jr. "Family-Structure in Seventeenth-Century Andover, Massachusetts," In Katz, Stanley N., Murrin, John M., and Greenburg, Douglas, *Colonial America: Essays in Political and Social Development.* New York: McGraw-Hill, Inc., 1993.

Hambleton, Else L., "Playing the Rogue": Rape and Issues of Consent in Seventeenth-Century Essex County Massachusetts. In Smith, Merril D., *Sex Without Consent: Rape and Sexual Coercion in America.* New York, New York University Press, 2001.

Hambrick-Stowe, Charles. *Early New England Meditative Poetry.* New York: Paulist Press, 1988.

Hammatt, Abraham. *The Hammatt Papers, Early Inhabitants of Ipswich, Massachusetts, 1633–1670.* Baltimore: Genealogical Publishing Company, Inc., 1980.

Henretta, James A. *The Evolution of American Society, 1700–1815.* Lexington: D.C. Heath and Company, 1973.

Hoyt, David W. *The Old Families of Salisbury and Amesbury, Massachusetts, with Some Related Families of Newbury, Haverhill, Ipswich and Hampton, and of York County. Maine.* Baltimore: Genealogical Publishing Company, Inc., 1982.

Ingram, Martin. *Church Courts, Sex and Marriage in England, 1570–1640.* New York: Cambridge University Press, 1987.

Karlsen, Carol F. *The Devil in the Shape of a Woman.* New York: Random House, Inc., 1987.

Koehler, Lyle. *A Search for Power: The 'Weaker Sex' in Seventeenth-Century New England.* Urbana: University of Illinois Press, 1980.

Leites, Edmund. *The Puritan Conscience and Modern Sexuality.* New Haven: Yale University Press, 1986.

Levine, David and Wrightson, Keith. "The Social Context of Illegitimacy in Early Modern England." In Laslett, Peter, Oosterveen, Karla, and Smith, Richard M., *Bastardy and Its Comparative History.* Cambridge: Harvard University Press, 1980.

Lindemann, Barbara S. "To Ravish and Carnally Know: Rape in Eighteenth-Century Massachusetts," *Signs,* (1984)1:63–82.

Lockridge, Kenneth A. *A New England Town: The First Hundred Years, Dedham, Massachusetts, 1636–1736.* New York: W.W. Norton & Company, 1970.

McElrath, Joseph R., Jr., and Robb, Allan P., eds. *The Complete Works of Anne Bradstreet.* Boston: Twayne Publishers, 1981.

McLaren, Angus. *Reproductive Rituals: The Perception of Fertility in England from the Sixteenth Century to the Nineteenth Century.* London: Methuen, 1984.

McManus, Edgar J. *Law and Liberty in Early New England: Criminal Justice and Due Process, 1620–1692.* Amherst: University of Massachusetts Press, 1993.

Main, Gloria L. "Gender, Work, and Wages in Colonial New England." *William and Mary Quarterly,* 3d. Ser. LI (1994), 39–66.
Main, Gloria L. *Peoples of a Spacious Land: Families and Cultures in Colonial New England.* Cambridge: Harvard University Press, 2001.
Malmsheimer, Lonna. "Daughters of Zion: New England Roots of American Feminism." *New England Quarterly L (1977),* 484–504.
Massachusetts Statutes and Laws. *The Charter and General Laws of the Colony and Province of Massachusetts Bay.* Boston, 1814.
Mather, Cotton. *Warnings from the Dead. Or Solemn Admonitions unto all People, but especially unto Young Persons to Beware of such Evils as would bring them to the Dead.* Boston: 1693.
Miller, Perry. *The New England Mind: The Seventeenth-Century.* Cambridge: Harvard University Press, 1939.
Morgan, Edmund S. "The Puritans and Sex." *New England Quarterly,* XV(1942),591–607.
Morrison, Samuel Eliot. *Of Plymouth Plantation, 1620–1647, by William Bradford, Sometime Governor Thereof.* New York: Alfred A. Knopf, Inc., 1852.
Murrin, John M. "'Things Fearful to Name': Bestiality in Colonial America." In *Pennsylvania History: A Journal of Mid-Atlantic Studies,* Special Supplemental Issue, 65(1998).
Noble, John. *Records of the Court of Assistants of the Colony of the Massachusetts Bay, Volume 1, 1673–1692.* Boston: Suffolk County, 1901.
Noble, John. *Records of the Court of Assistants of the Colony of Massachusetts Bay, Volume II, 1630–1644.* Boston: Suffolk County, 1928.
Norton, Mary Beth. *Founding Mothers and Fathers: Gendered Power and the Forming of American Society.* New York: Alfred A. Knopf, Inc., 1996.
Oberholzer, Emil Jr. *Delinquent Saints.* New York: Columbia University Press, 1955.
Parkes, Henry Bamford. "Morals and Law Enforcement in Colonial New England." *New England Quarterly,* V (1932), 431–452.
Perley, Sidney. *The History of Salem, Massachusetts.* Three Volumes. Salem: Sidney Perley, 1924–1928.
Porterfield, Amanda. *Female Piety in Puritan New England: The Emergence of Religious Humanism.* New York: Oxford University Press, 1992.
Powers, Edwin. *Crime and Punishment in Early Massachusetts, 1620–1692: A Documentary History.* Boston: Beacon Press, 1966.
Reis, Elizabeth. *Damned Women: Sinners and Witches in Puritan New England.* Ithaca: Cornell University Press, 1997.
Saxton, Martha. *Being Good: Women's Moral Values in Early America.* New York: Hill and Wang, 2003.
Shurtleff, Nathaniel B. *Records of the Governor and the Company of Massachusetts Bay in New England, Volume II, 1642–1649.* Boston: William White, 1853–4.
Silverman, Kenneth. *The Life and Times of Cotton Mather.* New York: Columbia University Press, 1985.
Smith, Daniel Scott and Hindus, Michael S. "Premarital Pregnancy in America, 1640–1971: An Overview and Interpretation." *Journal of Interdisciplinary History,*v:4 (Spring 1975),339–372.

Sommerville, Margaret R. *Sex and Subjection: Attitudes to Women in Early Modern Society.* London: Arnold, 1995.

Stone, Lawrence. *The Family, Sex and Marriage in England 1500–1800.* New York: Harper and Row Publishers, Inc., 1979.

Stone, Lawrence. *Uncertain Unions: Marriage in England 1660–1753.* Oxford: Oxford University Press, 1992.

Taves, Ann. *Religion and Domestic Violence in Early New England.* Bloomington: University of Indiana Press, 1989.

Thomas, Keith. "The Double Standard." *Journal of the History of Ideas,* XX(1959), 195–216.

Thomas, M. Halsey. *The Diary of Samuel Sewall.* New York: Farrar, Strauss, and Giroux, 1973.

Thompson, Roger. *Sex in Middlesex: Popular Mores in a Massachusetts County, 1649–1699.* Amherst: University of Massachusetts Press, 1986.

Thresher, Mary G. *Records and Files of the Quarterly Court of Essex County, Massachusetts, Volume IX, 1683–1686.* Salem: The Essex Institute, 1975.

Torrey, Clarence Almon. *New England Marriages Prior to 1700.* Baltimore: Genealogical Publishing Company, Inc., 1985.

Trask, William B. *Suffolk County Wills.* Baltimore: Genealogical Publishing Company, 1977.

Ulrich, Laurel Thatcher. *Goodwives: Image and Reality in Northern New England, 1650–1750.* New York: Oxford University Press, 1980.

United States Bureau of the Census. *Historical Statistics of the United States.* U.S.: GPO, 1960.

Unknown Author. "John Dane's Narrative." *New England Historical and Genealogical Register Volume 8, April 1854.*

Unknown Author. *Letter Book of Samuel Sewall.*

Unknown Author. *The Holy Bible Containing the Old and New Testaments.* Oxford: Oxford University Press, 1900.

Verduin, Kathleen. "'Our Cursed Natures,' Sexuality and the Puritan Conscience." *New England Quarterly,* LVI (1983), 220–237.

Walker, Garthine. "Rereading Rape and Sexual Violence in Early Modern England." *Gender & History,* 10 (1998), 1–25.

Wilson, Chris. "The Proximate Determinants of Marital Fertility in England 1600–1799." In Bonfield, Lloyd, Smith, Richard M., and Wrightson, Keith, eds. *The World We Have Gained: Histories of Population and Social Structure.* Oxford: Basil Blackwell, 1986.

Zuckerman, Michael. "Pilgrims in the Wilderness: Community, Modernity, and the Maypole at Merry Mount." *New England Quarterly,* L (1977), 255–277.

Index

For Product Safety Concerns and Information please contact our EU representative GPSR@taylorandfrancis.com
Taylor & Francis Verlag GmbH, Kaufingerstraße 24, 80331 München, Germany

www.ingramcontent.com/pod-product-compliance
Ingram Content Group UK Ltd.
Pitfield, Milton Keynes, MK11 3LW, UK
UKHW022119190926
475702UK00013B/1532
* 9 7 8 0 4 1 5 6 4 9 0 2 5 *